FAMOUS FRONTIERSMEN
AND HEROES OF THE BORDER

DANIEL MORGAN.

Famous Frontiersmen

AND HEROES OF THE BORDER

Their adventurous lives and stirring
experiences in Pioneer days

By
CHARLES H. L. JOHNSTON

Illustrated

Essay Index Reprint Series

BOOKS FOR LIBRARIES PRESS
FREEPORT, NEW YORK

Originally published as part of the Famous Leaders Series

Copyright 1913 by L. C. Page Co., Inc.

Copyright renewed 1941 by Charles H. L. Johnston

Reprinted 1971 by arrangement with
Farrar, Straus & Giroux, Inc.

973.099
JOH

INTERNATIONAL STANDARD BOOK NUMBER:
0-8369-2231-X

LIBRARY OF CONGRESS CATALOG CARD NUMBER:
72-152178

PRINTED IN THE UNITED STATES OF AMERICA

Thanks are due the Librarians of Congress, The Boston Public Library, and Harvard University, for numerous courtesies extended to the Author during the preparation of this volume.

PREFACE

My dear Boys; and particularly the Boy Scouts: As so much interest was displayed in my book " Famous Scouts " and requests for more tales were made by many of you, I have collected some interesting stories of valiant and daring adventurers, who were among the early settlers of the wilderness. These men were real scouts and trappers, for they lived in the wilds and had to know how to shoot a rifle; how to trap; and how to camp in whatever place night happened to overtake them. Savage men and wild beasts were frequently encountered, and desperate were the fights which these fellows engaged in. Some of them lived to a happy and prosperous old age; some perished from exposure, or by the hands of their red enemies.

You, yourselves, are playing at scouting in cities, in villages, and in a country which long since has been populated by the whites. These hardy, old fellows did not play at scouting, for it was their real existence, and they had to know the game from boyhood. Their deeds may seem to be atrocious and bloodthirsty, but were they not surrounded by implacable enemies who had no mercy upon them when they caught them unawares?

When I was in Harvard College our Professor of

English — Dean LeBaron Russell Briggs — used to advise us to " browse in the Library." I followed his advice in regard to these stories, and, after brushing away the cobwebs from many a forgotten volume, have been able to give you the accurate histories of several important frontiersmen and heroes of the border. These tales are all true and are vouched for by early historians. All that I hope is that I have served them up to you in a manner that is interesting and is not dull. Believe me,

Yours very affectionately,

CHARLES H. L. JOHNSTON.

THE FRONTIERSMAN

HE stood 'neath the whispering pines, by his cabin,
Lanky and gaunt, his face seamed and scarred,
Knotted his hands and blackened with toiling,
Bronzed well his face; his palms rough and hard.
Strangely he gazed in the dim, filmy distance,
Gazed, as the smoke from the fire curled and swayed,
Rapt was his look, for a voice from the forest
Spoke — and in accents disquieting — said:

Come! freeman! come! to the swirl of the river,
Come! where the wild bison ranges and roams,
Come! where the coyote and timber wolves whimper,
Come! where the prairie dogs build their rough homes.
Come to the hills where the blossoms are swaying,
Come to the glades where the elk shrills his cry,
Come — for the wild canyon echoes are saying,
Come — only come — climb my peaks to the sky.

A thrill shook the frame of the woodsman and trapper,
A strange light of yearning came to his eye,
Restless and roving by nature, — this wanderer,
Shuddered and paled at the wild, hidden cry;
Trembling he turned towards the hut in the shadow,
Shaking he strode to the low, darkened door,
Then stopped, — as sounded the voice from the meadow,
Mutt'ring the challenge — o'er and o'er.

Come, will you come, where the brown ouzel nestles,
Come, where the waterfall dashes and plays,
Come, where the spike-horn rollicks and wrestles,
On a carpet of moss, in the warm Autumn haze;
The cloud banks are blowing o'er Leidy and Glenrock,
On Wessex and Cassa the sun hides its head,
Come, will you come, where the trout leaps in splendor,
Come, only come, let the veldt be your bed.

ix

By the rough, oaken chair lay the grim, shining rifle,
On a nail o'er the fire swung the curled powder-horn,
With a smiling grimace he seized on these weapons,
Wild emblems of conquest, — storm-battered and worn.
" Stay," whirred the loom, as it stood in the shadow,
" Stay," purred the cat, as it lay near the stove,
" Stay where the woodbine and iris are trailing,
Stay, only stay, calm this spirit to rove."

But, " come," shrilled the voice on the dim, distant prairie,
" Come, where the Cheyennes are roving and free,
Where the beaver are damming the wild, rushing ice stream,
Where the lean puma snarls in the shaggy, pine tree.
Come — for the call of the wild is resounding,
From Laramie's peaks rolls the smoke of the fire.
Lighted by scouts, where the herds are abounding,
Fattened and sleek, for the red man's desire."

. . . .

Thus came the call, and thus trekked the plainsman,
Westward, yet westward his grim step led on,
By the wide, sedgy steppes, where the Platte curled and whispered,
By the brackish salt lake, stretching gray 'neath the sun,
Where the purple, red flowers in clusters lay glist'ning,
Where the wild kestrel whirled o'er the precipice sheer,
He conquered the wild, while the grizzly stood list'ning,
And growled, as the white canvased wagons drew near.

CONTENTS

LIST OF ILLUSTRATIONS

Famous Frontiersmen
AND HEROES OF THE BORDER

DANIEL MORGAN:

THE FAMOUS VIRGINIAN RIFLEMAN, AND HIS ADVENTURES WITH THE INDIAN BEAR

DANIEL MORGAN was a famous Virginian rifleman. As a young man he enlisted in the French and Indian War, and joined an army under Colonel St. Clair, who, as you remember, no doubt, was so signally defeated by Little Turtle.[1] The bravery of St. Clair sometimes amounted to rashness. His enemies have even accused him of indiscretion. At any rate, when camped near the head waters of the Mississippi, on the plains of the Chippewa, he placed his men near a dense forest, in which his redskinned enemies could easily pick off his sentinels without exposing themselves, in the least, to danger from return fire.

For five nights his army lay in this position, and for five nights a sentinel was posted near the gloomy borders of the forest. Alas! Every man who had held the place was shot. This struck terror to the hearts

[1] See "Famous Indian Chiefs."

1

of the soldiers, and, when a sentinel was to be posted upon the sixth night, no one would come forward to take the position, without a serious protest. St. Clair knew that it was only throwing away men's lives to place a sentinel in such an exposed situation, so he insisted upon no one occupying it. This pleased his followers mightily. " Colonel," said many, " you are a sensible man."

Upon the evening of the sixth day, however, a rifleman from the Virginia corps appeared before the Colonel's tent. His name was Daniel Morgan.

— " Sir," he remarked, saluting, " I feel that I can take charge of this post. Put me there and see what I can do."

St. Clair looked at him dubiously.

" I think that you are rather rash," said he. " But you can have what you desire. Go, and good luck to you, my son."

Soon afterwards, the new guard marched up. The scout fell in behind, shouldered his rifle, and went forward.

" I'll return safely," said he, as he followed the leading files. " And, Colonel St. Clair, I will drink your health in the morning."

The new guard marched on, arrived at the place which had been so fatal to the sentries, and here halted. Bidding his fellow soldiers " Good night," the sentry brought his gun to order arms and peered about him. The night was a dark one. Thick clouds overspread the heavens and hardly a star was to be seen. Silence reigned, save for the beat of the retiring footsteps of the guard. The frontiersman paced slowly up and down, then stopped, for in the far distance came the cry of "All is well!"

Seating himself upon a fallen tree, the soldier fell into a reverie, but, hark! what was that? A low, rustling sound came from out the bushes. He gazed intently towards the spot whence the noise seemed to proceed, but he could see nothing but the impenetrable gloom of the forest. Nearer and nearer came the strange rustling and a well-known grunt informed him that a large bear was approaching. Slowly the animal came on — then quietly sought the thicket to the left of his position.

At this particular moment the clouds drifted away from the face of the moon, so that the soldier could plainly see the lumbering brute. What was his surprise, when he viewed a deer-skin legging and two moccasined feet sticking out from the bottom of the animal, where should have been two furry legs. He could have shot the strange beast in a moment, but he did not know how many other quadrupeds of a like nature might be at hand. His fingers dropped from his rifle trigger, and, taking off his hat and coat, he hung them to the branch of a fallen tree, then silently crept toward the thicket. Crouching low behind some scrub bushes, he heard the twang of a low bow-string, and an arrow, whizzing past his head, told him that he had guessed correctly when he supposed that other redskins were near by. A low murmur of voices came from the bushes on the right.

The sentry gazed carefully about him. Pressing the

brush aside, he saw the form of a man, then of several more. He counted their numbers and found that there were twelve in all, some sitting, some lying full length upon the thickly strewn leaves of the forest. Believing that the whizzing arrow had laid the sentinel low, and, little thinking that there was any one within hearing, they conversed aloud about their plans for the morrow.

"These men are few," said one. "We will have forty warriors ready in the evening. We will shoot an arrow into the sentry, and then will attack the camp."

"Ugh! Ugh!" said another. "It will be easy to overcome these palefaced warriors. This will be done. There are but a few men who come out with the sentry, and these we can readily take care of."

"Ah!" said a third. "How pleasant it will be to see the palefaces running homeward. It will be good. It will be good."

Eagerly the sentry scanned these men. He watched them as they rose, and saw them draw the numerous folds of their robes about them. He trembled, as they marched off in single file through the forest, in order to seek some distant spot, where the smoke of their fire could not be seen by the whites, and where they would not be followed, when the supposedly dead sentry was found by his comrades. Then, rising from his crouching position, the frontiersman returned to his post. His hat had an arrow in it, and his coat was pierced by two of them.

"By George," said he, "I was lucky to escape."

Wrapping himself in his long coat, he returned immediately to the camp, and, without delay, demanded to speak to Colonel St. Clair.

"I have something very important to say to Colonel St. Clair," said he, to the guard before his tent.

When the soldier reported his request, his commanding officer ordered that he be immediately admitted to his presence.

"You have done well," remarked St. Clair, after hearing his story. "Furthermore, I commission you Lieutenant of the Virginia corps, to take the place of your unfortunate comrade, Lieutenant Phipps, who died three nights ago. You must be ready to-morrow evening, with a picket guard, to march to the fatal outpost, there to place your hat and coat upon the branches, and then to lie in ambush for the intruders."

"I shall be glad to carry out your commands," replied the newly appointed Lieutenant, smiling broadly.

According to order given out by Colonel St. Clair, a detachment of forty riflemen, with Lieutenant Morgan at their head, marched from the camp at half-past seven on the following evening. Putting up a couple of stakes, they arranged a hat and coat upon them so as to resemble the appearance of a soldier standing on guard, and then stole silently away in order to hide in the bushes.

For an hour they lay quiet, intently listening for the approach of the redskins. The night was cold and still. A full moon shed its lustrous radiance over field and forest. Snow was upon the ground, and becom-, ing chilled by contact with the cold sprinkling of fleecy white, some of the soldiers began to grumble quite audibly.

"Silence!" whispered Lieutenant Morgan. "I hear the rustling of leaves, and it is evident that either a bear, or some red men are approaching."

All crouched low and watched intently. Presently a large, brown bear emerged from the thicket and passed near the ambush.

"Hist!" murmured a soldier. "Look at his feet!"

Sure enough, moccasins were sticking out below. The bear reconnoitered; saw the sentinel standing at his post; retired into the forest for a few paces; then rose and let fly an arrow which brought the make-believe sentinel to the ground with a crash. The animal stood there looking at his handiwork with interest. So impatient were the Virginians to avenge the death of their comrades, that they could scarcely wait until the Lieutenant gave the word to fire. Then, rising in a body, they let drive a volley. The bear dropped instantly to the snow-covered ground, and a number of red warriors, who had crept up behind him, were also dispatched. Quickly loading, the frontiersmen made a dash into the forest, again fired, and killed, or wounded, several more of the enemy. They then marched back to camp, highly pleased and elated at their easy victory. Ten savages had fallen before the deadly aim of their rifles, and there was wailing and lamentation among the women of the Chippewa nation.

But how about Lieutenant Morgan?

This doughty soldier rose to be a captain, and, at

the termination of the French and Indian campaign, returned to his home, near Winchester, Virginia, where he lived on his farm until the breaking out of the War of the Revolution. Then, at the head of a corps of Virginian riflemen, he attained great fame and renown; was present at many an important battle, and rendered signal service to the American cause. But he never forgot the bear who walked with the feet of a man.

JAMES HARROD:

FOUNDER OF HARRODSBURG
KENTUCKY, AND FAMOUS SCOUT OF THE
FRONTIER

DANIEL BOONE — the founder of Kentucky — was revered, respected, and admired by the early pioneers. He was, as you know, a man of much skill in woodcraft, and was also an unexcelled rifle shot. Another early settler of this border state was James Harrod, of whom we have but little record, for he was a lover of solitude and his expeditions into the wilderness were usually taken alone. Furthermore, he was the most modest of men and never wrote or spoke of his own deeds. A little knowledge of his adventures, however, has come down to us, and we are sure that he was one of the bravest of the brave. To a noble courage was added a great gentleness of manner which, in another, might almost be called effeminacy.

What drove this valiant soul into the wilderness of Kentucky? What spirit moved his restless footsteps into the virgin forest? How came he to penetrate into that " dark and bloody ground? " Who knows? His was the restless spirit and his was the soul which loved

JAMES HARROD.

the vast solitude of the wildwood; for — even earlier than Daniel Boone — we know that this sinewy frontiersman built a log cabin for himself at the present site of Harrodsburg. When Boone went to the assistance of the surveyors of Lord Dunmore, who were surrounded by the red men, Harrod returned to Virginia and joined a force of whites sent to repel the Shawnees and other savages at Point Pleasant on the Great Kanawha. He was under General Lewis in the bloody affair, and then, having done his duty by his white brethren, returned to Kentucky in order to make Harrodsburg a place of refuge for the immigrants, who were beginning to turn their steps towards the setting sun.

One day, as he sat before his cabin busily engaged in cleaning his rifle, a man ran up to him. He was plainly excited, and was breathing heavily, as if laboring under a severe mental strain.

"Bad news, comrade!" said he, when he had partly recovered his breath. "Jim Bailey's cabin has been attacked by the red men and no one is alive to tell the tale, save his two daughters, who have been carried away by the savages in the direction of their village. Unless a party hurries immediately in pursuit, they will be taken to the tribe and will be never seen again. Their fate will not be a pleasant one."

The frontiersman jumped to his feet immediately.

"I will go at once," said he. "You warn the other settlers and send all that you can after me. Now, there is no time to be lost!"

Seizing his powder-horn and pouch of bullets, he

was soon speeding through the forest. He knew well where the cabin lay, and, as he burst through the tangled woodland, saw that a terrific fight had occurred around the little log fortress in the wilderness. Smoke still came from the chimney. The windows were battered and broken. The door was a splintered wreck. And, as he gazed inside, he saw the evil work of the vindictive redskins. The tracks of the murderers were plain, for a rain had fallen and it was evident that eight or ten had been in the party.

"Curses upon you, Shawnees!" cried Harrod, in loud tones. "You will pay for this ere many days are o'er!"

It was near midday. The scout took one lingering glance at the wreckage of that once peaceful home, then turned and followed the trail of the savages. It was clear, and he saw — after an hour's travel — that the Indians had separated. One half had gone toward the Indian towns. One half had sheered off toward a settlement, about fifteen miles below. Presuming that the Indians would take the girls to the settlement by the nearest route, he followed the first trail, and, as night came on, was delighted to see a camp-fire before him, in the dense woodland.

With true woodsman's cunning, the scout dropped to his knees and cautiously wormed a way toward the glimmering embers. Peeping over a fallen log, he saw that there were five Indians lying near the blaze. His heart now beat tumultuously — for there, also, were the two captive girls. They were bound with deer thongs, and, even at that distance, he could mark the misery expressed upon their pale countenances.

It was too early for the lone woodsman to attempt to make an attack. With the courage of a lion he intended to do this single-handed. You think it a hazardous adventure, no doubt? Wait, and see how he fared!

Creeping to a large oak, he put his back against it and went to sleep " with one eye open," as the hunters call it. He slumbered peacefully until about twelve o'clock — then rose and again wriggled towards the fire in order to see how matters stood. All the savages were lying down, save one, who seemed to be keeping guard over the others. But even he was sleepy. His head nodded drowsily upon his breast.

The scout watched him intently, while his right hand grasped his tomahawk. The savage seated himself, then got up, yawned, and lay down by the side of his companions. Harrod saw his opportunity, and, leaning his rifle against a tree, began to crawl towards the camp.

You can be well assured that the seasoned frontiersman made little noise as he did so. But he was suddenly forced to stop. The Indian sentinel arose, stretched himself, and walked towards the place where the scout lay prostrate upon some green moss. Every nerve in the Kentuckian was a-quiver. He was all prepared to make one desperate leap upon the foe. But, as he was about to spring upward, the Indian turned back and lay down.

The avenger of Jim Bailey's family now began to crawl towards the camp. Luck was not with him. A stick snapped beneath his left hand, and, as it cracked like the report of a pistol, the Shawnee sentinel sprang hastily to his feet. Looking furtively around, he stirred the fire and squatted down beside it. Harrod, meanwhile, crouched close to the moist earth, praying — beneath his breath — that the Indian would again lie down. Minute after minute passed. The redskin still stirred the embers with a long twig, and, fearing that day would break before he would accomplish his object, the bold pioneer began to retreat towards the tree where he had left his rifle. As he wormed his way backwards, he saw the guard stretch himself out by the side of his companions. The scout breathed easier.

Reaching the tree where his rifle stood, he took it up, and again began his cautious wriggle towards the fire. This time luck was with him, for he crept right up to the side of the sleeping savages.

Lest you think I am exaggerating this affair, I will here quote an authentic historian. He says: " To draw his tomahawk and brain two of the sleeping Indians was but the work of a moment, and, as he was about to strike the third one, the handle turned in his fingers, and the savage received the blow on the side instead of the centre of his head. He awoke with a yell. It was his last. Grasping his weapon more firmly, the frontiersman struck the fellow a surer blow and dropped him lifeless to the ground. With a terrific whoop he now sprang for his rifle just as the two other Indians rose to escape, and, firing hastily, one of them fell to rise no more."

The other red man scampered into the forest as fast as his sinewy legs could carry him. The scout was after him as hard as he, too, could go, but the savage could run like a deer and proved to be too fleet for the trapper. Harrod stopped, and, taking careful aim, threw his tomahawk at his enemy. So sure was his missile hurled that it lopped off one of the Indian's ears and cut a deep gash in his cheek. In spite of the grievous wound the savage did not halt, but bounded away like a Virginian deer. Harrod stood for a while, laughing at the running brave, then slowly turned and made his way back to camp. Here he found the two captive girls, crying bitterly. He unbound them, received their joyous thanks, was embraced by both; and then took them upon the trail to the settlement. Imagine the joy of the frontiersmen when they saw them return, and, although a party had started out to track the Indians, they had only travelled about three miles from Harrodsburg when they met the triumphant pioneer.

"Hurrah! Hurrah for Harrod!" they shouted. "You are indeed a worthy scout! Hurrah! Hurrah!"

The two girls were carried upon the men's shoulders into camp, and there were given a feast of welcome. They were embraced by the women, hugged by the children, and were presented with a wreath of flowers by the men. As for Harrod, his modesty forbade him taking part in the ceremonies, and, leaving the next day upon a hunting excursion, he was not heard or seen until a week later, when he returned with several deer and bear skins.

Shortly after this thrilling adventure the scout went into the forest in search of game. Not far from the settlement he spied a fat deer. He drew a careful bead on him, and was just about to raise his rifle for a shot when he heard the buck whistle and saw him raise his head. He knew from this that the forest rover had scented some hidden foe, and, sure that it was not himself that the animal smelled — as the wind was blowing from the deer toward him — he crouched down to await developments. He had not long to remain in this position. In a few moments he heard the crack of a rifle and saw the noble buck leap high into the air. He fell prone upon his side, and, as he lay quivering in the grass, three Indians came up and began to skin him. They were laughing and talking in loud tones.

" Ah ha," said the scout to himself, " they are skinning my game for me. Let them go on."

He crouched low in the brush, and when they had about completed this operation he rose, took careful aim, and killed the one he judged to be the leader of the party. Believing that he was too well concealed to be detected, he crouched behind the brush, and, turning his back, reloaded his rifle in that position. The redskins, meanwhile, climbed into some trees, but one of them exposed himself to the keen view of the scout. Harrod took careful aim, and, at the discharge of his flint-lock, the savage tumbled to the ground. The third Indian now saw where he was concealed, and, leaping to the ground, made at him with rifle raised. Harrod put his cap upon a stick and poked it above the brush. The redskin fired, thinking that he was aiming at the trapper, and, as his bullet whistled by the head of the man of the frontier, the scout knew that the advantage was now on his side. Drawing his tomahawk, he leaped from his hiding place, and, in a few bounds, had swung his weapon above the head of the now terrified brave. In a second it was all over with the red man.

The scout sat down and laughed loudly, for he had won a glorious victory. Then he rose, gathered up the arms of his enemies, loaded himself with deer meat, and made his way back to his cabin. He was well satisfied with the day's work.

This was but one of many adventures. He continued upon his solitary hunts, and, while searching for game, often was surrounded by roving Shawnees, so that his life was in constant danger.

A month after the first affair he was chasing some deer on Cedar Run — a tributary of a stream now named Harrod's Creek, in honor of this intrepid pioneer. He had shot a fat buck and was bending over him in order to get the choicest bit of venison, when a bullet whizzed suddenly by his ear. A loud and triumphant yell sounded in the forest at the same instant, and, looking up, he saw that he was confronted by a dozen red men. His only safety was in flight.

Scout Harrod was no mean runner. Inured to hardship, and with muscles of steel, he bounded away like one of the very deer which he had just dispatched. The Indians were in hot pursuit. As they came on, their leader cried, at the top of his voice:

"Come on! Here is the lone panther — Come on! Come on!"

So hotly did they push the running trapper that Harrod did not keep a proper lookout for what was in front of him. To his dismay, he found that he almost ran into a party of savages coming up to join the others. What was he to do? In a moment he had made up his mind.

Dashing right up to the oncoming braves he began to yell at the top of his lungs: "Come on, boys — here they are — Come on! Come!" He then followed this with an exultant whoop.

The Shawnees could not see their friends, — the pursuers. They were therefore of the opinion that this was a war party of whites, in considerable numbers, which is just what Harrod wished them to believe. Those in front became panic stricken, and turned without firing a shot. Those in the rear followed, while Harrod — racing after them — struck two to the earth with his tomahawk. One was a celebrated Shawnee chief, called Turkey Head, who was noted for his cruelty to the unlucky settlers who fell into his hands.

The scout kept on, plunged into a ravine, and seated himself in some thick brush. Peeping through the leaves, he saw his pursuers go on in full cry. Their wild yelping finally died out in the distance, and, turning around, the famous woodsman retraced his steps towards the settlement. He arrived there in due time, much overjoyed to have thus safely escaped from his vindictive enemies.

This was certainly a narrow escape, but another adventure — some days later — was about as thrilling as the last.

While at Harrodsburg he learned that a marauding expedition was about to start for the settlements, led by a famous warrior called Turtle Heart. He must stop it if he could, but, should he know their plans it would be far easier to head off the wild band, which would fall upon the log houses of the pioneers like a cloud of fire.

The scout set off alone in order to visit the Indian town, and, reaching it about noon, secreted himself upon an eminence from which he could watch the gathering savages. Here he lay until nightfall, then — carefully hiding his gun — stole noiselessly into the town and approached the council house. Worming his way up to it, he crouched near a hole — looked through — and saw many of the chiefs in close consultation.

"We will attack in two days," said one big, fierce-looking fellow. "The palefaces shall not possess the land given to us by the Great Father."

"Ugh! Ugh!" uttered several. "The palefaces must go home to the land of the rising sun!"

This was enough for the scout, and, rising, he began to beat a retreat. Suddenly he started back, for before him stood a giant redskin who seized him by the shoulder. Harrod saw that he was about to give a

whoop of alarm.   There was not a moment to be lost.
Catching the warrior fiercely by the throat, the pioneer stunned him by a terrific blow of the fist.   So
strong was he that he broke the neck of the brave,
and, without waiting an instant, bounded forth into
the darkness.   A single cry, or even the sound of a
struggle, would have brought a hundred infuriated
savages to the scene.   His nerve and gigantic strength
had saved him from an awful death.

Not many weeks after this affair he married a
young and beautiful girl, was given a Colonel's commission for his many services upon the frontier, and
retired to the peace and seclusion of a small log hut
near the town which he had founded.   But his charm-
ing wife could not prevent his long and solitary excur-
sions into the wilderness, where were deer, bear, wild
turkeys, and lurking redskins.   One day he went upon
one of these hazardous trips, and from it he never
returned.   Parties of friendly pioneers scoured the
woods in every direction, but he had " gone on and
had left no sign."   No trace of this gallant scout was
ever found — no word of him ever came from woodsman or savage.   Whether he met his end in manly
combat, or whether he was tortured at the stake, no
tongue could tell.   His fate is wrapped in impenetrable mystery, and the silence of the forest broods over
the spirit of James Harrod; frontiersman, **pioneer,
and hardy woodland adventurer.**

BATTLE OF FALLEN TIMBERS.

ROBERT McLELLAN:

PLUCKIEST OF THE EARLY PIONEERS

WHEN " Mad Anthony " Wayne was furiously battling with Little Turtle at Fallen Timbers, a daring adventurer was with him who was subsequently to play a most important part in the exploration of the then unconquered and unexplored West. Hardy, utterly fearless, and possessed of wonderful agility, — such was Robert McLellan, one of the most noted scouts that ever operated upon the border, and a rifleman whose aim was both quick and marvellously true.

In the summer of 1794 the celebrated " Mad Anthony " was pushing his way into the Indian country and was most desirous of securing a red prisoner, so that he could learn the force and strength of his savage opponents. Calling McLellan to him, he said:

" Bob, I wish you to take two trusty companions — Miller and Wells will do — and leave to-night for the Shawnee country. Secure a prisoner, as soon as possible, and return to camp with the fellow alive, for I am extremely anxious to get information in regard to the whereabouts of the large force of redskins which I know to be in my front."

McLellan was delighted.

" All right, Captain," he replied with enthusiasm.

"You leave the matter to me and I will guarantee that I and my friends will return with the desired captive. Only give us time and we will deliver the man of the woods, right side up and with care."

The General laughed.

"Very good," said he. "Go in, now, and win out."

Next morning McLellan and his two companions started forth with confidence and were soon far in the hostile country, where many prints of moccasined feet warned them that the savages were in the vicinity. One day they followed a fresh trail, and, upon peering around a projecting clump of bushes, saw three savages sitting upon a log near a great fire, at which they were cooking some venison. They crawled softly towards them, and decided, in a whispered consultation, that Wells should shoot the redskin upon the left; Miller, the one upon the right; and that McLellan, leaving his rifle against a tree, should run the other fellow down and capture him.

At the given signal the rifles spoke in unison, and the two redskins who had been marked, fell prostrate to the earth; for both of the pioneers could hit the eye of a squirrel at fifty yards. The one in the centre leaped swiftly to his feet, and, darting through the thicket, was soon bounding away to safety. But McLellan was after him in a jiffy, and the redskin realized that he was running away from one of the speediest frontiersmen in all Ohio. On, on, they rushed, but, seeing that he was being rapidly overtaken, the savage turned in his course, headed for the stream, and, with one furtive glance at the oncoming man in buckskin, leaped from the high bank into the eddying current.

Raising his tomahawk in his right hand, the trapper made the venturesome leap with quite as much readiness as his opponent, and landed with a resounding splash. The water was very shallow in this spot. To his disgust, he found himself stuck up to the waist in the heavy mud. The redskin, too, was mired, but, brandishing a long knife aloft, now endeavored to strike it into McLellan's body.

He was dealing with a crafty antagonist who had parried many a knife-thrust before, and, quick as a flash, the pioneer grabbed the right arm of the Shawnee. In an instant his tomahawk was raised as if to brain the red man, who cried, " Ugh! Ugh! Paleface, you too strong. I surrender."

In a moment more the other two pioneers had reached the bank, and, leaning over the edge, pulled both savage and frontiersman out of the mud. Each was vigorously washed. To the surprise of all, the redskin was discovered to be a white man; the brother of Trapper Miller, himself, who had been captured by the savages when young, and had preferred to remain with them, although his kinsman had early left and had returned to his own people. " Ugh! Ugh! " he muttered. " I hate all of you."

In spite of his protestations he was taken to the headquarters of " Mad Anthony; " was confined to the guard-house; and was questioned very closely in regard to the numbers of his Shawnee allies. He was

extremely moody and resisted all attempts at con-
ciliation, even from his brother, but at last some memory of his former relatives seemed to return; he began
to grow more amiable; and, joining the company
captained by a noted Ranger, served in the ranks of
the whites against the people of his adoption.

So much for the ability to run, which was exhibited
by this celebrated woodsman.   Marvellous feats of
strength and agility are also told of McLellan.
Amongst other stories, it is related that one day, in
Lexington, Kentucky, a yoke of oxen blocked the narrow street down which he was going, so that it was
impossible to pass on either side.   Instead of turning
out of the way, or waiting for the team to move on,
the famous man of the frontier made a few rapid
bounds, and — with a mighty spring — cleared both
of the oxen with the greatest possible ease.

Another yarn is also narrated concerning his wonderful ability to jump, for it is said that he was
excelled only by one William Kennan, a Kentuckian,
and noted scout of the border.   It is currently reported, and a historian of the period quotes two unim-
peachable witnesses to back his statement, that at a
trial of strength and agility with several other scouts,
McLellan was asked if he could leap over a covered
wagon.

" I feel like a colt," he is said to have replied, " and,
if you will but watch me, I am sure that I can clear
this obstacle.   Now, boys, look at me ! "

With a run, a short step, and a tremendous spring,
the trapper shot into the air, and — to the astonish-

ment of all — lighted softly upon the ground, on the other side of the wagon. He had leaped over an obstacle at least eight and a half feet high, is reported by an old chronicler of these early days, but this is hardly possible in view of the fact that the world's record for the high jump is but six feet nine inches. At any rate, he had made an extraordinary performance.

In the year 1806, the famous adventurer Meriwether Clark met Robert McLellan ascending the swift and muddy waters of the Missouri in a canoe. Clark was returning from his long and dangerous expedition up the Mississippi and to the Pacific coast, which he had taken with Lewis ("the undaunted one"). Accompanying the valiant McLellan were numerous companions; all of the same hardy stamp as their leader, and all bent upon trading with the redskins.

"Where are you bound?" asked Clark.

"To fix up a trading post," answered McLellan, "where I can meet the red varmints on equal terms, trade with 'em, and get rich."

Clark smiled dubiously.

"You'll have a hard time," he answered, "for the French and Spanish are very jealous of you English. They operate mainly from St. Louis, and are endeavoring to monopolize the entire trade of this western country."

"Well," answered McLellan, with some show of anger, "I intend to hold this place against all the frog and garlic eaters in creation. Let them try to force out Robert McLellan, an' there'll be as tough a fight as any man ever looked for."

From his former acquaintance with this trapper, Clark fully believed that any attempt on the part of the rival traders to drive him from the ground would certainly result in a sharp and bloody battle.

"These French and Spanish traders," continued McLellan, "are like a dog who has had far too much to eat, and who is determined not to allow any of his fellows to share in the viands which he has before him. They want it all."

Clark could not help laughing.

"Look out for these Indians around here," said he. "They are treacherous devils and will betray you when you least expect it."

"I'll be on my guard," McLellan replied.

The explorer now gave him valuable information in connection with the various tribes of Indians who occupied the ground adjacent to the banks of the river. He again warned him of their treacherous character, but felt more at ease when he learned that his old-time friend had recently been an Indian trader for some time upon the frontier. Parting company at this point, the two hardy pioneers were destined never to see each other again, for Clark turned towards the peaceful East, while McLellan faced towards the savage frontier, where lay danger, toil, and thrilling adventures.

Pushing up the turbid waters of the Missouri, the hardy scout soon saw that his progress was not going to be any too easy. Suddenly hundreds of red men crowded the steep bluffs, which jutted high above the sides of the narrow stream, and brandished their spears and tomahawks in the faces of the whites. There were but forty trappers, so it could be plainly seen that it was wisest to submit to the demands of the hostiles. A solitary chieftain — splendidly mounted — now dashed up to the bank and held up his hand in token of a parley.

"Ugh! Ugh! Palefaces," said he, "you cannot come further into our country, for you will drive off all the game and we desire it for ourselves. But, if you want to build big house for trading you can do so down the stream."

"I reckon they've got us, boys," said McLellan. "We'll retreat and put up our tent lower down. I'll guarantee that this hold-up didn't originate with the redskins. There's Spanish blood behind this affair, or else my name's not Robert McLellan."

The savages supposed that the whites were perfectly contented with this enforced arrangement, and drew off, leaving a guard to watch the traders. But McLellan was a past master in outwitting Indians and had fooled too many in former years. No sooner had the army of savages moved well towards their villages than he hastily loaded up his boat, and, by pulling it very rapidly, passed the cliffs, where the red men had held him up before. He soon reached a spot suitable for his establishment, there built several log huts, and prepared to spend a considerable time in peaceful trading. He also swore to have revenge upon a Spaniard, called Manuel Lisa, as soon as he could catch him. For he learned that this opposition trader had been the cause of his detention.

McLellan lived here for several years in partnership with an adventurous borderer named Crooks, who was an expert in trading with the savages. They prospered, but soon the Sioux grew very troublesome. One day, when the trappers were off on a hunt, the red men surrounded the post, overpowered the trappers left behind, and began to carry off all of the valuable stores. McLellan returned before the work of spoliation was quite completed and burst in among the savages, exhibiting terrific anger.

" You curs! " he shouted, " bring back everything that you have taken away, or I'll blow you all to pieces with my cannon! "

The Sioux well knew the ungovernable temper and desperate character of the infuriated trapper.

" He heap angry! " said they.   " We do as he say."

They returned much that had been taken away, but much that had been carried to the Indian village never came back, and the valorous trader had to pocket a loss of about three thousand dollars. Heaping curses upon the heads of the savages, the Spaniards, the Frenchmen, and all the other " unmitigated rascals," as he called them, the outraged trader now fitted up his boats and started down the Missouri River to engage in business at a place where his competitors would be more honest and honorable.

Crooks had parted company with McLellan some time before this outrage.

" I can do better for myself down stream," he had

said. " The Indians here are too troublesome, for
they are under the influence of the rascally Spaniard,
Manuel Lisa."

What was the surprise of the disappointed frontiersman, when floating down the Missouri on his
way to St. Louis, to find his former partner at the
mouth of the Nodaway River.

" I'm delighted to see you, Crooks," he cried, and,
rounding to, he ran his canoe upon the bank. While
their men mingled together the partners had a long
conversation, and from Crooks it was learned that
the organization, with which he was now connected,
was under the command of a Mr. Hunt — one of John
Jacob Astor's partners in the American Fur Company.

" We are bound for the mouth of the Columbia
River," said Crooks, " where we are to meet another
part of the expedition which has gone by sea. We
will be camped here until spring, so will you not join
us? I am sure that you will have better luck in trading and trapping in this new field."

McLellan could not withstand the temptation.

" By George," cried he, " I'll be with you. I'll
begin a new life and see if I cannot have better success than here upon the Missouri."

Throwing away all of his worldly possessions, except his trusty rifle, the unfortunate trader joined the
expedition.

" I am determined to begin the world anew," he
wrote to his brother. " And I trust that there will be
no Spanish traders in the country to which we are
going."

His hopes were in vain, for they heard that Manuel Lisa was on the way to impede their progress and would use every effort to pass them by and prevent them from gaining any trade benefits with the Indians above. Sure enough, an emissary soon appeared from the crafty Spaniard, holding a message in his hand.

" If you wait for my party," it ran, " we can enter this territory together and share the trade. This will be better for all concerned."

" Don't give in to him," cried McLellan, when he heard this message. " The lying Spaniard can't tell the truth if he tries to, and cannot be honest if he wishes. He'll trick you after he has made you believe that he is your friend."

" I believe that you're right," Hunt answered. " I'll send him no definite reply."

So he returned a missive which did not commit him to any particular course of procedure.

In a few days — it was the thirty-first of May — immense bodies of savages gathered on the bluffs of the river, armed and painted for war. They screeched their defiance and yelled like demons, so it was easy to see that the tricky Manuel had been influencing them. Every trapper seized his arms and stood ready for action.

" Load up the artillery!" cried Captain Hunt, for he saw that it was dangerous both to retreat and to advance. " We will first fire off some blank cartridges and see if we cannot scare these pesky varmints into submission."

In a few moments smoke and flame burst from the

mouths of the cannon and the redskins beat a precipitate retreat. But soon they gathered again and made peace signs.

"We would make big talk," cried one painted brave. "We love our white brothers."

"Load the cannon with grape and cannister," said McLellan to his men. "Hunt and I will go ashore, and, if the redskins show any signs of treachery, blaze away."

His men smiled, as the daring trapper now approached the bank, where the Indians welcomed him with much show of good will, for they saw that the white men meant business. They smoked the pipe of peace together, and, finding that the trappers were determined to advance at any cost, the red men suddenly evinced a perfect willingness to allow them to go on. Their hearts were warmed by the gift of several hundredweight of corn, and — what they loved still more — a quantity of tobacco. "Ugh! Ugh!" grunted the chiefs. "We love our white brothers."

Seeing that the red men were now peaceful, McLellan ordered his own followers to advance up the river, but he was soon surprised by seeing another band of Indians, who rode along the bank of the stream but seemed to be friendly.

"By George!" cried McLellan, "these fellows are the same ones that robbed my store, when Crooks and I were in partnership! They mean trouble."

But the children of the plains realized that the whites were in force, and, fearing that they might attempt to punish them for their former actions, peacefully accepted several presents which were offered them. Again the trappers forced their way up the swift waters, but again they were surprised by a group of red men, who rode up the bank, and, in a lordly and insolent manner, demanded presents similar to those which had recently been given to their brethren. This angered the trappers, for they appreciated the fact that the redskins wished to frighten them.

"You shall not get a single thing from us," shouted Hunt, — a man of great firmness. "Furthermore, if you make any more insolent demands, I will treat you all as enemies and turn our cannon against you."

This did not please the savages, as can be well imagined. Vowing vengeance, and shaking their fists at the trappers, they rode off across the prairie, while the whites were now divided into two forces; one going up one bank, and the other taking the opposite side. Thus they proceeded for several days, until they came to a spot where the stream was very narrow and was filled with sand bars. A vast number of redskins were camped upon the western bank, and Hunt was fearful that they would soon attack. He and McLellan were in one of the boats.

"I know that they are peaceful," said the former, "for their faces are painted. Row to the shore!"

As they approached, the savages dropped their bows and arrows, came to meet them joyfully, and proved to be a band of Arickaras who were at war with the Sioux, and were thus anxious to have the white trappers assist in fighting their battles for them. "How! How!" said they. "We glad to see our white brothers. How! How! We wish to have sticks which speak with the voice of thunder."

The adventurers looked forward to rich trade with the red men but were much surprised and angered by receiving word that the boat of Lisa — the Spaniard — was rapidly approaching.

"That rascally fellow will ruin our work!" cried McLellan, with considerable heat. "We must let him know, now, that we will stand no trickery from him. If he tampers with these redskins and sets them against me, I will let my rifle do the work of vengeance."

The Indians, meanwhile, showed no disposition to trade, knowing that the presence of a rival trader would ensure them better bargains. Lisa soon arrived and was not long in discovering that he was an unwelcome guest. McLellan had difficulty in restraining himself from wreaking a just vengeance upon this artful "Greaser," but fearing that he might involve Hunt and his other friends in a quarrel, kept his own counsel. It was, however, not for long.

Lisa agreed that he and Hunt would go to the Indian village and would trade there, but that no advantage should be taken of one another in the transactions with the wild riders of the plains. After a short delay they proceeded together up the river. But the crafty Spaniard was soon up to his old tricks and attempted to induce a certain French Canadian, in Hunt's employ, to leave his master.

" I will give you better wages and treatment," said
he. " Come — boy — be one of my followers."

This was overheard by McLellan and infuriated
him. Seizing a gun, he gave the Spaniard to understand that he had old scores to settle with him, and
that he had better get his own pistol and defend himself, for he was soon to be shot down like a dog.
" You thieving, sneaking Greaser!" he shouted.
" Now you will go to Kingdom Come in a hurry.
You should have been beneath the sod long
ago."

Fire flashed from the Spaniard's eyes and he
reached for his pistol, but, before he could draw, the
angered McLellan was seized by both Hunt and
Crooks, who took his weapon away from him and
pinned him to the ground, until he promised that he
would not touch the Spaniard. Lisa himself was careful not to again rouse the ire of the pioneer, and, as
a result, did not attempt to underbid the trade offers
to the Arickaras. Successful bartering was soon accomplished, and Hunt's party set about the difficult
undertaking of crossing through the Rocky Mountains and traversing the dry table-land to the Pacific
coast.

You can well realize that this was a hazardous
undertaking, for, not only did the trappers have a
hazy and undefined conception of the route to follow,
but there was little water in certain parts of this
country, and a great scarcity of game in others.
There were sixty-two in the adventurous band, with
eighty-two pack-horses to carry luggage, guns, and

camp equipment. All were well armed and were full of determination to succeed.

As the adventurous little body of trappers filed silently towards the West — a few days later — the Indians collected in order to bid them good-by. Many an old chief was seen to shake his head, as they wended their way towards the beetling mountains, and the treacherous, though adventurous, Lisa was heard to exclaim: "These men are fools! They are all dead! All dead! None will ever return!" But these pessimistic remarks did not seem to worry the followers of Hunt and McLellan. With cheerful looks and smiling faces they kept onward towards their goal.

Soon they were in the glorious Big Horn range and were in the vicinity of the tepees of many Indians, who were not slow in discovering their approach. Contrary to every expectation, the red men greeted them most hospitably, gave them dried buffalo meat, and told them how to find a way through the rugged hills before them. These were the Cheyennes — a war-like tribe — which had its name from the Cheyenne River. They were soon to be driven from their hunting-grounds by the steady, westward emigration of the whites, but were now rich in both ponies and buffalo robes, and were much feared by the neighboring denizens of the plains: the Crows and Ogalala Sioux.

The pioneers kept on, traded with the redskins whom they met, and found increased dangers and difficulties in their path. It was summer, and thousands of gnats and mosquitoes attacked both men and horses, rendering life miserable and making it most disagreeable to proceed. I, myself, travelled through this country in the summer of 1899, and have never seen so many pests as here. Swarms of green-headed horse-flies attacked our pack animals, so that they would sometimes be bloody from their bites. Often the horses would roll upon the ground in order to get rid of the flies, and thus would dislodge the packs, which had taken some time to adjust. Their sting was most poisonous. Mosquitoes were here by the millions, and we had great difficulty — even then — of getting through the fallen timber, which sometimes extended for many miles. These pioneers picked their way through the forests, forded the rushing streams, ascended and descended the deep canyons, and finally reached the headwaters of the Mad River, or Snake River, as it is called below its junction with Henry's Fork.

An adventurous trader named Henry had here established a trading-post, the year before, but becoming disgusted with the Indians, who refused to barter with him, had abandoned it. Hunt, McLellan, and their little party, reached this spot on the eighth day of October, where they stopped to recruit their strength. Then they engaged Indians to look out for their horses, which they concluded to leave behind them, and built a number of canoes with which to commit themselves to the current of the river. They embarked, and, for a hundred miles found their progress easy, but all at once they saw to their dismay that below them were dangerous falls and treacherous rapids. Their journey was blocked.

It was impossible to return to Henry's Fork, where were their horses, and to go on meant the destruction of all their supplies. What was there to do? To the North was the Columbia River, but an unbroken wilderness lay between. They must cross it, trust to luck that game would come their way, and that their rifles would not miss it when found. There were but a few days' provisions left, so it was decided to divide the party into four sections: the first, under Crooks, was to make its way up the river to Fort Henry; the second, under McLellan, was to continue down the Snake; while the third, under McKenzie, was to traverse the wilderness towards the Columbia. The fourth section was to remain for a time where it was. And it was further understood that any party which should come across assistance or supplies should return to the main body under Hunt, which would hold the present camp until their leader became convinced that all had failed in their efforts to reach their destination. Let us see how they fared.

McLellan continued his way down the rushing Snake with three companions, but, finding that it was almost impossible to make further progress, he deflected his line of march so as to follow the detachment under McKenzie. Their course was over a bare and arid country where there was no game and little water. Occasionally a jack-rabbit scampered between the clumps of sage brush, but no one seemed to have sufficient ability with the rifle in order to bring one down. A lean coyote would now and again be seen, and often the weird wailing of one of these creatures would make night hideous. The jerked buffalo meat which they carried was soon exhausted and the adventurers began to suffer from the gnawing pains of hunger, but on they walked with grim and steadfast determination. Weary, footsore, and nearly exhausted, they finally came upon McKenzie and his five companions. These fortunately had food, which they gave to the gaunt trappers, who rested for a full day before they could go on.

McLellan was undaunted. Trained in a hundred combats with the savages of the West, and hardened by years of exposure, he saw no cause for despondency. Some of the trappers, however, gave way to despair. They were among the barren drifts and extinct craters of gigantic volcanoes, while, through the winding fissures of its canyoned walls, the furious torrent of the Snake River dashed, foamed, and roared beneath them. Like a snow-white ribbon it plunged onward upon its wild career, and, in the sobbing roar of its cataracts, some of the more weak-hearted fancied that they heard the voices of those departed, who called to them to follow where they had gone.

It grew cold. A fierce snow-storm came upon them. As the food supply was gone, a dozen beaver skins were cut into strips and roasted, but this provender only sustained life for a few days. At length the trappers became exhausted, and, crouching under the protecting ledge of a wall of rock, shivered before their fire, and gloomily looked forth upon the blinding snow. All was sadness and despondency. Some contemplated death, which they thought to be inevitable, and even the lion-hearted McLellan lost that undaunted courage which had never before deserted him. Could it be that they were to die before they saw the roaring waters of the Columbia? Could it be that they were to perish before they reached the trader's post upon the green-gray stretch of the Pacific Ocean?

Peering into the gloom from his rocky shelter, the keen eyes of McLellan suddenly perceived a buffalo, which, driven to the rocky wall by the desire to get away from the blinding snow, was crouching under the lee of a high bluff. What could be more fortunate? Taking note of the direction of the wind, the trapper left his hiding-place and crawled against it, until he came within thirty yards of the beast. Carefully he wormed his way behind a jutting ledge of rock and sand, then — taking a good sight — touched the trigger of his rifle, and the great lumbering brute fell dead. With a wild and hilarious cheer the old scout dashed to where he lay and cut joyful capers around him in the snow. "Hurray! Hurray!" he cried. "Now we will have enough food to last us for many days. Hurray! Hurray!"

Seizing upon the carcass of the beast, the old scout rolled him down the hill towards the cavern in which his own companions were shivering. With a wild yell he announced his triumph and this was answered by a hoarse cry from the half-famished trappers, who rushed upon the beast, and, but for the warning of the old frontiersman, would have gorged themselves upon the raw flesh, so great was their hunger.

" Hold back, my friends," cried he.   " Wait but a moment and I will give you some cooked food.   Restrain yourselves, for a few seconds, and I will see that you get enough to save your lives.   Eat the raw flesh and you will all perish."

It was difficult to hold back the starving trappers, but soon a fire was lighted, the choicest parts of the buffalo were broiled upon a ramrod, and the gaunt spectres were allowed a feast.   This saved their lives. With renewed strength they again made their way towards the Columbia, and, meeting with an occasional buffalo which they had the good fortune to kill, at length reached the swirling river, where a band of roving red men supplied them with a number of canoes.   They also secured sufficient jerked meat to last them until they should reach the coast, where the trading-post of Astoria had already been established. To that lucky shot of McLellan's they owed their lives.

Hunt, meanwhile, had decided that the three parties had successfully made their way to the coast, so he had started for the Columbia.   Crooks had reached Fort Henry, where he spent his time in trapping and in trading with the redskins.   As for the trappers who had left for Astoria by sea, they had met with an adverse fate, for the savages had induced them to enter the mouth of a small river, when they reached the neighborhood of the trading-post, and here had surrounded and massacred all of the voyageurs, after the vessel had been run aground. It took Hunt over a month to arrive at the coast. Crooks eventually followed. He met the other trappers after a separation of five months' duration.

After frightful privations and suffering the four parties were now safe at Astoria; a trading-post which was to create a fortune for its founder, John Jacob Astor, a shrewd merchant of New York, who was a dealer in furs and peltries of wild animals. But there was still travelling to be done, for Hunt determined soon after his arrival to send a party overland, in order to notify Astor of the loss of the detachment which had come by sea.

Strange to relate, the lion-hearted McLellan announced that he intended to go back with this party to St. Louis. "For," said he, "I have not been given a sufficient share of the profits of this company. I am entitled to more." His friends begged him to remain and not again to plunge into the wilderness, where were dangers just as great as those from which he had escaped. But he was obstinate in his purpose. "To St. Louis I shall go," said he, "and not all the redskins on the earth will stop me. I have been treated most unfairly." Thus, on the twenty-second day of March, 1812, he turned his back upon Astoria, and set out upon the hazardous trip towards the East. The detachment was under the command of John Reed, clerk of the Fur Company, a man of undoubted courage and experience in frontier warfare.

There were seventeen in this particular expedition, all men of well tried courage and resource in wilderness adventure. Ascending the Columbia in canoes, they reached the falls and were preparing to make the portage when a band of redskins surrounded them and began to shoot arrows at their ranks. The trappers crouched behind the protection of trees and boulders, and made a stand, sending many a humming bullet into the ranks of the savages, who suddenly ceased hostilities, and, holding up their hands in sign of peace, came towards the white men. Mingling with the travellers, the Indians offered to carry their luggage around the rapids.

" The redskins only want to steal all that we've got," whispered McLellan to his men. " But we can let them carry the canoes around the falls. Then we can get the baggage over during the night, and, when morning dawns, we'll be off before the varmints know what we're up to."

The redskins seemed to be well satisfied. They carried the canoes upon their broad shoulders, and, as night fell, retired to their village across the river, leaving a few upon the same side as the whites. McLellan waited until the moon rose; then waking the others, he told them to get their baggage around the falls as soon as they could. The trappers worked industriously, and just as day was breaking, they deposited the last sack of provisions at the head of the rapids. This had been done without waking the redskins, who were upon their side of the river.

But now was an uproar, for the savages across the stream learned what was going on, and, in a few moments, came swarming to the attack. A hundred of them rushed upon the nervy band of trappers, crying out, " You no go on. You stay here. You no go away."

Brandishing aloft an immense club, a red warrior rushed upon Reed and felled him to the ground. Another ran towards McLellan, who, with rifle in hand, stood watching the affray. As he approached, the trapper was ready, and, although the redskin attempted to throw a buffalo robe over his head in order to blind his vision as he made a thrust at him with his knife, the old scout was too wary a bird to be caught napping. Stepping quickly aside, he shot the savage dead. As the redskin rolled over, a noise sounded from behind, and, wheeling around, he was just in time to hit another Indian who was about to shoot him with a rifle. The trappers now rallied to the defense of their leader. The savage who had attacked Reed was dispatched just as he was about to brain the trapper with his tomahawk. The rifles of the men from Astoria spoke in unison, and terrified by the desperate courage of the rangers, the savages dropped back. McLellan urged his followers to the charge, and, with a wild yell, they rushed upon the redskins, who took to their heels, leaving many of their number prostrate upon the ground.

The unfortunate Reed had lost his dispatches to Astor, for he carried them in a bright, new, tin box which immediately attracted the attention of the Indians. They fancied that it must be of great value, because of the care which the leader took of it. But this put an end to the expedition. Reluctantly and sadly the trappers returned to the trading-post, where the wounded recovered from their injuries received in the little skirmish with the red men.

Hunt was greatly disappointed. " Boys! " said he, " I must absolutely get my dispatches through to Saint Louis, — Indians or no Indians. Astor must know of the fate of his other division. I will start a second expedition in June and Robert Stuart will be its commander. He will take only four good men with him."

McLellan announced that he would be a member of the party, and Crooks also declared that he would leave Astoria, because he had become dissatisfied with the method in which Hunt had treated him. They soon launched their canoes in the Columbia; began to paddle up the stream, and, before long, reached the mouth of the Walla-Walla, where they hid their frail craft, and started across country to the Snake River. Horses had been purchased from the red men, and with these they made good time, although again their food supply became exhausted so that they were forced to scrape the fur from beaver and buffalo skins and eat the hide in order to keep from starving. Fortunately game was now met with and this provender saved their lives.

At the place where they had last camped on Snake River they had buried a quantity of dried meat and other food, but when they arrived there they discovered that the redskins had found out its whereabouts, had dug it up, and had carried it away. It was growing cold, but they pressed forward with renewed courage, and entered a country which was free from game, so that again they were threatened with the dangers of starvation. Besides this, it was the land of the Crow Indians, who were terrific thieves and who soon discovered the presence of the little band of trappers. The sharp eyes of McLellan — well used to watching game — were not long in discovering the presence of the Indians.

"Look out. boys," said he. "I notice some of the red varmints hovering near by and suspect that we will be attacked before long. Look to the priming of your rifles and have plenty of ammunition handy. Be on your guard!"

The trappers gave good heed to this warning and redoubled their guards around the camp at nightfall. It was well that they did so, for, on the very next day, a large band of red men rode up to their halting-place, all fully armed with spears and arrows.

"Ugh! Ugh!" said the spokesman. "Where are my white brothers going?"

McLellan answered for the trappers that they were upon a peaceful errand and would not molest the red men, if they in turn would do them no harm. As he spoke, the redskins looked carefully at the men of the frontier, and, seeing them well armed and ready for business, decided not to attack. But they travelled with them for six whole days, quietly stealing any little articles that they could find, and, on the evening of the sixth day, ran off all the horses of the trappers in a mad stampede. The white adventurers were in a desperate situation.

Stuart, the commander, now spoke vigorous words.

"We must cache everything which we cannot carry, and push on," said he. "Let winter overtake us in this God-forsaken country and all is lost. On! On!"

As the men were busily engaged in digging a hole in which to bury the supplies, one of the trappers interrupted them.

"Two of those thieving Crows are watching us," said he, "and they will dig everything up just as soon as we disappear."

McLellan grew furious at this information.

"No thieving Crow will ever get anything of mine," said he, "unless they get my scalp first. I'll burn everything which we leave behind, and then let Mr. Redskin hustle for the white man's food."

"You're right!" answered all. "Burn it we will!"

Their stores were soon piled up into a heap and were consumed by the flames.

They now headed for the Mad River, where they built rafts, and floated them down these turbid waters, for several days. Then they again struck off across country towards the East, crossing a wide plateau to the base of the Rocky Mountains. They were in the land of the Blackfeet Indians, who were as hostile towards the whites as were the Crows, and who were as arrant thieves; but they kept on towards the high land, hoping thus to elude the red men. As they proceeded into the mountains, McLellan bitterly complained against their course and begged them to remain upon the plateau. "For," said he, "I've already had enough mountain climbing to last me a lifetime, and I'd rather be comfortably killed by the Indians than break my neck falling down a canyon. You boys would rather climb mountains than fight the redskins."

To these remarks Stuart and his companions paid no attention, but kept on their way. McLellan was liked by all, and one trapper offered to give him a load of jerked meat to carry, instead of the traps.

"A hunter should be able to kill his own meat without carrying any," said the old pioneer, who was now thoroughly angry. "Who wants to carry a whole horse-load of dried beef on his back? As for me, I'll go no further with you. Fools! Good-by!"

This burst of temper seemed to relieve his mind, and, starting down the mountain, he set out alone without once looking behind him. His companions kept on, and as they reached the top of the eminence, gazed over the plain, where a dark spot marked the form of the angered man of the frontier.

"Boys," said Stuart. "There goes the last of the old pioneers of the Kentucky border. You will never see him or his like again."

As he said this, the eyes of many of his companions filled with tears.

Events were not to go smoothly with either McLellan or Stuart, for the former lost his way; became so weak from lack of food that he was unable to go further; and wandered aimlessly about. The latter also suffered terribly from hunger, but kept on, hoping to meet with game at every mile. His men were footsore and dejected, for they entered upon a barren region where there was no game, and where even the coyotes seemed to have disappeared. They became desperate, and determined to throw themselves upon the mercy of the malicious Blackfeet, should they come across them.

With this end in view, the voyageurs kept a sharp lookout for Indian fires, hoping to gain food and assistance from the red men. Suddenly, in the far distance, they saw the twinkle of a little light and knew that some living being was near them. But it was late in the day. So they dispatched one of their number to see who it was, while the rest went into camp for the night. The messenger did not return.

Upon the day following, the exhausted plainsmen hastened in the direction of the fire which they had seen the evening before, and met their companion running towards them.

"Boys," said he, "'Old Bob' McLellan is lying by that fire in an absolutely exhausted condition. He is so weak that unless some stimulant is given him he will expire. Hurry and give him food from our meagre supply!"

This hastened the feet of the trappers, and reaching the place where the stubborn-minded old pioneer was lying, they discovered that he was in a desperate plight. A cup of hot coffee, however, soon revived him, so that he was able to struggle to his feet and join in their weary march. His rifle was carried by one of his companions.

The little party pressed on, luckily came across a "solitary," or bull buffalo, which had been driven

from the herd because of old age and infirmity, and
had the good fortune to kill it.   Strengthened by this
repast, they stumbled forward, and, by great good
chance, came upon a band of Snake Indians, who fed
them, gave them buckskin for moccasins, and, at their
departure, not only presented them with a goodly
quantity of jerked meat, but also with an old horse
to carry it.   Winter was coming on.   Small flurries
of snow announced the advent of the season, but they
were now nearing the river Platte, where was an
abundance of game.   The old scout had recovered
from his exhaustion and was once more the leader of
these heroic plainsmen, who had twice been upon the
verge of starvation.   Their emaciated forms had
filled out; their faces were sunburned and glowed
with health; while their spirits and their strength was
as of yore.

It was well into November when the party reached
the river Platte, where were quantities of antelope
and buffalo upon the grassy plains which rolled from
either bank.   They had a big hunt and collected sufficient buffalo meat to last through the winter.   Then
they built a hut of logs and plastered it with mud,
determined to remain here until the warmth of spring
made it possible for them to move further upon their
long journey to the settlements.   The days passed
pleasantly, but one morning they were awakened by
the wild screeching of a band of savages, and rushing
to the doorway of their cabin, found that they were
surrounded by fully a hundred painted braves.

" Well," said McLellan, " I — for one — am all

ready for a brush with the redskins, whom I hate as
much as I do old Lisa: the dastardly Spanish trick-
ster. So, my fine fellows, look to your rifles and we'll
have a little picnic."

"Not so fast," Stuart interrupted. "I believe that
these fellows are peaceably disposed towards us."
And — so saying — he stepped forth from the door,
rifle in one hand, the other extended towards the Indians. Several of them came forward, shook his hand
with heartiness, and intimated that they wished to
have peace and not warfare. One of the chiefs could
speak good English.

"We are on the war-path," said he. "We are
Cheyennes and our enemies are the Crows, who have
raided one of our villages, have stolen many ponies
and much dried meat. They shall be punished."

This was cheerful news.

"Well," murmured Stuart, "here we are between
two fires. On one side are the Cheyennes, on the
other are the Crows. As they are both upon the war-
path, we are in continual danger from each of them.
If a war party is defeated, it will doubtless wreak
vengeance upon us when returning from the fray.
The only thing for us to do is to take our chances and
move towards the East."

The situation was presented to the rest of the trappers, all of whom were of the opinion that they should
decamp. Winter was upon them and snow was deep
upon the ground, but, if they would save their lives,
they must leave at once. The raw-boned old horse
was loaded up, their packs were slung on their own

shoulders, and, upon the thirteenth day of December, the band of adventurers set off down the Platte. Snow-storms and bitter winds assailed them, but on they struggled until well beyond the range of the war-like savages. Here they built another hut, passed the winter in peace, and in March, 1813, started down the river in canoes which they had made from hollowed stumps of trees. After an uneventful trip, they finally reached the Missouri and were soon on their way to the frontier trading-post of St. Louis. Astor then learned what had happened to the adventurous souls who had attempted to reach his trading-post by sea.

The hazardous trip was over at last. "Old Bob" McLellan and his companions had crossed the wildest portion of an unexplored continent; had endured terrific hardship and exposure; but had brought home an accurate description of the virgin West to the hearing of many adventurous souls, who — thronging upon the border — were anxious and eager to press into the unknown prairie and mountain land. Two or three times the trappers had just escaped death by starvation. Twice they had barely missed a massacre by the redskins. Yet their courage and fortitude had carried them through every peril, and at last they were among their own kind, where appreciation of their nerve and valor was freely shown.

What of "Old Bob" McLellan, as he was affectionately called? Alas! The sinewy plainsman had been much broken by the hardships of this arduous journey to Astoria. Exposure and starvation had done its work upon the frame of the hardy man of

the frontier, and now he was unable to again venture
into the unknown.   Purchasing a stock of goods suitable for a trader, he opened a country store at Cape
Girardeau, near St. Louis, but the angel of death even
then hovered over the soul of the stalwart man of the
plains.   In a few months he quietly passed into the
great beyond.

Thus peacefully ended the career of one of the last
of the valorous scouts and pioneers who had forced
back the savage hordes from the Alleghanies to the
Mississippi, and who, even as old age advanced, had
plunged into an unexplored and unpeopled country,
to risk both life and limb among savage men and
beasts.   Red ran the blood in the veins of this vigorous Kentuckian, and he is to be remembered as a
good type of the venturesome pioneers who explored
and opened to white civilization the vast and unknown
regions of western America.   The hazardous journey
to Astoria quite equalled in danger that eventful pil-
grimage of Lewis and Clark, the first white adventurers to cross the Rocky Mountains to the Pacific.
Hats off to " Old Bob " McLellan.

COLONEL BENJAMIN LOGAN:

THE INTREPID FIGHTER OF THE KENTUCKY FRONTIER

"**M**OTHER, I know that the law allows me to have all of the property which my father left, but I do not want it. You can have your share, and to my brothers and sisters I give the remainder. I, myself, will move further West, into the wilderness."

The youth who spoke was about twenty-one years of age; tall, slender, and graceful. His face was open, frank, and expressive. As he ceased, he waved his hand towards the West and left the room in which his parent was sitting upon an old-fashioned horse-hair sofa. His name was Benjamin Logan.

Although the old English law of primogeniture prevailed in Virginia at this time, which gave the farm, horses, and farming utensils to young Logan (upon the death of his father) he refused to accept them. Instead of this, he nobly partitioned the estate between his mother, his three brothers, and two sisters, and removed to the Holston River. Then he began to farm a rough piece of ground, only part of which had been cleared of timber.

About this time the Indians upon the Ohio frontier became very troublesome, and Logan enlisted as a private in the army of Lord Dunmore, Governor of Virginia. Marching into the Indian country was a rough experience, but the youth enjoyed it, and when the red men signed articles of peace at Chillicothe, Ohio, the stout Virginian was among those who stood near the chiefs and saw them put their names to the agreement. Kentucky was now fairly peaceable. So the energetic young man moved his family to Harrodsburg, where a stockade had been erected called Logan's Fort.

"You must look out for the redskins," said a comrade to him. "Although they have signed an agreement to let us alone, my friends report that there are many of them in the vicinity, and they are all daubed up with paint, because they are upon the war-path."

"I will be on my guard," replied the young pioneer. "We must all run to the fort if there is danger of attack." The test was to come sooner than he expected.

Upon a balmy day in May, when the women were milking their cows near the gate of Fort Logan, and a few men were standing by, in order to assist them, a small band of redskins appeared at the edge of a thicket. *Crash,* a volley woke the stillness, and one of the frontiersmen fell dead while two staggered behind the log breastwork, with mortal wounds. A third — a stout fellow called Harrison — was unable to reach the gate, and dragged himself along to the shelter of some bushes.

Within the fort, all gazed with sorrow at the wounded pioneer, who, although in range of the Indian rifles, was so protected that the balls could not quite reach him. Those in the fort kept up a fusillade in the direction of the red men, making them get below cover, and thus the battle continued; the leaden balls zipping and whizzing across the place, where Harrison lay partially concealed. The man's family, in the fort, seemed to be in an agony of distress at his terrible condition. To save him would require great nerve and heroism. There were but fifteen men in the stockade; two were badly wounded. Should they sacrifice any of this small number in the endeavor to rescue a man, who, even should he be retaken, would be unable to fight in defense of the fortification? This question confronted the beleaguered pioneers, and it was a serious one.

At this moment young Logan stepped forward and said:

"Who will go with me to the rescue of this poor fellow?"

It was strange to see the effect of these words upon the besieged frontiersmen. At first every one refused.

"I'm not a fast runner," said one, "and know that they will easily catch me on the return trip, even if I am not shot before I reach the wounded man."

A second — a fellow of giant build — quavered: "I am a weakly chap. I never was no good, nohow, on liftin'. Perhaps you'd better git ernother stouter feller than I be."

Still a third remarked that, "he wuz plum onlucky with Injin bullets, an' never wuz known tew git amongst 'em in the open without havin' one uv 'em nick him."

Ben Logan could not help smiling at this.

"What, are you all afraid to follow me?" said he.

At this, a trapper called John Martin stepped towards him, and said:

"I will go with you, for I can only die once and I am as ready now to go to my Maker, as I ever will be. Come on! To the rescue!"

"You are a man after my own heart," answered the bold pioneer, grasping him warmly by the hand. "We will start at once."

Throwing open the gates to the stockade, both dashed towards the prostrate frontiersman. They had proceeded about five yards from the fort when Harrison made an effort to rise. As he got to his hands and knees, Martin turned and fled to the stockade.

"This is fine treatment," mused Logan, but he kept on under a veritable shower of bullets from the redskins. Fortune favored him; he was not hit, and reaching the wounded frontiersman in safety, clasped him in his arms, and began to lug him back to the fort. The deed was a noble one.

Bullets from the red men fairly poured around the struggling backwoodsman, as he staggered towards the stockade of logs. His hat was pierced by a ball; one even penetrated his hunting-shirt, but, in spite of this, he finally reached the doorway. Hurrah! As he deposited the body of the wounded man safely upon

From an old print.

"BEGAN TO LUG HIM BACK TO THE FORT."

the ground a mighty cheer welled from the throats of all. Hurrah! Hurrah, for Benjamin Logan!

Even the Hercules who had complained of being "a weakly fellow" threw up his hat in the air.

"Well, by Gum! Logan," said he, "if yew ain't th' plum luckiest feller I ever knowed. I believe that yew be charmed, so ez an Injun bullet can't hit yew. Ez fer me? Why, I would hev been struck er dozen times in thet hazardous journey. Huzzah! says I. Here's tew yer!"

But all danger was not yet over by any means. The red men were in numbers, and besieged the fort with a tenacity that made matters take a decidedly ugly look, for the few men of the garrison were not able to put up a very stiff fire against the increasing bands of Indians. Another danger also threatened, for the supply of ammunition became exhausted. How was more to be obtained?

Distant, about a hundred miles, was the frontier settlement on the Holston River, to which Logan had first moved when he left his farm in Virginia. Here was ammunition in abundance, and also supplies of food and clothing. Would any one have nerve enough to creep through and relieve the beleaguered garrison? This required the greatest judgment and unbounded courage, for the intervening country was swarming with savages, all upon the war-path. It was a region full of deep ravines, tangled thickets, and treacherous swampland.

Again all were asked to undertake the journey, but there were as many excuses as before. Again Benjamin Logan stepped into the breach and offered to bring relief. That night he clambered to the top of the stockade, dropped softly to the ground outside, and soon his form was lost in the shadows of the encircling forest. He passed through the Indian lines in safety, and, by daybreak, was headed for the post at Holston. His last words to the garrison were: "Hold fast! Hold on! I will be sure to return within a fortnight and you will all be saved!"

For several days the garrison returned the fire of the Indians with spirit, but, as the hours fled by, a terrible feeling of despair came over them. Their water began to give out; their ammunition was so low that they had to use it sparingly, and the food supply was in such a condition that there was danger of starvation if help did not soon arrive. Logan, meanwhile, was toiling upon his way through by-paths, swamps and cane brakes, having deserted the beaten trail through Cumberland Gap. Fortune favored him. He met with no prowling red men, and, within six days, had covered the distance to the frontier post.

The intrepid pioneer now procured ammunition, food, and a company of backwoodsmen. With these, he hastened onwards towards his beleaguered companions, and, upon the tenth day after his departure, suddenly appeared before the stockade. There were not twenty rounds of ammunition left in the fortress. Gaunt and hollow cheeks were here. Noble women upheld the fainting spirits of the men, but now, with little hope of succor, it was with difficulty that they kept up their fire upon the redskins, and put out the flaming brands which they kept throwing into the stockade. A wild and exultant cheer greeted their leader as he ran across the clearing to the door of the side wall. " At last you have come! " they shouted. " We had given you up for dead! "

A few days later Colonel Bowman arrived, with a large body of men, at which the Indians raised the siege and fled. But they had not gone for good. On the contrary, they fairly swarmed over the borders of Kentucky and their marauding parties committed some frightful outrages. There was nothing now to be done but to defeat them in a battle and burn their villages, if the white settlers were to have peace.

It was the year 1779. The Revolution was over. England had lost her colonies to her own sons. Now the Colonists were beginning the great struggle to free themselves from the curse of Indian invasion. An expedition was therefore organized to invade the Shawnee territory and to raze to the ground the famous town of Chillicothe. Benjamin Logan — now Colonel Logan — was second in command. Bowman, who had come to the rescue at Logan's Fort, was to lead the expedition; which was to consist of one hundred and sixty men. They advanced in the heat of July, and marched with such precaution that they reached the neighborhood of the Indian town without having been discovered by the enemy.

A plan for assaulting the village was now decided upon. It was very simple, for the force was to be divided into two parts; one, under Logan, was to march to the left: the other, under Bowman, was to march to the right. The men were to spread out in single rank, and when the leading files of the two columns had met, then, they were to attack. It was dark when the backwoods soldiers began the advance. Logan's men quite encircled the town, but where was Bowman? All through the night the leader of the left flank waited for the coming of the other column, but not a man in buckskin appeared. Hour after hour passed away and the darkness gave way to dawn. Still Bowman was strangely missing.

"Had you not better attack?" whispered one of his men. "The Shawnees will soon be awake and will discover our whereabouts."

"Let us wait another hour or two," answered the courageous leader. "I believe that the advance of Bowman's column will soon be here."

Logan's men were secreted in ambush. Here they remained until an Indian dog began to bark, arousing his master, who came out of his tepee in order to see what was the matter. An imprudent trapper had exposed his head above the underbrush, and the keen eyes of the redskin quickly discerned an enemy. He raised a loud war-whoop.

As he did this, a gun went off on Bowman's side of the village, and, seeing that further concealment was useless, Colonel Logan cried out to his men:

"Charge into the village, my boys. You must drive the redskins through the town, for Colonel Bowman will surely support you."

His buckskin-clad rangers defiled quickly into the village, and, advancing from cabin to cabin, soon had reached a large building in the centre. The Indians fled swiftly before them, but later, recovering from their surprise, endeavored to turn the right flank of the Kentuckians, whom they perceived to be in small numbers. Where was Colonel Bowman?

The Shawnees had now seized their own rifles and were pouring in a hot fire upon the advancing frontiersmen, who tore the heavy doors from the Indian cabins, formed a breastwork, and protected themselves from the whizzing balls. They were holding their own and were making progress towards the Indian citadel, where most of the braves had collected, when an order came from Colonel Bowman to retreat. His ranking officer had spoken, so there was nothing for Logan to do but to obey.

As soon as the men were told that they must go to the rear, a tumultuous scene commenced. Dispirited and disheartened by the order to turn their backs upon the enemy, they rushed away from the tomahawks and balls of the savages, as best they were able. The Indians were astonished and jubilant over the turn which matters had taken and pursued the rangers with wild and exultant yelping. The frontiersmen scattered in every direction, dodging and twisting in order to avoid the balls which whistled around them, and ran from cabin to cabin, in confusion. Suddenly they collided with Bowman's soldiers, who, because of some panic of their commander, had stood stock still near the spot where Logan had left them the night before. The redskins soon surrounded them on all sides, and kept up a hot fire.

What was the matter with Bowman? He sat upon his horse like a pillar of stone; gave no orders; and was in an apparently helpless mental condition. His men paid no attention to him, but swarmed to the protection of trees and stumps, took aim at the yelping red men, and soon held them at a safe distance. When they seemed to be quieted, the frontiersmen resumed their march. The Indians, however, came back to the attack, but were beaten off. They followed, and made an assault every half mile, or so. Their tenacity was due to the fact that they expected reinforcements and hoped to annihilate the whites.

"Keep together, my brave men," shouted Colonel Logan, at this juncture. "Do not let these redskins stampede you, for then you will all be massacred."

The crisis was a terrible one. The retreat would become a rout, unless the soldiers were kept together.

At this juncture Colonel Logan and a few of the boldest souls, dashed into the brush, on horseback, and cut down some of the nearest red men. As they performed this bold feat, the savages held back, and thus allowed the fleeing soldiers to get away. Only nine Kentuckians were killed, a few were wounded, and the rest escaped to the settlements. As for Colonel Logan, his gallant conduct, when under stress and fire, greatly increased his reputation, and at the next gathering of the Kentucky troops he was unanimously elected to lead them against the red men, when again they should need chastising.

The Indians remained quiescent until the summer of 1788. Then the frontier was again attacked by marauding bands, and so destructive was their advance that the pioneer militia had to be called out. Colonel Logan was asked to lead the troops against the enemy.

"Boys, I shall be delighted to do so," said he. "But this time there must be perfect discipline and no retreating. If you break in the same way that you did in our attack upon the Shawnee town I will not answer for your scalps. Let us have order, or we will never succeed."

"Lead on, Colonel," cried many. "You have the right idea, and none of us will go back on you."

The advance through the wilderness was most successful. Eight towns were burned, twenty warriors were killed, and seventy-five prisoners were taken. The son of a chief named Moluntha was carried off as a prisoner, and because of his brightness and promise was kept in Colonel Logan's family. He was called Logan, after his distinguished captor, and grew to be a majestic-looking man, six feet in height.

As for the Colonel, he returned to his farm after this campaign fully satisfied with his work, and determined to lead a quiet existence. This he was well able to do, for the red men had been so signally chastised that they no longer attempted to rob, burn, and plunder upon the border. His namesake, however, came to an untimely end.

During one of the campaigns by General Harrison against the Maumee Indians, Logan — the redskin —

was dispatched by his superior officer upon a scouting expedition with several companions. They met a large force of hostile Indians and were driven in to their own camp, where one of the white officers was heard to remark:

"Logan is a treacherous scoundrel. I believe that he will desert to those of his own color at any moment."

This was heard by the red man and he was stung to the quick.

"I shall prove this to be a falsehood," said he. "I am true to my white brothers."

Next morning he started towards the enemy with some companions and had not gone far when he found himself in an ambuscade, formed by the famous chieftain called Winnemac. Logan had the same cool courage which distinguished his white namesake.

"We are deserting to our enemies, the British," said he. "We no longer care to fight with the Americans. We are at heart your brothers."

Chief Winnemac grunted, but kept a watchful eye upon his captives as he carried them away. After the first day, however, he decided to return the rifles and other arms to the prisoners. He had counted too much upon the words of the savage, for Logan had determined upon escape.

"We will attack our captors to-night," he whispered to his two companions, Bright Horn and Captain Johnny. "There are seven. We will wait until some leave and will then gain our liberty."

As he had expected, after the camp-fires had been

lighted, four of the British sympathizers left, in order to collect fire-wood. They had not been gone over five minutes before the three captives had fired upon those left behind, killing all three. They reloaded, as the others came running to the camp, fired upon them, and forced them to take refuge behind some trees. As they stood confronting each other, one of the most wiry and skillful crept around to the rear of the American red men, pointed his rifle, and shot Logan in the shoulder. He fell forward, badly wounded.

Lifting him to the back of a pony, his friends carried him to the American camp, where he was placed upon a litter. Captain Johnny, who had left them upon the return trip, arrived next morning, bringing with him the scalp of Chief Winnemac. Logan lingered for a few days, and then succumbed to his wound. "I have removed all suspicion upon my honor," said he. "Now I am willing to die. My two sons must be educated by the people of Kentucky.

Thus perished the namesake of the noble-hearted Colonel Logan, who helped to clear Kentucky of the savage tribes, and who soon afterwards rounded out his life of splendid activity, and died universally lamented. To such pioneers the state owes a deep debt of gratitude.

GEORGE ROGERS CLARKE:

FAMOUS LEADER OF THE BORDERLAND OF KENTUCKY

O NE of the foremost of the pioneers: one of the noblest of men: one of the most daring of fighters: such was George Rogers Clarke of Virginia. Like Daniel Boone of Kentucky, Clarke was not only a brave warrior in the rough and ready armies of the Middle West, but was also a potent factor in the destinies of the American people.

Born in Albemarle County, Virginia, he early made his way to Kentucky. At twenty-three we find him engaged as a surveyor in this virgin land, and as he was a large and powerful man like George Washington, he could easily contend with the difficulties of his profession. So inspiring, in fact, was his appearance, that he was entrusted with the command of the militia upon his first visit to the border. He had a soldierly bearing and a grave and thoughtful mien.

After remaining for a time in Kentucky, this noble borderer returned to Virginia in order to settle up his affairs. He saw that a conflict would soon take place for the possession of the Middle West between the Americans, the French, the English — who had a chain of forts extending down the Mississippi from

Detroit, Michigan, to Vincennes, Indiana — and the redskins. Which party would win? That remained to be yet settled. Clarke, of course, sided with the American pioneers who were pressing westward from Virginia and Tennessee.

"The Indians," said he, "are incited to burning, scalping, and murdering our peaceful settlers upon the border, by the tongues of the British soldiers, who, supplying them with food from their forts, are continually egging them on to rapine and murder. Our only salvation, as settlers, lies in organization and military training. We must equip ourselves with arms and ammunition and must press against them before they grow so strong that they can crush us."

He suggested that the Kentuckians assemble in convention, and that there they should discuss the affairs most dear to the hearts of all. To this the people readily assented, and at this meeting chose Clarke, himself, and a man named Jones, as delegates to the Virginia Assembly. They were to go to the older state and were to ask for five hundred pounds of gunpowder for purposes of defense against the redskins.

When they expressed their wants they were met with a cold reception.

"We will *lend* you this important supply," they were told by those in authority. "But you must guarantee its repayment and must defray all expenses connected with its carriage across the mountains."

Clarke was indignant at these terms.

"This is not the treatment that brave borderers deserve," he said. "This should be a free offering to the men who stand as a breastwork between you yourselves and the redskins. If you allow your outlying posts to be swept away by the British and Indians, then the tide of warfare will roll over your own settlements, and you will realize — too late — the folly of your refusal."

To this remonstrance the council replied that they could not better their offer.

But Clarke was a fighter.

"You do not realize the dangers of your position," he again stated to them. "We apply to you for aid because you are nearest and dearest to us. But — if you refuse us — we can go to New York and there obtain our supplies. We have pushed into this country. We have settled it. We are of your own blood. We claim it. A country which is not worth defending is not worth claiming."

This was the way to talk to the hard-headed Virginians. After an earnest debate it was decided to recall Clarke and to comply with his request. An order for five hundred pounds of powder was given to him. It was to be delivered at Pittsburgh, subject to his demand, and for use by the borderers of Kentucky.

"I am deeply grateful to you, my brothers," said Clarke. "This gift will be well used and my people will be very thankful to you for it. God bless the noble settlers of Virginia!"

With a small force of seven men, the daring pioneer

now went to Fort Pitt for the powder, and carrying it in canoes, safely transported it to a place called Limestone, Kentucky.   Indians were thick in this country, and all were hostile.   But he came safely through the wild places and carefully secreted the powder at various points, where it could be found by the borderers when needed.

Daniel Boone was now an old man and was so modest that he refused to thrust himself forward and become a leader around whom the settlers could rally. All eyes, therefore, turned to Clarke, whose merits were now recognized as a gallant fighter and able commander.   The borderers saw that they here had an unselfish fellow who had their own interests in view, and who had obtained well-needed assistance for them. They knew that, without powder, they must be swept back before the storm of Indian invasion.   The time for a leader had now come, and destiny had sent to the Kentuckians George Rogers Clarke — the brave and the noble.

This soldier now addressed the settlers upon several occasions and in several different places.   He told them that they must assume an aggressive attitude and must attack the Indian villages, destroy their crops, burn their habitations, and teach them the horrors of invasion.

"We must not wait to be attacked ourselves," said he.   "We must do the attacking.   We must strike before we are struck, and must hit hard."

The Kentuckians were stirred by these speeches of Clarke and swore to follow him to the death.

" Lead on! Lead on!" cried they. " We will follow and will do our best to clear the land of our red enemies."

This pleased the leader of the borderers, for he saw that his own spirit animated his men. He therefore wrote to the Governor of Virginia, telling him of his plans for border warfare, and requesting aid. Men and ammunition were sent him. An expedition was speedily organized at Louisville — then called the Falls of the Ohio — and the border soldiers started down the stream in boats. At the mouth of the Tennessee River a party of hunters were met with. From them Clarke learned that the garrisons at Kaskaskia and Kahokia were fully aware of his coming and were quite ready to give his men a hot reception.

" The greater portion of the French," said the guides, " prefer American to English rule. You will find no difficulty in winning them over to your cause."

These men were taken along as scouts, and, creeping quietly through the wilderness, they surrounded and captured Kaskaskia without shedding a drop of blood. So kind were Clarke's followers to the inhabitants that many accompanied them on the march to Kahokia, — a town just opposite St. Louis, Missouri. Both places were populated mainly by people of French extraction who adhered to the cause of France in America.

Clarke was a diplomat. Some one has said that " he eked out the courage of a lion with the cunning of a fox." At any rate, he knew enough to make a firm friend of the parish priest, Monsieur Gerbault, who consented to go to Vincennes — in the absence of the British commander, who had gone to Detroit — and induce the garrison there to embrace the cause of the Kentuckians. He was successful. After a lengthy harangue the fort went over to the Americans and its command was given to a Captain Helm, one of Clarke's Lieutenants.

Clarke had accomplished what was thought to be the impossible. Without any difficulty whatsoever he had captured three forts and had persuaded all the inhabitants to join his standard. But these were the French. There were still the redskinned devils who would soon be burning, plundering, and massacring upon the borders. Clarke needed more men. So he promptly organized the French into militia companies with which to garrison the captured fort, appointed French officers to command them, and was thus able to use all of his Kentucky backwoodsmen in dealing with the redskins.

The French and Spaniards never asked for peace from the Indians but always harshly demanded whatever they might desire. Clarke determined to adopt their course. This kind of diplomacy is that which usually wins with the American Indian, for the red man could never comprehend why the whites would offer peace if they felt at all certain that they could accomplish their purpose by means of war. The Indians never made treaties unless they had met with a reverse and were in the presence of a superior enemy. When Clarke *demanded* like a warrior it suited their ideas much better than if he had *asked* like a squaw.

We now come to the most extraordinary event in his career: an event which marks him as a man of courage and capacity. When things were going against him he managed to turn the tide in his own favor with remarkable ability.

Braving great dangers and privations, he met the redskins in their own villages and conferred with them. Two attempts were made upon his life, but he escaped all harm and managed to secure a treaty of peace upon terms which the red men had first spurned. The treaty was signed and Clarke's eyes looked hungrily at Detroit — the great stronghold of the British. He had not sufficient men to take it.

Two detachments from his small army captured a British post on the upper Wabash, garrisoned by forty men. This aroused the British to greater activity. The Kentuckians and French were coming too near for either pleasure or safety. Besides this, the savages had begun to waver in their allegiance to the British flag as they saw the success of the pioneers from across the Ohio River.

Vincennes, as you know, had gone over to the Americans, and there was but a small force there of French militia. Two Americans were in charge: a Captain Helm and a Mr. Henry. On the fifteenth day of December, 1778, the English Governor of Detroit appeared before the town with a large body of rangers and demanded its surrender. The French militiamen immediately ran up a white flag.

Hamilton approached the fort, and as he neared it,

was surprised to find himself confronted by a cannon, behind which stood Captain Helm with a lighted match in his hand.

"Halt!" cried Hamilton. "My foolish fellow, I demand your instant surrender!"

"I'll never surrender," answered Helm, "until you settle upon the terms with me."

"You'll be allowed to march out with all the honors of war," said the British Governor. "And you will be held a prisoner until exchanged. The militia will be disarmed and paroled."

"All right," answered Captain Helm. "These terms suit me exactly.

Imagine the feelings of the good, old Governor. Instead of seeing a great body of men debouch from the fort, preceded by a brilliant staff, out marched a few ragged militiamen headed by Captain Helm, with one solitary private. It is said that the noble soldier could not help laughing. At any rate, he felt so well over the affair that he did not attempt the reduction of Kaskaskia and Kahokia — as he should have done — but was content to send parties of his men on forays against the settlements along the Ohio River. News was soon brought to Clarke of the capture of Vincennes. The old war-dog was much disconcerted. Hamilton in possession of Vincennes! It was almost past belief, yet runners soon came to him from the frontier, who confirmed the ill tidings. What was he to do? He had only two hundred men. Hamilton had three or four times that number. It was the middle of winter and he was short of all manner of supplies. The entire country was flooded. He had a single flat-bottomed batteau. Should he wait to be attacked, or should he attempt the seemingly impossible and endeavor to re-take Vincennes? He answered the question by turning, one day, to his compatriots, and saying:

"Whether I stay here or march against Hamilton — if I don't take him, he will take me. By Heaven, I'll take him!"

And to this his men cried:

"Lead on! Where you go we will follow!"

Now was such a march as the world had seldom seen before. The brave and valiant Arnold, who took his rangers through the depths of the Maine forest to the attack on Quebec at the outbreak of the American Revolution, was such a one as this lion-hearted pioneer. Arnold lost a great many men: Clarke did not lose any; but the difficulties of the journey were severe. Through the cold of winter, the chilling rain, the mud and icy water, — the latter often three feet deep, — marched the Kentucky rangers. They reached a miserable country called "the drowned lands," and for miles were waist-deep in the water. The way was full of crevasses and mud-holes into which some of the men sank up to their necks. Clarke was always in the front, sharing the hardships of his followers, and outdoing them in the contempt for peril and suffering. An occasional spot of dry ground — a few yards in extent — was a welcome sight to the half-drowned rangers. Still they pressed onward upon their mission.

" On, boys! " said George Rogers Clarke.   " We will take this post or die in the attempt! "

Splashing forward, the scouts and rangers soon reached the two branches of the Wabash River.   Ordinarily three miles of solid ground lay between the two streams.   Now there was a continuous sheet of water before their eyes.   The command stopped, amazed.   They had come to an apparently unsurmountable obstacle.   But there were no obstacles to George Rogers Clarke.

Striding to the front, and holding his rifle aloft in order to keep the priming dry, he dashed into the stream.   The rest followed with songs and with cheers.   But the chilling water soon made these cease, for it became an irksome task to breathe.   They staggered with fatigue, but their leader never faltered, and there was not a man who would have deserted him.   On the seventeenth day of February they reached the eastern shore of the Wabash and came to the lowlands of the Embarrass River.   It was nine miles to their goal: the fortress of Vincennes.   Every foot of the way was covered with deep water.

The situation seemed to be desperate.   Clarke, however, was not the one to despair.   Taking a canoe, he made soundings to see if some path might not be discovered through this inland sea.   There seemed to be none — the water everywhere reached to his neck.   The men were alarmed.   Their faces looked blanched and pale.   Was their march of untold hardships to end in death by cold and starvation?

A surprising thing now took place.   Whispering to

those nearest to him to follow his example, Clarke poured some powder into his hand, wet it with water and blackened his face as a sign that he would succeed, or die in the attempt. Then — uttering a loud whoop — he dashed into the water. The frontiersmen gazed wonderingly at him. Then they broke into song, rushed after him, and made for a ridge of high ground, which was followed until an island was reached. Here they camped, but next morning the ice had formed to the thickness of three-quarters of an inch. You can well imagine what were their prospects!

But Clarke was never daunted or dismayed. Making a speech to his half-starved and half-frozen command, he again plunged into the water.

"We must do or die!" said he. "On to Vincennes!"

With a rousing cheer his followers dashed in after him — pushed through the broken ice — and waded ahead. The water became more and more deep. Clarke feared, therefore, that the weaker members of the party would be drowned. Luckily he had a few canoeists with him, and these picked up the fainting ones and carried them to hillocks of dry land. The strongest were sent forward with instructions to pass the word back that the water was getting shallow, and they were told to cry "Land! Land!" when they got near the woods.

This cheered the drooping spirits of the fainthearted. The water *never* did get shallow. Woodland was certainly ahead, but when the men reached

it water was up to their shoulders and they had to
hang to the trees, bushes and logs, until rescued by
the canoes.   Some gained the shore in safety, some
were so exhausted when they reached a small island
that they could not climb up the bank and lay half in
and half out of the water.   Luck was with them, for
a canoe came down the river in which were some
Indian squaws and their children.   They were captured, and with them was some buffalo meat, tallow,
corn, and cooking utensils.   Oh, lucky find!   The
weak were now rejuvenated by a hearty meal.

They were upon an island of ten acres.   It was
truly an Eden for these half-drowned frontiersmen.
A long rest soon strengthened the weakest, and by
means of the Indian canoe, and a few batteaus which
had been brought with them, they ferried over to
Warrior's Island, within two miles of Vincennes, and
within plain view of it.   Every man feasted his eyes
upon the log fortress and forgot that he had suffered.

Let me here quote from Clarke himself.   He says:

" Every man forgot his troubles.   It was now that
we had to display our abilities.   The plain between us
and the town was perfectly level.   The sunken ground
was covered with water full of ducks.   We observed
several men out on horseback, shooting them, and
sent out many of our active, young Frenchmen to
decoy and take one prisoner, — which they did.

" We learned that the British had that evening
completed the wall of the fort, and that there were a
good many Indians in town.   Our situation was now
truly critical.   There was no possibility of retreat in

case of defeat, and we were in full view of a town with six hundred men in it, — troops, Indians and inhabitants.

"We were now in the very situation that I had labored to get ourselves in. The idea of being taken prisoner was foreign to almost every man, as they expected nothing but torture. We knew that success could be secured only by the most daring conduct. I knew that a number of the inhabitants wished us well: that the Grand Chief — Tobacco's son — had openly declared himself a friend of the Big Knives (Americans). I therefore wrote and sent the following Placard.

"TO THE INHABITANTS OF POST VINCENNES:

" GENTLEMEN : — Being now within two miles of your village with my army, determined to take the fort this night, and not being willing to surprise you, I take this method to request such as are true citizens to remain still in your houses. Those, if any there be, that are friends to the King, will instantly repair to the fort, join the 'Hair buyer' general, and fight like men. If any such do not go, and are found afterwards, they may depend on severe punishment. On the contrary, those who are true friends to liberty may depend on being well treated, and I once more request them to keep out of the streets. Every one I find in arms on my arrival, I shall treat as an enemy.

"G. R. CLARKE."

This was written by a pioneer general with two hundred half-starved, half-frozen, and undrilled troops. Behind the walls of the fort were twice this number of well-drilled, well-fed, well-clad men. We can but admire his audacity and impudence. But did he fulfil his promises to his people at home. And did he take Hamilton?

The frontiersmen were soon in motion and marched upon the town. A hill intervened, and when he reached it, Clarke deployed his men across it several times. When they would get over, Clarke would run them around the base to the rear of the knoll — where they would be out of sight of the people in the fort — and then would march them across again. In this way he made the inmates of the fortress of Vincennes believe that he had a much larger force than was really his. The borderers soon seized all the positions which commanded the fort and waited until dusk before beginning the assault. " I fear that they will know my numbers, if I attack during daylight," said the Kentuckian, "and this I do not want them to know."

As night began to draw near, the crashing of rifles awoke the echoes of the forest and the fort was hotly assailed from every point of vantage. The Kentuckians were able marksmen and soon silenced the cannon of the redoubt. No sooner would a porthole be thrown open than the gunners would be shot down as they stood. After an hour of such work the firing ceased, and the garrison was summoned to surrender.

Hamilton was dumbfounded at the audacity of the Kentuckians. He was also much disconcerted by the actions of one hundred of his redskin allies, who, seeing the boldness of the frontiersmen, immediately transferred their allegiance to them and were anxious to join in the assault upon the post. In spite of this he refused to surrender.

A far heavier rifle fire was now opened upon the fort, so that no defender could look out of a porthole or expose himself in any manner whatsoever, without being shot down. An assault was determined upon.

At this juncture a couple of figures emerged from the principal gateway of Vincennes, bearing a flag of truce. When the emissaries arrived before Clarke, they brought word that Hamilton proposed a three days' truce and an immediate conference. Clarke did not wish the British to know his real numbers, so he declined the truce. But he assented to have a talk with the English commander, some distance from the fort, at a place where the Englishman's eyes could not see the small numbers of the Kentuckians.

After a long interview nothing came of the pow-wow. Hamilton asked to march out with all the honors of war and to be allowed to depart to Detroit, after giving the assurance that neither he nor his men would ever again bear arms against the Americans. Clarke was afraid that the soldiers would not keep their word and demanded a greater amount of money and stores than the Britisher was willing to allow him.

" I have sufficient force to take the fort by storm

at any time I choose," said Clarke. " Furthermore,
I propose to capture all the detached parties that are
now in the woods and are headed for Vincennes.
Having put them out of the way, I intend to take
the fort at my leisure. I will thus — at one stroke —
put an end to all of those people that have been har-
assing the American frontier. In case I take you
by storm, I intend to shut my eyes and let my men
do their own pleasure, for such is the treatment that
has been accorded to our own people by the officers
of the Crown."

The conference broke up, and so terrified was a
Major Hay, who represented the English commander,
that he could scarcely make his way back to Vincennes.
As he wobbled along, a party of redskins — led by a
white man painted as an Indian — was seen to approach the town. The newcomers apparently had no
knowledge that the Kentuckians were foes, for they
walked up as if they were nearing their own people.

When they had approached within a few yards of
the men under Clarke, they were fired upon and two
were killed. Three others were badly wounded. The
remainder — six in all — turned in flight, but were
soon taken prisoners. They were tomahawked by the
red allies of the Kentuckians; their bodies were
thrown into the river; and wild war-whoops announced this fact to the red men in the fort. These
became enraged and frightened when they discovered
that Hamilton was unable to protect them.

Clarke only smiled, for he had hoped that they
would bring on a mutiny within the walls of Vin-

cennes, and it is exactly what occurred. Seeing that
he was unable to hold the allegiance of his own red
adherents, the once bold Hamilton decided upon capit-
ulation. On February twenty-fourth a white flag was
displayed over the log walls, and, after a short parley,
a truce was decided upon. The Kentuckians secured
fifty thousand dollars' worth of military stores. Besides this they detached the Indians from the English and took away from the Britons the entire northeast territory, which would otherwise have been held
by them when peace was concluded. Clarke, with his
two hundred raw Kentucky riflemen, had won a nota-
ble victory.

Think of it! The long march, the terrible rivers of
frozen ice, the lack of proper food, the toilsome journey through deep forests! Then the cheek and gall
of that saucy message to Hamilton, safe in a strong
fortress with twice the number of men as those half-
frozen backwoodsmen outside! Then the daring attack, the wonderful accuracy of the rifle fire, and the
final victory! Such men were heroes. Whether your
sympathies be with Kentuckian or Britisher, you must
admit it, and you must — I own — take off your hat
to Clarke: the twenty-seven year old leader of this
gallant band.

But what of the subsequent career of this wonder-
fully successful man? Alas! What we know of his
thereafter does not abound to his credit. To the
enthusiasm of youth he joined the daring ambition of
the born soldier: never satisfied. Always anxious to
move forward and on, he asked the Kentucky Assem-

bly for men and agreed to capture Detroit; to destroy the English power for all time; and to prevent further combination of unfriendly tribes of red men. He was promised both soldiers and ammunition, but they never came. It is said that in disgust at his forced inaction he took to drink for relief from his worries. He became dissipated, morbid, and a recluse.

For some time he rested in inactivity near the Falls of the Ohio, and about the year 1780 built Fort Jefferson on the Mississippi. He then journeyed to Richmond, Virginia, in order to appeal in person for the necessary means for taking Detroit. His plans were thought well of and were approved. But the measure never passed the legislature. Before it could be put into effect he was appointed to command a body of troops who were to check the aggressive operations of Benedict Arnold. He was made a Brigadier-General and was authorized to collect a large force, which was to meet at Louisville (the Falls of the Ohio) and was to fall upon Detroit and destroy this strong citadel of British authority.

Misfortune seemed to follow upon his footsteps. The force was never collected and the projected campaign had to be abandoned. He and his men had several brushes with marauding bands of Ohio Indians, and in 1782 took part in the unfortunate battle of Blue Licks, in Kentucky. Rallying a detachment of one thousand men, Clarke invaded the Indian towns, but the savages fled from their villages and scattered, so that there was no one to fight when the borderers entered. Fortune had forsaken George Rogers Clarke,

and, although in 1786 he led another expedition of
one thousand men against the Indians on the Wabash
River, it resulted in an absolute failure. His followers were mutinous. The campaign had to be abandoned. The hero who could inspire a march of two
hundred miles through half-frozen forests had lost his
former magnetism. He had begun to go down hill.

Dispirited, somewhat broken in health, and fainthearted, the bold frontiersman sought the seclusion of
his hut near the Ohio River. Here he was offered and
accepted a commission in the French armies west of
the Mississippi, for this land was then under the lilies
of France. An expedition was about to be made
against the Spaniards upon the lower reaches of the
river, but a revolution in France overturned the party
in power and destroyed all the plans of those in America. Clarke was soon no longer Major General, and,
forced to a life of inactivity, he returned to an isolated and lonely existence in his log hut. At forty
years of age he was a prematurely old man, and in
1817 he died at Louisville, Kentucky: a town which
was growing rapidly in size and which had been the
scene of many of his early triumphs. Exposure and
neglect of the proper laws of living had done their
work.

George Rogers Clarke was a remarkable man. As
a youngster he was brimful of enthusiasm, of vigor,
of magnetism. He carried an expedition through to
success in the face of fearful obstacles. Had he shown
the white feather for an instant he would have met
with ignominious failure. His courage, his cheerful-

ness, his optimism impelled him on to victory.   Had
he been able to govern his appetite for liquor he would
have been a man of splendid usefulness in his later
years.   His collapse at the early age of forty is full
witness to the deplorable effects of the inability of a
strong man to curb his passions.   One can but look
upon his career with sadness and regret.

JOHN SLOVER:

SCOUT UNDER CRAWFORD AND HERO OF EXTRAORDINARY ADVENTURES

TWO red men paddled down the White River, far in the western portion of the state of Virginia, one bright morning in the month of May, 1765. As they rounded a bend in the stream before them was a little trapper's son, apparently with no one with him. He was throwing pebbles into the water and was laughing as they splashed upon the surface of the stream.

"How!" grunted one of the braves. "I like to have young paleface in my lodge. I make him take the place of my own papoose, whom the Great Spirit has stolen from me."

"You can get him," suggested the other. "Come on, let us paddle towards the little one and capture him."

As the redskins approached, the boy looked at them with no sign of fear, and laughed at their solemn-looking faces. But they did not laugh. Instead of this, the one in the bow leaped upon the shore, seized the youngster, and carried him to the canoe, where he was bound by deer thongs and was quickly paddled down stream. His parents looked for him in vain that evening, and for many evenings, but their little

JOHN SLOVER.

son never returned. Thus John Slover became a ward of the redskins.

The Indians were then living at Sandusky, upon the Ohio River, and here the little white boy grew up to be a man. Adopted by the Miami tribe, he learned to love their ways, to live the wild, roving life as a trapper and hunter, and to be more at home in the forest than in the houses of those of his own race. In the autumn of 1773, a treaty was made at Pittsburg, Pennsylvania, between the Miamis and the whites, and at this place was a big gathering of the savages and frontiersmen, with their families. Jack Slover was interested in the affair and hung around the clusters of talkers, who were eagerly discussing the terms of the articles of agreement.

"Hello!" came a voice, as he was near one animated group. "If this isn't little Jack Slover grown to be a man! Turn around, son, and see if you don't recognize me."

The adopted ward of the Miamis spun about upon his heel, and there saw a raw-boned trapper, who was gazing at him with an inquiring eye.

"I certainly do not recognize you," he replied. "Who are you, anyway?"

The young fellow knew of his kidnapping, when a small boy, but had never cared to go back to his own people.

The frontiersman now seized him by the shoulders. "Why, I'm your father's brother, Tom Slover! I saw that you were not a Miami the minute I looked at you, and I found out that you had been captured many years ago by the Indians. Upon closer inspection it was easy to perceive that you were my brother's son. My boy, we have been waiting to find you for years. You will now come back to us, won't you? "

Young Slover hung his head, for he was loath to part from the friends and companions of his youth. He was on the point of refusing, but, just then, another frontiersman approached who announced that he was his father. The meeting between son and parent was not demonstrative; in fact, the youth rather drew away from his own flesh and blood. Soon, however, he became more reconciled, and, after an hour's conversation, agreed to accompany his kinsmen to their home in Westmoreland County, Pennsylvania.

The conference was soon over, both Indians and whites were agreed upon the terms of the treaty, and the captured son of the pioneer went back to his own country, where he seemed to be contentedly abiding at the outbreak of the American Revolution. He was one of the first to enlist, and, because of his experience in woodcraft, was made a sharpshooter. In this branch of the service he did good work, and was honorably discharged at the close of the struggle with the Mother Country.

Some years after the Revolutionary War — in 1782 — the redskins of the Middle West became very bold, and made frequent incursions upon the white settlements of Ohio, Pennsylvania, and West Virginia. Prompt vengeance was demanded by the pioneers who had penetrated into the wilderness and had there built their homes. An expedition was determined upon, and Colonel William Crawford — a brave officer of the Revolutionary War — was selected as its commander. The time and place of rendezvous were fixed for May 20th, 1782, at a point on the western shore of the Ohio, forty miles above Fort Pitt. There were four hundred and fifty volunteers; among them an accomplished surgeon, Dr. Knight.

Just before the expedition got under way, Colonel Crawford approached Slover, and said:

"My good friend, we are in need of a scout and guide upon our expedition. You know this country like a book, so I would like to engage you as one of our forerunners and assistants. Will you go with us?"

The adopted ward of the Miamis was reluctant to accept.

"I have lived with these Indians whom you intend to attack," said he. "I have slept with them; hunted with them; have eaten with them. Surely you would not have me turn upon all of my old friends?"

The Colonel smiled.

"Yes, but what sort of friends?" he answered. "Here they have been murdering innocent women and children. Have been burning homes, killing cattle and horses. They have been subjecting their prisoners to horrible tortures. You are too much of a man not to appreciate the need of checking these onslaughts upon our people."

"The whites are gradually encroaching upon their lands, — the lands which they believe that the Great

Spirit has given to them," replied Slover, in a deliberate tone. " Can you blame them for resenting these advances? They are children, too, of the wilderness and they fight like the wild beasts who surround them."

" Then you refuse to accompany us?"

" No, not so. Upon thinking over the matter, I believe that it is impossible for the two races to live side by side, unless one race is supreme. That the whites will overrun the country is only too evident. I will go with you, for I certainly do not approve of the manner in which they have conducted their warfare, and I believe that they must be punished."

The march was soon commenced, but, in a few days, some of the volunteers broke ranks and started for their homes. It was impossible to hold them. Further signs of insubordination were soon in evidence, some of the men demanding that they be sent back to their cabins, declaring that their horses were jaded and that their provisions were almost exhausted. Not long afterwards two skulking Indians were seen spying upon the advance. They were fired upon, but escaped. It was now evident that all secrecy was out of the question. The men grew mutinous and were so unruly that the officers requested them to continue for only one day longer, and then if no Indians were found they were to return. This was being discussed when one of the advance pickets dashed in, crying out: " The Indians are ahead of us about a mile. They are drawn up in the timber and are waiting for us!"

At this news a loud whoop came from the lusty

throats of the frontiersmen, and they discontinued their complaints. Priming their rifles and fingering their powder-horns, they pressed forward to the attack, while their leader, Crawford, who had fine military judgment, saw that the enemy had seized a position of great strength, from which they must be driven at once. He therefore urged on his men to the charge.

As the order came, the pioneers dismounted and rushed boldly upon the redskins in front and upon the flanks, hunting them from the woods, across an open field, and into some dense forest-land in the rear. Here the savages were heavily reinforced, and Crawford's Rangers were almost driven from the timber by the wily braves, who were now fighting from every bush, stump, hillock and tree. The battle waged with great fury until dark, when the savages withdrew, and the trappers slept upon the ground, ready to resume the affair in the morning.

As daylight appeared the battle was renewed at long range, neither side being anxious for a hand-to-hand engagement. It was plainly evident that the Indians were constantly being reinforced. Their whooping and yelling grew more and more derisive, and they began to extend their lines so as to flank the men of the frontier. For this reason, the officers decided upon a retreat.

Slover, the scout, was far over to the right, watching some horses, and no news of the intended movemen was brought to him. Soon the uproar of retreat came to his ears and warned him of his danger. He therefore selected the finest horse among those under his charge, mounted it, and fled after his comrades, who became rapidly disorganized. The red men fired a volley in the direction of the frontiersmen, at which one of the Crawford Rangers shouted: " The enemy have found out our design! Save yourselves! Save yourselves! "

Panic now became general, and so great was the disorder that it was plainly heard in the lines of the Indians, among whom was the famous renegade, Simon Girty. " Out, men," he cried, " and pick up the stragglers, for these Americans have whipped themselves! "

Those who had been wounded were dropped at the beginning of the rout and were speedily dispatched by the tomahawks of the savages. The rest fled in whatever way they could, without semblance of order or discipline, and, as they ran helter-skelter through the forest, were pursued by the exultant redskins with wild and blood-curdling whooping. Slover galloped along with some difficulty, as the ground was very rough, and soon found further obstructions in his path, for a wide bog lay before him, which extended for a great distance in either direction.

Some of the fugitives were unable to get across the bog on foot, but Slover and a few others were able to cross on their horses. As they fled on through the darkness of night, behind them echoed the horrid yells of the savages, the rifle shots of the whites, and the shrieks of the wounded. Six fugitives joined the fleeing scout, two of whom had lost their rifles, and, as the Indians were pressing them furiously, they headed for the settlement of Detroit, hoping to elude the red men as they went. They ran into another portion of the swamp a few hours later, and halted there for a slight repast of cold pork and corn bread — of which they had a small supply in their haversacks.

As they were seated upon some stumps, and were munching their repast, they were startled by an Indian whoop very close at hand.

"We are discovered," whispered Slover. "Hide yourselves, my men, in the tall grass."

Not many moments afterwards, a band of Shawnees passed by, laughing and talking among themselves, apparently with no idea that the pioneers were near. They were well satisfied with the signal defeat which they had administered to Crawford and his men; had many scalps and much plunder. When they were gone, Slover and his companions continued on their way, entering upon a sea of waving grass, which made it evident that any skulking red men would soon discover their whereabouts.

Silently they plodded across the prairie, but suddenly the man in advance called their attention to the fact that some moving objects were approaching.

"Lie low, boys!" he shouted. "I think that a crowd of redskins are just in front of us."

He was right, and, as they hid in the tall grass, a troop of Indians passed by, moving rapidly and noisily along. Fortunately the red men did not discover their trail, and with great shouting and singing had soon walked out of hearing. The trappers arose, continued their flight, and kept a sharp lookout for enemies. They were soon to meet with more children of the forest.

Two of the fugitives now became very lame and were unable to keep up with the rest of the party. One had a bad attack of rheumatism; so bad, in fact, that he fell way behind the rest and did not come up, although they whistled, called, and strove to attract his attention in every possible way, in spite of the danger of being discovered by lurking redskins. They finally went on without him, and gave him up for lost. He at length reached Wheeling in safety, having passed through many dangers and hair-breadth escapes from capture by roving Indians.

Slover and his friend were hurrying towards the settlements, and naturally left a well-defined trail behind them. This was followed for several days by a band of Shawnees, who finally decided that the whites would be easy to capture and determined to ambush them.

This they did, and, as the frontiersmen were quietly passing between some high bluffs, a volley rang out from either side and two of their number fell dead. The rest sprang immediately to the shelter of trees, where Slover took aim at one of the Indians who could be seen raising his hand.

"Do not fire," said he, in excellent English. "If you surrender to us, you will be well treated. We will take you to our houses and will allow you to leave, in a short time, for your own people."

Slover and two of the frontiersmen gave themselves up immediately, but a young fellow named John Paul refused to do so, and, rushing to the rear, managed

to get away. The redskins peppered the air with bullets, but none hit the fugitive and he got safely beyond
range.   After a long and arduous trip through the
wilderness, he at length reached the frontier settlement
at Wheeling, West Virginia.

As John Slover and his companions were being
taken along by the Indians, one of them recognized
him as the young paleface who had been brought up
by the Miamis.

" You no good, Mannuchcothe," said he. " You
fight against your own brothers. You kill your own
people. Ugh! Ugh! We fix you for this."

John Slover began to think that perhaps what the
savages had promised was not to take place, and when
once they came in sight of their town, their whole
demeanor changed. They began to howl and cry out:

" You are some of those who wish to drive us from
our country. Death to you! Death to you!"

The squaws, warriors, and children came running
to meet the captives and began to whip and beat them.
Then they took the oldest of the frontiersmen and
blackened his face with charred sticks.

" Are they going to burn me, Slover?" the poor
fellow gasped.

" Do not answer, Mannuchcothe!" shouted the Indians. " Do not answer! We will not hurt him! We
will adopt him!"

The red men now took the prisoners to Waughcotomoco, another of their towns, about two miles off,
but sent a runner in advance to announce their coming. As the captives came in sight of it they saw

hundreds of Indians in a double line, ready to make them run the gauntlet. This they did, and although Slover got through safely, the frontiersman whose face had been blackened, was knocked down, kicked, beaten, and shot full of arrows. He reached the council chamber, where he thought that he would be safe, and, although he seized one of the posts with both hands, he was torn away from it and was soon dispatched with a tomahawk.

Slover, meanwhile, was left alone, but he had no cheerful thoughts, for before him lay the bodies of Harold, the son of Crawford, the American leader; of a Colonel Harrison; and of several other prominent soldiers of the American army. They had all been killed during the retreat. His remaining companion was led away to another town and was never again heard of; while the gallant scout, himself, was now confronted by a young Miami buck, who said in the Indian language:

" Mannuchcothe, you must come before a council and must explain to the old men why you deserted our tribe. Mannuchcothe, it will go ill with you."

The sharpshooter did not worry, for he did not believe that his old friends would go back on him. In this he was correct, for there seemed to be no great amount of malice towards the ex-Miami, until the appearance of a white renegade — James Girty — the brother of the famous Simon. This scoundrel made an impassioned speech, in which he said:

" My Indian brethren, this white captive should suffer death. For not only has he deserted you for your enemies — the palefaces — but when I asked him how he would like to live with you again, he told me that he would care to remain only long enough to take a scalp and then escape. He is your enemy at heart and has even now been fighting against you. Death, and torture before death, would not be too severe for him."

The scout was outraged and angered by these remarks.

"What you say is not true," he replied. "I have never in my life made the statement that I would only remain long enough with my red brethren to take a scalp and then escape. I entered this war with reluctance, and I had not fired a shot up to the time that I was captured by my old companions. I am a friend of the Miamis and always will be their friend."

To these remarks the red men grunted an assent and allowed him to move, unbound, around the village. He was assigned to a lodge with an old squaw, who became very much attached to him, and, not many days afterwards, came to him and said: —

"That James Girty is influencing my brothers against you. If you have a chance to escape, you must do so, for I fear that they intend to put you out of the way."

Not long afterwards a council of Shawnee, Wyandot, Delaware, Chippewa, Miami, and Mingo braves decided that Slover had been untrue to their race, and that he must suffer punishment and death. Two warriors appeared before his wigwam in order to carry him away, but the old squaw covered him with her blanket and said that he should not go. When the two bucks endeavored to enter, she threw a pot of boiling water at them.

This was too much for the warriors, who retreated before the scalding fluid, but they soon returned with James Girty and forty Indians, who overpowered the fighting squaw. Slover was seized, bound, and his body was painted black. This was a sign that he was to be tortured and eventually killed.

Five miles from Waughcotomoco was another Indian town, to which the scout was marched. A vast number of red men greeted his coming with fierce cheering, and formed in two lines in order to make him run the gauntlet. As he raced between them, they struck him with clubs, with spears, and with their hands. In spite of this he was not badly hurt and could walk without assistance to another small town, two miles further on, where — in an unfinished council house — he was fastened to a stake. Brush was piled around his feet and this was lighted for his torture. " I will meet death like a brave man," said Slover to himself. Then, turning to the Indians, he cried out: " You shall rue the day that ever you put an end to John Slover. My white brothers will avenge me a hundredfold."

An Indian orator arose, and, with a fierce and vindictive speech, sought to fan the flame of the red men's passions to the highest pitch.

" How! How! " cried many voices. " It is well that the white man should die. How! How! "

Slover glowered upon the yelling mob as the crackling flames began to creep nearer to his feet. But now an unexpected interposition of nature occurred, which was greatly in the victim's favor.

A high wind arose; dense, black clouds covered the sky; the growling of thunder drowned the words of the orator and the yelling of his hearers. A sheet of rain burst upon the fire at the stake, extinguishing it completely, and Slover saw the Indians scatter to the cover of their wigwams, where they called out to him:

"We will burn you to-morrow. The Great Spirit has helped you, but he cannot save you."

The shower lasted for over an hour, and when it had concluded the red men gathered around the stake, where they beat and kicked their captive until eleven o'clock at night. Then a brave called Half Moon asked him if he did not want to go to sleep.

"I am exhausted," replied the scout. "If you intend to kill me to-morrow, loosen my bonds and let me rest."

Half Moon untied the strands which bound the weakened frontiersman, carried him to a log hut, and there bound him to a pole in the centre, with deer thongs which cut tightly into his flesh. A rope was placed about his neck and was tied to a rafter of the house. Three guards were placed to watch him, and, as Half Moon departed, he said:

"Get a good sleep, paleface. You will need it, for to-morrow you will eat fire. This is what comes to you for fighting against your own people."

The scout had not yet lost all hope of making his

escape, and carefully considered the possibility of getting away. Two of his guards were soon asleep; the third (an aged brave) smoked a long, clay pipe and told him that he had seen many palefaces tortured at the stake. " Some weep like squaws," said he. " Others bear it like men. You have once been a redskin and should be able to stand the fire without crying. You should come through without a bit of trouble."

On and on he thus rambled until he became worn out — his head dropped upon his breast — and he began to snore loudly. As the noise of his heavy breathing came to the ears of the scout, he began to work vigorously at his bonds. By wriggling, tugging, and pulling, at last his hands were free. He reached for the thong about his neck and began to chew it with his teeth.

As he turned and twisted in an endeavor to free himself from this remaining bond, day began to break and the pale light of dawn flooded the cabin. The talkative old Indian awoke; yawned; stretched; and looked around at the captive; but Slover clasped his hands behind his back as if they were still tied, and stood perfectly still. The red man turned over upon his side and again composed himself in sleep. It was now or never with the captured frontiersman.

Again seizing upon the rope, Slover gave it a few strong jerks, and, biting it with his jaws for a second time, suddenly parted it. With his heart bumping against his side like a trip-hammer, he stole noiselessly from the lodge. Not an Indian was stirring,

INDIANS TORTURING A PRISONER.

and, darting toward a corn field, he narrowly missed stepping upon a squaw with her two children, who were asleep beneath a tree. He crept through the growing stalks, and upon the other side saw quite a number of ponies. Taking the rope from his arm, he made a slip-noose of it; selected a fine, young horse; threw it over his head; mounted, and rode away like mad. His life depended upon his exertions.

As he dashed off, he heard a door open in an Indian lodge and knew that the red men were astir. They would soon discover his absence. He would be followed by all of the swiftest and hardest-riding men of the encampment. No wonder that he dug his heels into the flanks of his pony and urged him to do his very best.

At ten o'clock he reached the Scioto River, — now much swollen by the recent thunder shower. But his horse was winded and he had to stop in order to give him both water and breath, for he was blowing from his exertions. He plunged into the stream, crossed it, and continued his flight at the fastest pace which his horse was able to make. Finally the faithful animal began to pant and stagger. He was done for.

As the Indian pony fell upon his side, Slover leaped to the ground and heard a wild yelping behind him in the forest. He thus knew that the Indians were hot upon his trail. The horse had carried him seventy miles at a fast pace, which is extraordinary. But the animal was now lying prostrate, with the glaze of death showing in his eye. He had run a good race.

The scout bounded forward, loping through the

underbrush, timber, and tall grass, and leaving as
little trail as he could. But his exertions were wearing heavily upon him, and, about ten o'clock that
night, he fell exhausted to the ground. He lay in a
stupor for two hours.

When he was again able to move, a full moon cast
its silvery light over the dense woodland, where he
had fallen, and no sound broke the stillness of the
night save the weird call of a whippoorwill. The redskins could easily have captured him had they been
close upon his track, but his care in leaving little trace
of his flight had thrown them from the pursuit.
Breathing more easily, he again continued his race for
life, and, as day came, abandoned his trail for a low,
rough ridge, where was little grass or soft earth. On,
on, he continued, occasionally stopping to listen at the
sounds of the forest, but, except for the occasional
call of a bird, no voice came to his expectant hearing.
The red men had lost heart and had returned to their
wigwams.

As evening came, the frontiersman reached the
banks of one of the creeks which empty into the
Muskingum, and again sank exhausted to the earth.
The mosquitoes swarmed upon him, biting him un-
mercifully, and as his hunting suit (which the red
men had allowed him to put on when tied) was torn
to tatters by the nettles and briars, they had a splendid opportunity to get at his bare flesh. Some wild
berries furnished him with much-needed food, — the
first he had eaten since his escape, — and, if we are
to believe his word for it, he says that he was so terri-

fied with fear, that he had forgotten to feel hungry
during his flight. " I was fairly peeled from head to
foot by briars and mosquitoes," he has written. " And
I was now so hungry that I fell upon two crawfish
which I found behind a rock in the Muskingum, and
ate them raw."

The scout was now refreshed, and plunging into the
Muskingum, swam to the other shore. Two days
later he reached the Ohio River, opposite Wheeling,
West Virginia, and seeing a man in a skiff who was
apparently fishing, called out to him in a loud voice:

" Hallo! Hallo! Comrade! I'm a fugitive from
the Indians and was one of Crawford's men. Come!
Take me over to the settlement!"

The fellow did not seem anxious to hasten to his
relief, for he was afraid that Slover was one of the
white renegades who had joined the redskins and was
anxious to trap him. After a long harangue he finally
rowed to the place where the tattered scout was
standing. The refugee fairly hugged him for joy,
and, in a few minutes, was again safe in the settlement, where he was greeted with warm and affection-
ate regard by the other men of the frontier, who had
received many stragglers from the ill-fated expedition
under Colonel Crawford.

The escape of John Slover was one of the narrowest
of which there is any record in the annals of war
upon the frontier. No wonder that for many years
the story of this famous affair was the favorite topic
of conversation, when the after-dinner pipes were
lighted, and the men of the forest would sit before the

glowing embers, there to tell tales concerning the heroism and courage of the gallant settlers of the wild and undeveloped West. Truly the adventures which befell John Slover were the most thrilling of them all.

LEWIS WETZEL:

HEROIC VIRGINIA FRONTIERSMAN AND IMPLACABLE ENEMY OF THE REDSKINS

"BOYS, watch your mother and grandfather for a few hours, because I am going out fishing. There is no danger of attack from redskins, for none have been seen for six months. If, however, any one comes to our cabin with news of prowling bands, shoot off your rifles three times. This will warn me of any danger to you, and I will hasten home."

So spoke John Wetzel, whose cabin was upon the far western Virginian frontier, and, turning from his two little boys, he plunged into the wilderness. This was the last that he ever saw of his wife and her aged father. He had not been three days in the forest before his cabin was attacked.

Stealing carefully through the brush, a marauding band of savages suddenly made a sortie upon the isolated house of logs. There was not time to warn the inmates of the stealthy approach before the tomahawk and scalping-knife were at work. In an hour's time all of the inmates had been dispatched, except Lewis Wetzel and his little brother, Martin, both of whom

were carried off into captivity. Lewis was about thirteen years of age and Martin was eleven.

" We will soon escape," whispered the older youth.
" Wait until evening arrives and then I will show you
how to creep away from these horrible savages."

Lewis had been severely wounded by an arrow, but
he stoically bore the pain, and trudged behind his captors with no show of ill humor. The Indian prisoner
who lagged, or who made a cry of distress, would be
speedily dispatched by the savages, and this he knew.
The other boy went bravely ahead and said nothing.

Through the wilderness walked the red men, and
on the night of the second day they camped twenty
miles beyond the Ohio River.

" Ugh! " spoke a brave. " These children cannot
escape us now. We will not bind them with thongs
this evening, but will allow them to go free."

The savages had underestimated the daring courage
which was in the heart of Lewis Wetzel. No sooner
were the red men fast asleep, when, touching his
brother with his hand, Lewis warned him to keep absolutely silent and to follow him away into the darkness. They were barefoot.

" It is impossible for us to escape without moccasins," said Lewis, after they had gone some distance.
" This ground is full of stones, and our feet will be
ruined. You wait here for me and I will return to
the camp and get a pair for each of us, and then we
can easily travel through the wilderness."

The brave boy not only secured the moccasins but
also returned with a gun and some ammunition. Then

on they plunged through the forest. Just as the first streaks of dawn began to light up the gloomy depths, behind them echoed the shouts of their enemies, the red men.

" Walk backward upon your trail, brother," said Lewis Wetzel. " Then turn to the right and secrete yourself in the dense undergrowth. These red men will soon catch up to us and we must be thoroughly hidden."

This advice was followed, and it was well, for the boys had lain in the covert but a few minutes when their captors came bounding past. They were yelling to each other and were furious with anger at having lost their prisoners. The two Wetzels waited until they were out of sight. When the yelping had ceased they crept from their hiding-place and ran away to the right. In a few hours they heard the Indians again returning, and, secreting themselves in some underbrush, saw some savages dash by on ponies. They were not the same red men whom they had first seen, but these, also, could not find them. When the redskins were well beyond hearing, the terrified children ran to the river, fastened two logs together, and succeeded in crossing it. Not long afterwards they reached the house of a frontiersman and knew that they were safe. When they told him their story, he showed great surprise.

" Bully for you, boys! " cried the man of the clearing. " You, Lewis, showed particular courage and daring. You are a credit to your poor father, who is, I hear, terribly overcome by this butchery of the redskins. I trust that you will both live long and useful lives upon the border."

" Thank you!" cried the boys. " We will do our best, anyway, to avenge the terrible injury which the red men have inflicted upon our family."

Thus early was implanted in the breasts of the two Wetzels an implacable hatred for the savages.

It is said that Lewis was the strongest and most active of all of the youths upon the western borderland of Virginia, and by long practice had gained the ability to load his rifle while running at full speed. This was an immense advantage to him in his numerous affrays with the red men.

Not long after the terrible defeat of Colonel Crawford, in which John Slover was a participant, a pioneer named Thomas Mills arrived at Wheeling, West Virginia, where Lewis Wetzel was temporarily residing.

" I have left my good horse at Indian Spring, some five miles away," said he. " The country was so rough that I could not ride him here, for some redskins were upon my trail. Wetzel, I wish that you would accompany me to where he is, for I want to be able to hold my own with the savages, should we meet any of them."

" Mills, I'm your man," said Wetzel. So, upon the day following, they were on their way towards the spring.

When they arrived at the place where Mills had left his horse, they found the animal tied to a bush.

" That looks mighty suspicious," whispered Wetzel to his companion, " because I understand that you left him untied. Do not go near the animal until I circle around him and see if any savages are in our front."

The pioneer, however, neglected to heed this sage counsel and proceeded to untie the pony. As he reached down towards the bridle-rein, the head of an Indian appeared from behind a rock.

" Mills! Mills! Take to a tree!" yelled the scout. " There's a redskin drawin' er bead on yer!"

The warning was unheeded. The frontiersman continued to work on the bridle-reins; then a sharp crack was heard, and the red man fell back, shot through the forehead by Wetzel. At the same moment a series of quick reports came from the brush, and Mills sank to the ground, pierced by a half dozen bullets.

Wetzel started away on the run, for a number of top-knots rose from the bushes. Their owners hastened after him, but were uncautious enough to drop their own guns so that they could run all the faster. Knowing that he had discharged his piece, they expected to soon overtake him, tie his hands behind his back, and remove him to their own camp, to run the gauntlet and be tortured. They had counted without their host.

The lithe and sinewy trapper raced onward, exerting his utmost speed, and, finding that he could not get away from his pursuers, turned about and fired upon the nearest red man. The art of loading upon the run, which he had learned, was of tremendous assistance to him, for he was thus able to place a bullet in his adversary's chest, which stretched him upon the ground. Again he started forward, loading as he ran, and, turning a second time, was about to fire, when his nearest pursuer seized the muzzle of his rifle.

" Hah! Paleface! I have you! " cried the red man, for he had often been to the settlements and had learned how to speak excellent English.

" Not yet," answered the trapper, and he grappled with his antagonist. They were very evenly matched. By the greatest exertion, the white man succeeded in wresting the redskin's hold from his rifle, and in shooting him dead. It was a short struggle, but during it two Indians gained upon the man of the frontier, so that they were very close indeed. He now turned and ran as fast as he was able — loading as he went.

The Indians were whooping wildly, but they had knowledge of his skill in loading on the run. When he turned again in order to fire, they took hasty departure to the shelter of some large trees. He kept on going — the red men still after him. But he was a crafty fellow, as the following will show:

Having reached a clearing in the forest, he purposely stumbled and fell, as if exhausted by his race for life. The redskins thought that they now had him. They bounded forward with exultant shouts, but as they came nearer, the bold trapper rolled upon his side, raised his rifle, and brought one of them to the earth before he could get behind a tree. The second Indian turned and fled as fast as he was able, howling out in loud tones:

"HE NOW TURNED AND RAN AS FAST AS HE WAS ABLE — LOADING AS HE WENT."

"No catch dat feller. No catch him at all. He gun always loaded. He devil with the shooting stick."

At this the crafty trapper rose to his feet with a loud guffaw.

"These redskins have yet to learn a trick or two," said he, chuckling. "They should remember that some trappers can load their rifles when on the run. My fine fellows — Au revoir!"

So saying, he started upon his way to the settlements, lighting a corn-cob pipe on the way, and still chuckling softly to himself.

Not long after this affair, the father of the two Wetzel boys was returning from a hunting excursion into the Ohio wilderness. With him were his sons Martin and Lewis. The latter had just shot a brown bear, and carried the skin with him in the bottom of the canoe. As they were gliding down the river, a band of Shawnees suddenly appeared upon the bank.

"Come ashore, palefaces!" said one. "It is not good for you to go down the river!"

"Paddle to the other side of the stream," whispered the older Wetzel. "Hasten, boys, or their bullets will reach us."

Quickly they turned towards the opposite bank, but a volley of lead pursued them. They kept on doggedly. A missile struck the old pioneer, inflicting a mortal wound.

"Lie down, Martin!" cried he. "They will get you also, if you do not do so."

Then the heroic old man paddled forward, his life-blood ebbing at every stroke. Volley after volley zipped around the frail barque. Again and again the frontiersman was struck, so that when well beyond range of the Indian rifles he fell fainting to the bottom of the canoe. That evening he expired.

Standing over the body of their parent, both Wetzels took a solemn oath to avenge his untimely end.

"From now on," said Lewis, "I will use every endeavor to slaughter the red men. They have killed my dear father. Death shall be upon their own heads. Death and no quarter."

Not a week had elapsed after the sudden end of this staunch man of the frontier, when news was brought into Wheeling that the Indians were again upon the war-path. A scout came running into the settlement, crying:

"The Shawnees and Wyandots are approaching. They have slaughtered one man, and are burning, killing and scalping. Every able-bodied settler is needed to drive them away."

Immediately all turned out with rifle and powder-horn in order to repel the invaders. But before they started, a purse of one hundred dollars was made up, to go to the first individual who should take an Indian scalp. The trail of the marauders was soon struck; was followed for several miles; and was found to be very fresh. Then the advance scouts returned with the information that a large body of the enemy was encamped a few miles ahead.

"They are too many to be attacked," said the soldiers of the advance. "We must go back to Wheeling, or they will surround and annihilate us."

They set off upon the return, but they noticed, as they did so, that Lewis Wetzel did not move.

"Are you not going to accompany us?" asked some of the trappers.

The frontiersman scowled.

"I set out to hunt Indians and thought that this had also been your purpose," said he. "My object in hunting Indians is to kill them, and now that we have treed our game I do not intend to run off without a shot. As for you, I consider you to be a band of cowards."

"It is too bad about you," said they. "As for ourselves, we intend to return home."

Wetzel gazed after them with an amused smile, then stooped and examined his arms, for he was a man of caution.

"I will get a scalp of my own," said he. "Perhaps more. These fellows will see that I mean what I say."

There were plenty of Indian signs, but he could find no large bands of the red men; instead, he stumbled upon a camp with only two braves in it.

"There must be more in the encampment," thought he. "I will creep away; will come back this evening; and will then have an opportunity to get what I am after."

Turning again into the forest, he was soon out of hearing, and, by great good fortune, came across a red deer, which he killed. He had a fine feast. As night fell he hastened towards the Indian camp, crept close to it, and found only one red man, instead of a dozen or more, as he had expected. He waited until the redskin was fast asleep and then made good his boast. As he started upon the back trail for the settlement, a fresh scalp hung at his girdle.

Owing to his great strength and agility, he reached Wheeling just one day behind his companions, instead of three. They were delighted to see him.

" My boy," cried they, " you have certainly made good and are entitled to the greatest possible credit. Bully for you! "

The trapper in fact was more than a match for many redskins, as the following will show:

Not long after his return to Wheeling he went out into the forest in order to get some venison to dry and salt for winter use. He saw no game, but suddenly stumbled upon a camp of four Shawnees, who were busily engaged in tanning some deer hides. They did not see or hear him, so he determined to return at nightfall and single-handed to attack the party of braves. This he did.

First, resting his rifle against a tree so that it would be close at hand for any emergency, he drew his tomahawk, uttered a wild yell, and dashed in among the savages, cutting down one of them in a moment. Two more fell beneath his unerring weapon. The fourth darted off into the woodland with Wetzel close upon his heels. He was a good runner and got safely away, while the man of the frontier returned for the scalplocks of the three. He was back at Wheeling before two days were over.

"What luck did you have, Lewis?" asked a companion.

"Not much," answered the man-of-the-woods. "I treed four of th' pesky varmints. But one slick-ez-lightnin' feller got away. He had er close call."

At Marietta, Ohio, was a frontier fortification where a number of troops were stationed to protect the settlements from Shawnee invasion. Here General Harmer summoned several tribes to meet him in conference, and here Lewis Wetzel and a scout called Dickerson ambushed themselves near the Indian encampment with the intention of killing the first warrior who might pass. Wetzel, you see, was a vindictive fellow and did not even fight in the open.

The two assassins had not long to wait, for a redskin soon came by on the gallop without show or sign of fear, because a flag of truce had been delivered to the whites but a short time before. As he passed, both men fired, and, although the warrior reeled in his saddle, he clung to the mane of his horse with a tenacious grip and rode on into the fort. Here he dropped exhausted to the ground, and, before dying, cried out:

"My white brothers, I demand vengeance upon these hidden men who have driven me to the Great Spirit. You who have true hearts, see that I get what I desire, and my soul will then rest in peace."

When news of this was brought to General Harmer, he said, with much heat:

"Justice shall be done to this poor redskin. I hear from some of my men that Lewis Wetzel was respon-

sible for this affair.   Captain Kingsbury will therefore
take his company and scour the woods for the rascal.
Let him be brought to me, dead or alive."

Wetzel, meanwhile, had returned to his home in the
Mingo Bottom settlement and was engaged in a
shooting match for a turkey.   When the soldiers arrived, and the frontiersmen learned what they were
after, they gathered around their comrade with the
remark that:

"Whoever touches Lewis Wetzel will have tew
fight th' hull gang uv us."

Captain Kingsbury therefore withdrew, but Lewis
Wetzel was not careful to keep beyond the clutch of
his arm.   Some time afterwards he paddled down the
river to an island opposite Harmer's Fort in order to
spend the night with a friend, and news of his presence was brought to the soldiers within the stockade.
A company of men was soon headed for the island:
the frontiersman was surrounded at midnight; was
thrown into the guard-house, heavily ironed, and was
not only deprived of open air, but also of exercise.
He quickly sickened and grew pale.   When told that
he would shortly be hung, he sent for General Harmer, and said:

"General, I am not ashamed of my deed, for ever
since the day that my people were brutally slain by
the children of the forest, I have considered it perfectly justifiable for me to do unto them what they
have done unto me.   If you will grant me one request,
it is that you allow me to go loose among the savages
armed only with a tomahawk.   Then I will have one

chance in a thousand to escape, but I will take that chance."

The General shook his head.

" The scaffold is the proper death for you," he replied. " As an officer of the law I must see that you receive the fit punishment for your crimes. But, as I see that you are growing pale under strict confinement, I hereby order that the irons be taken from your legs. Your handcuffs must remain."

The trapper bowed his head, but as soon as the General had gone and he was allowed to move in the open air, he frisked about like a young colt. A number of soldiers guarded him closely, but as he walked and jumped around in front of them, he continually experimented with his handcuffs, in the endeavor to wrest his arms from their grip. Gradually he edged farther and farther from the guard. Finally he had moved to a position from which he felt that he could safely get away. With one mighty bound he had turned and was off into the forest. Volley after volley came from the soldiers, but he escaped untouched.

Wetzel knew well the woodland in which he found himself, and hastening to a dense thicket pushed through a close tangle of briars to a fallen tree. He wedged himself beneath this, and none too soon, for within a very few moments a number of Indians and soldiers approached. Twice some redskins sat upon the very tree beneath which he was crouching, and he heard one say:

" Ah, but the white dog would make good running

through the ranks of our red brothers. We must stick our knives into him when we find him."

At last darkness came. The trapper heard his pursuers returning, so he crept stealthily from his hiding-place and made for the river. He reached it in an hour, and by the light of the half moon, saw a frontiersman fishing from a canoe. He was afraid to call to him, for the woods were full of Indians, so he attracted his attention by beating upon the water with a stick. The fellow saw him; picked him up, and paddled him to the other shore, where his handcuffs were cut from his wrists. Next day he stood among his own friends.

Not long after this remarkable escape the trapper was at a fort on Wheeling Creek from which a number of pioneers had mysteriously disappeared.

" They have been killed by the redskins," said one of the backwoodsmen, who resided there. " How, where, and when, no one seems to know; but, my friend, there have been mysterious calls of turkeys in the woods. Turkeys, mark you, my friend, — wild turkeys! "

Wetzel pricked up his ears. He remembered that each of the men who had been killed had heard turkey calls near the fort: had gone out to shoot one for supper: and had never returned. The turkey calls had all come from one direction and here was a high hill covered with boulders. A small cave-like depression could be seen from the camp. Putting two and two together, he decided that Mr. Redskin had produced the call of Mr. Turkey and that it was Mr.

Redskin's unerring aim that had put an end to the lives of so many good frontiersmen. " I shall soon stop the twaddle of the fascinating tongue of Mr. Gobbler," said the scout to himself.

Setting out one morning, before day had broken, he soon drew near a hill, on the top of which was a small cave. It was an excellent spot in which to hide one's self, and, placing himself in ambush, he watched it narrowly. At sunrise he saw the tufted head of a Shawnee appear in the narrow opening, and the " gobble, gobble, gobble " of a turkey, sounded from the throat of the savage. The trapper bent low and watched the performance, for it was an exact imitation of the male bird. " Gobble, gobble, gobble," echoed again from the gloom of the cave, and, " crack " sounded the rifle of the bold pioneer. A wail of anguish arose from the cavern's mouth. Then all was still. The Shawnee gobbler had gone to the Happy Hunting Grounds.

Well pleased with himself, Wetzel started back to the fort with the scalp-lock of the enterprising brave, and, as he neared the stockade, met a soldier hastening towards him.

" Did you hear that turkey call? " said the enthusiastic sportsman. " I'm going out to get him, sure."

The scout pointed to his girdle.

" There is Mr. Gobbler," said he. " He was the kind of a bird that shoots a rifle. My boy, you should thank your lucky stars that I saw him first."

Not long after this event the frontiersman made a journey to the Kanawha River with John Madison, brother of James Madison, at one time President of the United States. They were busy surveying some land, and one day came to a hunter's cabin, which appeared to be deserted.

"No one is here," said Madison. "Let us take some of this jerked venison and also a pailful of this coffee. I do not believe that the camp will be again visited, and we may as well have the food, as to let the wood-mice eat it."

"All right," answered the trapper, and, without more ado, they appropriated what they wished, and continued upon their journey.

Early the next day, as they were crossing a small valley, many shots rang out, and wild war-whoops sounded from every side. Cries of "You give back our venison!" were heard above the din, and Madison reeled in his saddle, falling headlong to the ground. Wetzel did not wait to see what had happened to him, but, digging his heels into his horse's flanks, dashed off into the brush.

Now was a furious chase. Although well mounted, the scout soon saw that the red men also had good ponies, and he feared that they would catch him. Over the mountain paths they flew, for hour after hour. At last they neared a broad river, and leaping his horse into it, the scout swam to the other side. The red men had not the courage to follow where he had led, and thus he made good his escape.

The pioneer had a generous heart in spite of his vindictiveness to all savages, and not long afterwards had an opportunity to display his good feeling towards the weak and distressed. Going with a friend one day to pay a visit to a frontier house belonging to the Bryans, they found indications that the Indians had just been there, for the home was burned to the ground. Tracks in the moist earth led into the forest, and besides those of the redskins were the print of a woman's feet.

" Miss Betsy Bryan has been carried off, I fear," said Wetzel sorrowfully, pointing to the footprints. " We must rescue her even if it costs us our lives. Comrade, let us hasten to the chase."

His companion nodded, and, without more ado, the two men of the frontier followed the well-marked trail of the savages. Towards evening they crossed the Ohio River. Not far from the bank was a camp-fire, and, going towards it with great caution, they saw the girl seated near the flames. A white renegade and three Indians were her companions.

"Lie down, comrade," whispered Wetzel to his friend. " I will tell you when to rouse yourself, for we cannot attack until these redskins are asleep."

His companion obeyed, and waking him about two o'clock in the early morning, the scout told him to fire at one of the red men and then to rush into the camp in order to protect the captive. " I, myself, will attend to the renegade," said he.

Both frontiersmen fired at about the same time. The renegade was done for, as was one Indian, also. The two remaining savages took to their heels. Wetzel was after them in a jiffy, but, as they soon hid in the brush, he fired his rifle off, thinking that they might pursue him if they believed that his weapon were empty. He was not mistaken. The savages rushed from their hiding-places, gave close chase, and gained rapidly upon the running plainsman. They began to yelp wildly, as they thought that they had him cornered, but they did not know that this was the famous trapper who could load while on the run.

Turning about, Wetzel now shot the nearest red man, but the other kept on after him like a flash. The scout loaded while darting forward, as usual, then wheeling quickly, he dispatched this second assailant. His wonderful ability to load when at full speed had made it thus possible for him to thoroughly avenge the assault upon the frontier settlement and the capture of the inoffensive girl. Taking the scalp-locks of the two fallen braves and tying them to his girdle, he was soon back at the camp, where he was tearfully greeted by the rescued maiden. In a short time they were at home in the settlement.

Wetzel continued his life of hardship and adventure after this; made a journey south, where he was imprisoned at New Orleans, and, in 1803, joined Lewis and Clark in their expedition up the Missouri River. He left them after two months, and spent about two years near the headwaters of the Yellowstone, engaged in trapping and in hunting. From now on, until his death in 1818, he was a trapper and fur trader; his hatred for the redskins remaining unabated until his demise. He was camping near Natchez, Mississippi, when this occurred.

A braver man never lived than this famous scout,

who could load while on the run, and who had probably experienced more hairbreadth escapes than most
of the pioneers. His one great failing was his dislike
for the red men and desire to put them out of the
way, but, after one considers the distressing circum-
stances attending the death of the members of his
family, when he was a mere youth, one can pardon
this bloodthirstiness. There was much good in Lewis
Wetzel; the valorous frontiersman of the early days
of the settlement of the United States.

SAMUEL COLTER:

AND HIS WONDERFUL RACE FOR LIFE

WHEN Lewis and Clark were on their way to the Pacific coast they had with them two trappers, one of whom was to meet with extraordinary adventures. These were Samuel Colter and Lemuel Potts — both sturdy sons of the West — who obtained permission from the leaders of the expedition to remain near the headwaters of the Missouri River, in order to hunt and to trap. They intended to overtake the main body, after a short time, and hoped to obtain enough beaver skins to net them a good sum of money upon their return to civilization. You probably remember that Lewis had trouble with the Blackfeet, when near the Missouri, one of whom he had to kill because he began to run off the horses. For this reason these two trappers knew that they would have to use extreme caution or else they would fall into the clutches of some of these savages. The vengeance of an Indian is always swift and sure.

Knowing that the redskins were all about them, the trappers decided upon the following plan: they would lie hidden during the day, would set their traps late in the evening, and would visit them in order to remove the game in the gray of the early morning. Success met their efforts, and, before long, they had a goodly quantity of skins. No Indians were seen, although Indian sign was abundant, and they knew that there were plenty of Blackfeet in the vicinity.

One morning, while paddling up a winding stream where numerous traps were set, to their keen ears came the sound of heavy tramping.

"Those are redskins," whispered Colter. "Let's decamp at once, and get back to our starting-place."

But Potts thought differently.

"Those are buffalo," said he. "Wait until we round the corner and you will find out that I am right."

Just then they swirled around the bend in the stream, and to their dismay, found both banks fairly swarming with Blackfeet. Escape was impossible, and, although cold shivers began to run up and down his spine, Colter ran the bow of the canoe towards the bank.

The red men began to whoop loudly, as they saw them approach, and called to them to come ashore. This they did, and, as they stepped upon the bank, a burly savage jumped forward and snatched the rifle which Potts carried, from his hand. Colter was a man of great physical strength and courage, who was not afraid of twenty savages. He wrested the weapon away from the redskin, handed it back to Potts, and confronted the startled braves with a face filled with determination and fire. Potts jumped into his canoe, pushed out into the stream, and started to paddle away, in spite of the commands of Colter, who cried to him to come back and take him with him.

Suddenly an arrow whizzed from the bank and Potts cried out, " I'm wounded, Colter. I cannot come to your assistance."

In spite of this, he raised his rifle, fired, and killed the redskin who had shot him. A wild yelping now arose from the other savages, and, before five minutes had passed, the body of Potts fell into the water, riddled with hundreds of arrows.

Colter stood upon the bank, unarmed and alone. The Blackfeet swarmed around him; stripped him of his clothes and then held a pow-pow, while they determined what they should do with him.

" Let's skin him alive! " said one.

" No, whip him to death! " suggested another.

" Burn him at the stake! " shouted a great many.

The wrangling thus continued, until it was decided to let him run a race for his life. He was to get away if he could, but, if he could not, he was to be burned at the stake. All seemed to be much pleased at this decision.

A chief now approached the captive and said: " Paleface, you run fast, eh? "

" No, no, chief," answered the trapper, " I am very poor runner, I slow as the tortoise."

This was an untruth, for Colter was one of the swiftest foot racers upon the border, but his reply was hailed with loud shouts. Led upon a sandy plain by the chief, he was followed by six hundred armed red men, who gave him a start of three hundred yards, and then told him to go.

As Colter dashed away, a fierce whoop arose from

all the red men and they started in pursuit with continued yelping. In a few moments they saw that it would take their swiftest runners to overhaul the white man, for he sped along like a greyhound. They had, however, a great advantage over him, for his feet were naked, and there were prickly plants, sand bars, and sharp stones upon the plain. Their feet, on the other hand, were protected by stout deer-skin moccasins.

On, on, sped the gallant scout, although his feet were cruelly lacerated by the stones and shrubs. On, on, he went, while the shouting of the red men died away, as they perceived that he was out-distancing them. None caught up to him, in fact, he drew rapidly away from the very swiftest of them all.

After a run of three miles Colter glanced back over his shoulder and saw that one of his pursuers was holding his own with him. He had headed towards the Jefferson Fork of the Missouri River, and knew that if he once reached the water he could doubtless hide himself. The pursuing red man had a spear in his hand, and, so fleet was he, that he was soon within a hundred yards of the trapper.

"If I do not stop this Indian," said Colter to himself, "it is all over with me."

Straining every muscle in order to get away, Colter suddenly felt the blood gushing from his nose, and knew that a slight hemorrhage had been occasioned by his efforts. He was but a mile from the river, and, again looking back, saw the Indian within twenty yards of him. Escape was now impossible. Turning swiftly around, — he stood absolutely still and opened his arms.

The red man was astounded at this unexpected action, and, in endeavoring to check his headway, fell to the ground. The lance, meanwhile, flew from his hand and stuck into the earth a considerable distance from him, where it broke off. Luck was with the half-winded man of the plains, who now turned about, seized the broken spear-head, and darted swiftly to the side of the prostrate red man.

The trapper aimed the sharp lance at the Indian, and drove it into him with such force that he was pinned to the earth. A deep groan came from the helpless brave, as the backwoodsman again turned to run towards the river, although he was now exhausted by loss of blood and by the terrible race for life. His pursuers were still far behind, and he reached Jefferson's Fork so far ahead of them that they could not see him. One spring — he had leaped into the water — and was swimming towards a little island about a hundred yards from the bank.

Upon the edge of this had lodged a clump of sticks and floating brush. Colter made for it and dove beneath the tangled mass; emerging somewhere in its centre, with his head between two giant logs. Breathing with great difficulty, and faint from his exhausting run, he waited with throbbing heart for the red men to arrive. This they did very shortly.

They had stopped beside the body of their comrade and found that he was in his death-agony. Infuriated by this, and with terrific yells, they again set out in pursuit of Colter, who heard their vindictive screeching as they reached the bank. Some of them swam out to the island and punched about in the drift with their spears. As they did so, the trapper drew down in the water so that only his nose was exposed. He remained thus for about half an hour, when the redskins gave up their search and returned to the body of the fallen chieftain. Colter feared that they might set fire to the drift, but this idea did not seem to have entered the minds of the Blackfeet, who began a hideous wailing as they gathered around their leader. Carrying him upon their shoulders, they started back to their camp, and gradually their wild lamentations died away in the shadows of the forest.

The trapper was in a desperate predicament, for he was without either clothes or rifle. His feet had been lacerated by the stones and plants so that he could walk only with difficulty, and his body was chilled by his long immersion in the cold waters of the river. Certainly there was no brilliant prospect before him, for he was miles from any settlement. Would you not think that he would have become absolutely disheartened and would have given up in despair?

Not so with this bold follower of Lewis and Clark. After a day's rest and a meal of berries, grass and stalks from a shrub known as the sheep sorrel, he started for Lisa's Fort on the Yellowstone, a distance of a week's hard journey. Fortune favored this man of iron. Toads, frogs, and insects became his food, and with clothing of bark and reeds he finally reached the hospitable shelter of Manuel Lisa's trading station. He was scarcely recognizable.

Colter had suffered untold agony from thirst, from hunger and from cold. The evenings are chilly in this country — even in summer — and, although he made a fire by rubbing two dry sticks together, he shivered all through the night. The wild sheep sorrel had given him most needed nourishment, while the body of a dead rabbit, which he fortunately stumbled upon, had brought sufficient strength to carry him to the Fort. No wonder that the trappers there gave three rousing cheers for this frontier hero.

In ten days after his arrival at the group of log huts, Samuel Colter was again fit for service, but Lewis and Clark were already far away upon their transcontinental journey. He remained at the Fort, had several brushes with the Blackfeet, and eventually found his way back to the settlements, where he was much admired for his nerve and courage in eluding the wild denizens of the plains near the headwaters of the Missouri. Certainly he had good reason to be proud of his escape from the bloodthirsty hands of the Blackfoot warriors. Three cheers for brave Sam Colter! He well deserves to be remembered as a Marathon runner who ran a more thrilling race than the tame affairs of the present day, where no band of savages, who are thirsting for one's gore, pursue the struggling athletes.

MESHACK BROWNING:

THE CELEBRATED BEAR HUNTER OF
THE ALLEGHANIES

IN 1781 was born in Frederick County, Maryland, a pioneer who was truly entitled to the name of "The Mighty Hunter." The son of one of General Braddock's soldiers, who had settled in this beautiful country, Meshack Browning lived his life in the wild fastnesses of the then uncleared mountains of the Blue Ridge, and, at the close of a long and eventful career as a huntsman and trapper, could say with pride that he had killed from eighteen hundred to two thousand deer; from three to four hundred beaver; about fifty panthers; and scores of wolves and wildcats. He was the hero of every man's conversation in this mountain republic. All looked up to the hardy pioneer, and, after his long and eventful life was brought to a close, when well beyond eighty years of age, no one was more cordially missed than this sturdy old man of the mountains.

Young Meshack's father died when he was an infant of but two weeks of age, leaving his mother desperately poor, with one daughter named Dorcas, and three sons. It was a hard struggle to bring them up, but by working in the garden, by raising plenty of vegetables, and by spinning, saving and knitting, the good lady managed to scrape along somehow or other. Little Meshack had to learn how to use the rifle at an early age, for by this means only was it possible to supply the larder with fresh meat. Wild turkeys were abundant; deer, wildcats, wolves and bear roamed all through the rugged hills round about their home. Thus he quickly became expert in the use of the flintlock.

The hunting season usually began in October, and during this month the task was commenced of laying in the winter's provisions. Some days little Meshack would go out with a kindly uncle who had joined the family and would hunt for deer. On other days he would chase after bees, and as he and his uncle were most successful in this kind of hunting, they would often spend more time in searching for honey than in seeking venison. It would not be long before the table would be well supplied with both deer steaks and honey. The high, fresh grass which surrounded the log cabin would cause their cows to give a quantity of milk, from which little Meshack's aunt, who was an industrious woman, made plenty of butter; and frequently a fat turkey would be added to the store. Thus life was simple, easy, and healthful in the wild fastnesses of the Blue Ridge.

Things went on well enough until word came to the pioneers that General St. Clair's army had been defeated and cut to pieces by the redskins under Little Turtle, which you no doubt remember. This was frightful news, and little Meshack's mother was very much afraid.

" What if the Indians fall upon us here," said she.
" We could not protect ourselves against these terrible red men. Let us move further back into the
country where there are more white people. We can
thus combine for our own defense."

Meshack's uncle thought about the same way, so,
packing up their few belongings, the little family hurried to a place called the " Blooming Rose," where
there were thirty or forty other families. This was
in 1792 — long, long ago, it seems — and yet I, myself, have known old fellows of these mountains who
appeared to be well conversant with the terrible battles
of St. Clair, " Mad Anthony " Wayne, and the redskins under Little Turtle. These many struggles had
been often narrated to them by their parents; most of
whom had taken part in those stirring events.

Not long after coming to this settlement, the youthful Meshack had his first adventure with a bear.
While milking a cow one day, he heard a great deal
of noise at the house, and inquiring what it all meant,
was told by one of the girls who lived there that a
bear had just gone by. Running to the front portico
he there found that four or five gentlemen, who had
come to visit the owner of the house (bringing with
them their bird-guns, and several little dogs), had
gone in pursuit of the beast. The dogs were so small
that two of them would have made about a mouthful
for Brother Bruin.

The owner of the house, Mr. Caldwell, was a successful bear hunter and had two fine dogs which were
well trained to fight these animals. Meshack called

them, took the old man's gun, and ran in the direction of the noise, until he overtook the party of huntsmen, who had halted just as the bear reached a clump of woods. The little dogs would not leave their master, for they seemed to be afraid that the bear would tear them to pieces. But as soon as Mr. Caldwell's animals scented the bear, off they went, heads down and tails up. Meshack followed on behind.

On, on, coursed the dogs: on, on, went Meshack. Hastening towards the sounds of the fray, the young hunter saw both bear and dogs turning somersaults down a very steep hill. Over and over they rolled, Meshack after them as hard as he could tilt, and the way that the fur flew was most interesting. The fight became desperate, and the bear found that his hind-quarters were suffering severely; so severely, in fact, that he determined to climb a large tree. When half-way up to the lowest branches, he saw Meshack come puffing and blowing down the hill. This frightened him and he attempted to descend to the ground.

As he crawled slowly towards the sod, Meshack let drive and sent a small rifle ball through the middle of his body. The bear plunged to the earth, making two or three somersaults as he did so, but finding the dogs too ferocious for him, he immediately ascended a large oak tree. The oak being forked and very high, he went up to the first branch, and, lying down on it, refused to move. By this time the gentlemen who owned the little dogs had come up, and as many of them had never seen a bear before, they began to consult among themselves about what was to be done.

Meshack had no more balls for his little rifle and they had nothing but small shot.

After a lengthy discussion it was agreed to try and see what a load of shot would do for Mr. Bruin. Meshack agreed that it was impossible to kill the bear with that and told the other huntsmen to let the beast alone until he fetched some more balls, or else secured some one else to come and shoot him.

"Stand back and keep your counsel to yourself," cried one of the men. "We know how to handle this rascally bear. Let us finish him off!"

Taking aim at the animal's head, one of them again fired, but this only made the bear snort, scratch his face, and climb up the tree as far as he could go. Here he seated himself upon another fork, and, although repeatedly shot at, would not budge.

The bear hunters were feeling very much discouraged. After a long parley they decided to send for a certain pioneer called John Martin, who could shoot a squirrel off the highest tree in the woods. A scout was dispatched for him, and, at about nine in the evening, he returned with the famous marksman, who brought a rifle shooting an ounce ball. After the trapper had had full time to recover his breath, which climbing the high hill had rendered rather short, he placed himself in a good position and let drive. Mr. Bear remained in his place unscathed. Several more shots were fired by the old fellow, but Bruin simply hugged the limb in apparent comfort.

"Here, boys," cried one, "is a Mr. Morris — a Revolutionary officer — who has killed many an English soldier. Let him have a crack at this elusive mark!"

"Yes! Yes!" called several. "Give some one else a chance."

The new marksman cleaned and loaded his gun, took careful aim, and off went the musket. The bear snorted, groaned, and made a great fuss, but remained in its place. Another load was prepared and the Captain again tried his luck, when the bear, apparently provoked by such ill treatment, rose from his resting-place and started for the group. But upon arriving at the lowest fork of the tree, and seeing so many men and dogs, his courage failed him, and he again lay down. Mr. Martin tried two or three more shots without any result. Bruin seemed to be made of cast iron.

"Let me have a shot at him," said Meshack, at this juncture. "I believe that I can kill the old boy."

"Stand out of the way!" cried the Revolutionary soldier. "I am sure that I can finish him off, and I'll knock you out if you interfere with me."

It was getting dark by now, and Bruin was still unkilled. It soon was so dark that Mr. Martin could not see the powder in the pan. The gun missed fire.

"Here, Mr. Martin," cried young Browning. "Give me your gun, and I will finish this confounded rascal."

The old frontiersman passed him the piece.

"Take it," said he, "and good riddance."

Meshack felt for the powder in the pan and found it empty, but having some in a horn, he placed it carefully in the proper vent and was ready to try his luck. There were fourteen men now around the tree.

The young pioneer could only see the bear by getting him between himself and the sky, but he took the best aim that he could, and fired. Pow! Down came the bear this time with a thud; and, with a wild yelping and barking, the dogs made for him. A shout of horror arose from the bystanders as they all took to the trees, while over and over, down the steep hill, rolled the bear and the dogs, until they fell into a hole, where they stopped. A terrible snarling, yelping and growling now ensued.

The last shot had so disabled the bear that he lay upon his back defending himself valiantly as the dogs made for him. Meshack had now nothing to shoot him with, so he went in search of a club, and pulling a dry pole out by the roots, broke it off short, and went into the fray.

Creeping behind the bear, as he was reaching after the dogs in front, he struck him on the head between the ears, while down he went, the dogs attacking his hindquarters, meanwhile, and holding on to him tightly. The tough, old fellow uttered one despairing growl, then rolled over, stone dead. His end had come.

Meshack kept absolutely still, and, as he crouched near the bear, the back-track party began to come up. All had descended from their trees when they saw the bear rolling down the hill.

" Where is Browning? " asked one.

" Goodness only knows," answered another.

" I expect that the young fool has run on the bear and has been killed by him."

" Hello, Browning! Hello!" cried many.

Young Meshack would not answer.

" It's no use to call," said one of the tree climbers. " He's as dead as a door nail."

Still Meshack would not answer, because he wanted to hear what they would all say.

" Hello! Browning!" was repeated.

" What do you want?" at length cried the young pioneer.

" Where is the bear?"

" Here he is."

" What is he doing?"

" He is dead."

" Well, I reckon that isn't true, because you couldn't kill him without a gun or a tomahawk, and you haven't got either of them."

" I beat him to death with a club."

" By George! you are fool enough to do anything. We don't believe you."

So saying, they gingerly began to come nearer and nearer, until they were at the edge of the hole where the bear lay dead. They would come no closer until young Meshack took the bear by the foot and shook it in the air.

" By Jingo! he is dead!" said one. " Bully for you, my boy."

The young pioneer now held up the club with which he had dispatched the bear, and each took it and struck the dead beast on the head in order to say that he had helped to kill the long-lived animal, but no one congratulated Meshack. In fact, several let it be known that they themselves had killed the tough, old fellow.

The question now arose as to how Bruin was to be carried home. Some were for getting two oxen and a cart, but young Browning suggested that they carry him on a pole. This they did, and staggering and tumbling onward, the animal was gradually towed towards the house of Mr. Caldwell. The bear was laid in the kitchen, where the owner of the house came to view him and to taunt the back-trackers and the climbers for their cowardice. When closely examined, it was seen that Captain Morris's two shots had struck him, one passing through his ear, the other breaking two of his tusks, without doing any serious injury. No ball from Martin's numerous fusillades had touched him at all.

"Your shot killed the bear, Browning," said he, turning to Meshack. "If the bear's backbone had not been weakened by the last shot he would have undoubtedly killed many, if not all of them. As for these fellows who climbed the trees, it was a most cowardly trick, and the same thing would have occurred had they been in a fight with the red-skins."

This was very galling to the back-trackers, and they envied and abused young Meshack whenever they had an opportunity. When the bear was cut up they even did not wish to give Meshack a share of it, but Mr.

Caldwell insisted that he should have his just pro-
portion of the game.

" I have no use for the meat, sir," said the youthful
pioneer. " But if you will give me the skin, I shall be
glad to have it."

Mr. Caldwell immediately took up the hide and
presented it to him.

" It is justly yours," said he, " for my dogs treed
him, and you killed him. You have a right to the
skin, because it has always been a rule among hunters
that the first blood drawn takes the skin, be it bear
or deer."

Thus ended the young trapper's first bear fight.
It raised his reputation as a fearless boy, and made
him admired and respected by all the stout backwoodsmen of the Blue Ridge. Frequently, thereafter, when
he would be seated in the kitchen with the other children, they would induce him to tell the whole tale and
would ridicule the back-track huntsmen for their cowardly conduct. One of them, Miss Nancy Lee, said
to him one evening:

" Browning, I always thought that you were a
great coward, but I do not think so now. And I
heard father tell a strange man the other day that if
he had you in an Indian fight he knew that you would
attack the redskins as fearlessly as you did that bear.
Meshack, I have often wished that I had been born
a boy, then I would be some day a man and would
be able to kill or drive away the red rascals who followed General St. Clair, so that they would never
again come back to murder the whites. If you had

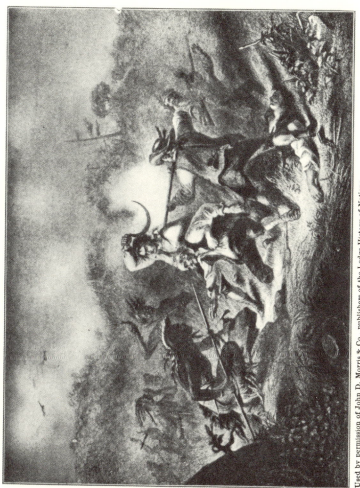

"THERE WAS EVER THE DANGER OF AN ONRUSH BY THE REDSKINS."

seen as much of their work as I have, you would feel
as vindictively towards them as I, myself, do. Let
me tell you a story about them:

"Some years ago, before General St. Clair lost so
many men in a great fight with the Indians, father and
mother were compelled to leave this place, and we
all went up to the Fort at Wheeling, West Virginia.
The neighbors were forced to vacate their farms, also,
and go into the stockade. My father and three or
four of his friends used to go out to hunt for game
sometimes, and a few pioneers always stood guard
while they were away. Others worked at planting
and harvesting corn and at chopping wood. There
was ever the danger of an onrush by the redskins.

"At length news came to us that the Indians were
in the neighborhood. The Fort was put in the best
possible condition for defense, and we awaited their
approach. But no attack came. Several days passed
by, no sound came from the depths of the forest and
it was supposed that the savages had given up the
assault. But such was not the case.

"One day two Indians made their appearance on
the high hill above the town, across the river, and
opposite the Fort. They fired their rifles at the stockade and then went slowly away, slapping their hands
behind them in token of derision and contempt for
the frontiersmen within the log enclosure.

"Many of the pioneers were outraged by such an
insult, for they were hot-tempered fellows. Several
began to run after the savages, and they would have
all gone had not the commanding officer stood in

the gateway and stopped them. Twenty-four of the boldest and most dashing ran up the steep hill after the Indians, who kept on retreating as if with no intention to offer battle. When the whites reached the summit, they suddenly found themselves surrounded. Crack! Crack! sounded many a rifle, and bullets began to whizz by on every side. They gazed about them in dismay. Fully four hundred painted redskins were on three sides of them. Their only hope was to turn and make a break for the Fort.

" The redskins, meanwhile, had moved to their rear, and, as the frontiersmen approached, put up a stern resistance to their assault. Many fell. Some escaped unhurt and dashed madly for their haven of refuge, pursued by the red men with wild, vindictive yelping. My father was one of the last to get through the lines, and, as he ran for his life, with a close friend of his before him, he saw his companion fall to the ground. As he passed him, the wounded man cried out, ' John, don't leave me to be scalped,' but my father ran on, as he knew that he could do nothing for him. A moment more and he saw a white renegade, who had gone to live with the Indians some years before. The fellow was close to him and carried a spear, mounted on a handle like that of a pitchfork. He was at my father's heels when they arrived at a narrow defile in the hill next to the Fort. A large tree was lying on the ground and another small one was standing very near it. Something tripped up my father's feet, and in he fell, between the two trees. As he went down, the white renegade made a furious lunge at him. The spear, however, glanced off the log, turned its point upward, and stuck so fast in the standing tree that the white savage could not withdraw it before my father leaped to his feet, escaped unhurt, and reached the Fort in safety.

" The poor fellow who had called out to him for help had had his thigh broken; but he crawled upon his hands and knees to a hollow log, in which he hid himself until dark, and then wriggled to the Fort. A short time later a frontiersman came in with his arm broken, but the rest all fell before the rifles, arrows and tomahawks of the redskins.

" Thus perished twenty-one of the best and bravest men in West Virginia. Their death was a great loss to the frontier settlements, as also to the strength of the Fort, which, in a few days, was hotly besieged by these same red men. Their success had made them bold. Having intercepted a boat loaded with cannon-balls, destined for the use of the garrison, the savages procured a hollow tree, bound it round with as many chains as they could, drove wedges underneath the chains in order to tighten them as much as possible; loaded it like a cannon, and, at a favorable moment, let go a most tremendous broadside. Whang! The whole thing exploded with a resounding boom, killing several, wounding others, and frightening the rest half out of their wits.

" They did not remain frightened, however, and soon renewed their attack upon the Fort. Near by was a log house belonging to Colonel Lane and the assault was mainly directed against this place, but the redskins were driven off. The powder became very scarce in the house, so it was proposed that some men should run to the log barricade for a supply. Among the volunteers for this dangerous task was a sister of Colonel Lane, who said that she, herself, would go. It was objected to, and the young men insisted on going themselves. But she was firm in her purpose, and replied that the loss of a woman would be felt less than the loss of a man. Pinning up her dress, so that her feet would have fair play, she started upon her dangerous mission.

" The Indians were perfectly astonished at this sight and did not fire a single shot at her. Thus she reached the Fort in safety, secured plenty of powder, which she tied to a belt around her waist, and off she bounded again for the house. The red men were not so lenient this time. Suspecting some mischief, they fired a volley of balls after her, all of which missed the fleeing woman, so that she reached the house in safety, with plenty of powder with which to withstand the future attacks of the savages.

" The Indians were now discouraged. Capturing a fat cow, they roasted her hind quarters, had a feast, and kept up a fusillade on the stockade while they ate the tender meat. When the repast was over, they all marched away in profound silence. As they disappeared, a settler at one of the port-holes drew a bead upon the last savage, but a random shot from somewhere in the forest dropped him like a stone. A wild war-whoop echoed from the sombre woodland and the Indians had vanished."

Thus ended the story of the attack. It was a thrilling tale, and Nancy concluded with the remark:

" I think, Browning, that if the Indians were to commence hostilities again, while you were living with us, you would fight for our family, wouldn't you? "

" Indeed," replied the young bear hunter, " no Indian would ever put hands upon you while life and strength was left in my body sufficient to save you from their accursed hands."

And he meant what he said.

Not long afterwards the young frontiersman was married, and desiring some bear meat for the winter supply, started into the forest in order to secure a quantity of this article. He knew where there was a swamp of black haws (trees of which bears are very fond) and so he walked rapidly for the bottom where these grew. When in sight of the place, he went around it in order to let his dogs have wind of the thicket. He had two excellent hounds with him, the older of which was sent into the swamp in order to raise the game. In he went, and he was scarcely out of sight before a loud snapping, howling, and yelping came to the ears of the eager huntsman.

The young dog was crouching at the heels of the trapper, but now he dashed into the thicket, also. Soon there was hard fighting going on. Meshack, himself, ran as fast as he could in the direction of the battle. When he came up with the dogs, the bear had taken to a tree, just out of their reach. He was a big, brown fellow; very sleek and shiny. As he heard the trapper rushing through the bushes he let go his hold, dropped to the ground, and was in an immediate battle with the dogs. Browning ran the muzzle of his gun against him and fired, but the bullet struck too far back to seriously injure Brother Bruin. As the musket went off, the dogs closed in and the fight became most desperate. The bear was giving them more than they could stand.

Meshack had dropped the gun in the weeds, and had no means of protecting his pets except by means of a large knife in his belt. It was now or never, for the bear had one of them on the ground and was biting him severely. In a few moments it would be all over with him. Therefore the trapper ran up to Brother Bruin and made a lunge at his side. The knife struck him far back, and did not cause a mortal wound. Still on he fought, though the blow released the dog, who arose and attacked the bear again with renewed energy, just as the beast attempted to crawl beneath a log which was raised from the ground. The young dog caught him by the nose as he went under, while the other seized him by his right hind leg. Both held fast, while Meshack ran upon him with his knife and dealt him two or three severe blows. Growling, snuffing, and breathing hard, the tough old Bruin rolled over dead.

This was one of many such adventures. There were also encounters with wildcats, panthers, wolves, and other denizens of the woods. With deer, also, there were many strange happenings, as the following will prove:

In February, 1800, the trapper and another young man, called Louis Van Sickle, went into the woods in order to catch a young deer, which Browning intended to raise as a pet. The Virginia red deer will become tame in two or three days, and even the oldest bucks will prove quite docile after a few weeks' confinement. Several had been so tamed by the trapper that they would come to him, put their nose in his pocket, would take apples or moss out of it; would eat this food, and would then search in his pockets for more.

The snow was about four feet deep as the two trappers went into the laurel swamps where the deer took winter refuge. As they drew near the edge of the swamp, they discovered many paths made by the animals as they came out of the thicket in order to browse upon the small bushes and on the moss upon the fallen timber. They struck off, down one of the paths, and soon saw seven large deer running and jumping up and down in the deep snow. They pursued as best they could, for they had snow-shoes on underneath their moccasins, and soon Meshack was far ahead of Van Sickle, who was unable to travel over the snow with any speed.

When the trapper reached the hindmost deer, the foremost ones, being tired out, had stopped to take breath. The last one attempted to pass by those in front and leaped into the deep snow, where he stuck fast. Meshack caught hold of him with the intention of tying him, but he was too fat and strong and fought viciously. They were struggling together, when Louis came up with a long clasp-knife and cut the throat of the buck. With the knife in his pocket, Meshack now ran after the others, and soon overtook them as they were crossing a small branch, with steep banks upon either side. A large tree, which had fallen over the stream, lay a short distance from the ground, where many leaves had drifted under it. One of the bucks, being hard pushed and greatly frightened, darted among the leaves, and thus escaped the eyes of the trapper, who had his attention upon the deer in front. Meshack passed by, pursued the others for some distance, caught a large buck, which he attempted to tie, but he fought him desperately, and was so strong that he could not handle him.

While engaged with this buck he heard Louis crying out from behind:

" Hello!   Browning!   Come to my assistance! Come quickly!"

Meshack left the buck and ran to the relief of his friend, thinking, as he did so, that he had probably fallen among the stones and had broken his leg, for the ground was rocky and full of holes. As he ran towards him, he said to himself: " If he has broken a leg, I will first take my ropes and will tie him to a tree, then I will pull it out straight, set the bone, and will tear up some clothes and wrap them around the limb, scrape a place clear of snow, build a good fire, and leave him here while I go for a horse and sled on which to carry him home."

He was to be agreeably disappointed. As he came in sight of his friend, he observed him lying upon his back with his knees drawn up towards his face, and his large, wide snow-shoes turned up to the sun. Before him stood one of the largest bucks, with his tail spread, his hair bristled up, and his eyes glowing fire. He was carefully watching the prostrate trapper, and every time that he moved the buck would spring upon him and would beat him over the head and face with his feet until he became quiet again. The irate deer would wait until Louis would make another move, then he would again jump upon him.

This was the same buck that had hidden underneath the log when Meshack had passed by. The animal had recovered his breath, and, as Van Sickle approached, sprang upon him suddenly. Striking the astonished trapper with his fore feet, he threw him backwards in the deep snow, and every time that the scout would attempt to arise, the deer would attack and strike at him until he would lie still.

How often the buck had repeated this chastisement before Meshack came in sight is difficult to say. When the trapper saw his companion lying motionless, and hallooing vociferously for help, he could not suppress a loud laugh. Van Sickle made several attempts to rise, but in vain; for the buck gave him a sound beating at every move. The prostrate woodsman was furious with rage. He cried out loudly:

"You intend to let me freeze here in the snow, Browning? That is death, anyway, and I am going to get out of this fix, or else lose my life in the attempt. Can't you drive this cursed buck away?"

As he ceased speaking, he made another move, and,

as the buck sprang upon him again with his fore feet, he reached up, passed one arm around the animal's neck, and then the other. Drawing the deer close to him, he vigorously endeavored to upset his valiant opponent. Meshack continued his laughter, for it was certainly a novel wrestling match, and the buck seemed to have the trapper at his mercy. He determined to let his friend fight it out to the bitter end, without any assistance on his part.

The buck seemed to be weakening after fifteen minutes of struggling, and Louis now raised his legs and threw them over the animal's back. The snowshoes were somewhat in the way, but he withdrew his right hand from the deer's neck, and, as he lay beneath him, began to strike him in the ribs with his closed fist.

" It's now your turn, you rascal," he called out. " You have had your innings, and it is now my opportunity. How do you like this — and this — and this ? "

Every time that he punched the buck the deer would grunt and endeavor to strike him with his fore feet.

Meshack had stopped laughing by now, and walking up to the fighting trapper, said:

" Let go of the buck, Louis, and I will finish him with my hunting-knife."

" No! No! " replied the woodsman. " I have a good hold on him now, and I refuse to let go until either he or I lose our lives."

He continued to strike heavy blows upon the buck's side, as Meshack seized the animal by the ear. Now determined to end the affair, he quickly dispatched him with his hunting-knife, and, as he dropped to the snow, the prostrate trapper drew himself to his feet with a loud shout of satisfaction and delight.

"Meshack," said he, "you have saved my life! If you had not come, I do not believe that I would have whipped this fellow, for he was the toughest customer that I ever tackled in my entire woodland experience."

Van Sickle was so upset by the beating which the buck had given him that he would never hunt any more unless Browning went in advance, and if a bush rattled, would jump back in deadly fear that another buck was coming after him. He was severely injured, having many black and blue lumps upon his head, and one very black eye. Two or three days later, he exhibited a long war-club, which he had made to defend himself with, as well as to attack the fighting bucks. It was eight feet in length, with a large knot upon the upper end, and was a deadly means of defense. He would never venture to the woods again unless Meshack went along, and, as the trapper would not go with him, he had no opportunity of trying his murderous instrument.

Shortly after this strange and novel battle in the woods, Meshack was asked by his wife to bring home some young turkeys for supper. Telling her that he could soon do this, he called his dog, Watch, and was off into the woodland. His faithful hound had been lame for more than a month from the bite of the last bear which he had tackled, and was still very stiff.

He frisked about his master in spite of this, and seemed to be all ready for anything that might turn up.

It was not long before the trapper saw three or four old turkeys with perhaps thirty or forty young ones. He sent Watch after them, in order to drive them towards him, but they flew into some low, white oak trees. When Meshack walked fast, as if he were going past them, they would sit still as they could for him to pass on. After taking twelve or fifteen steps the trapper would shoot off their heads. He thus kept on, until he had shot off the tops of nine young turkeys. This was sufficient for the larder, and whistling to his dog, he turned about for home.

Watch, however, seemed to be very much excited, and kept whining and sniffing, as if some species of game were near.

" What is it, my boy? " asked his master.

For answer the dog bounded away towards a large mass of rocks. Here he began to bark vociferously, so that the trapper felt sure that a bear was concealed near by.

" Fetch him out, boy! Fetch him out! " he cried.

Down went the dog, and into a crevice in the rocks, while Meshack raced to the other side. To his astonishment no bear came forth, but a huge panther bounded into the open, and, jumping from rock to rock, was soon out of sight. The dog followed along the rocks as best he could, and both quarry and pursuer were soon lost to view. After a few moments, however, the dog opened again, and seemed to be coming back on the other side of the stones and laurel bushes, which here grew in profusion.

Meshack turned to follow the dog. When he had gone a few steps he heard something moving, and wheeling about, saw the panther creeping close upon him. As he went behind some rocks Meshack levelled his rifle. When he came out the trapper fired, directing the ball, as near as he could, to the heart of the ferocious beast. The gun cracked. The panther sprang into the air, snapping at the place where the ball struck him. Then, turning towards the trapper, he came on, put his paws on a small, fallen tree, and looked his adversary full in the face.

Meshack drew his hunting-knife, and, as the panther made a lunge at him, struck at him again and again. The sharp claws ripped the hunting-shirt of the bold pioneer and gashed his arms, but the fierce thrusts of the hardened woodsman soon made the beast cease his attack. He crawled into a leaning tree, where he sat for a moment glaring at the man in buckskin, and then came to the ground. In spite of the fact that he was bleeding profusely, he soon disappeared into a rocky cavern.

The bold trapper has written:

"I was really glad of it, for I found myself so nervous that I could scarcely load my rifle, and, when the panther was looking at me, I was determined that if he made an attempt to come near me, I would seek safety in flight. He would have been obliged to ascend a steep hill, and, as I had at least five steps the start of him, I do not think that he could have caught

me. If any man would run at all, I think this would
have been as good a cause as any he could have
wished for. I know, furthermore, that I would not
have been distanced in the race."

In the meantime Watch returned.

"Heigh on, Watch!" cried the trapper. "Go
seek him out! Go seek him out!"

The dog was off in a jiffy, and descended to a large
mass of rocks where he could be heard worrying the
panther. The growling, snarling, and yelping soon
ceased, so Meshack hastened towards the sound. He
saw a den before him evidently in use for many years,
and in the opening lay the beast, stone dead. Watch
was licking his chops, as much as to say, "Now,
what do you think of me, old boy? Didn't I do a
good day's work, eh?"

Meshack was delighted, for the panther was evidently an old stager. He was of tremendous size.
Many a dead deer had been found in this particular
part of the forest in years past, so it was evident that
the beast had ranged the woods for a long time.
After his death no more half-eaten deer were seen
in the woods by the hunters and backwoodsmen, so
it was plainly evident that the mighty panther had
been the cause of all this loss. Certainly the trapper
had had a dangerous encounter, and had had a narrow escape from severe injuries.

Meshack had heard of a great den of bears on
Meadow Mountain, called the Big Gap, and on April
4th, 1803, he started out to hunt them with a friend
called Hugh. They were not long in reaching the

ground where the bears had denned, or "holed," as the hunters called it. "It was," says the trapper, "the greatest place for bear holes I ever saw in my life. I really believe that at least twenty had laid in one acre of rock. They had all left their holes when we arrived, in order to go out after acorns, except an old female and her younglings, which were located in a deep place in the rocks."

The dogs soon found this family of bears and attacked them, although the old one fought with great fury, while her cubs ran for their lives. As they passed by, Meshack shot at one and killed it, although Hugh missed the one at which he fired. The old bear had left her hole, meanwhile, and endeavored to follow after her young, but the dogs worried her to such an extent that she did not get out of sight of the hole before she was shot dead at the first fire. Two of the young ones escaped.

The two trappers continued their hunt, and in the evening of the same day fell in with another old female and two young bears. The dogs ran them all up the same tree, but the laurel was so thick that as soon as they shot the old one the young ones ran safely away, while the dogs were worrying the mother. The dogs soon finished the parent bear, and, setting off after the two young cubs, drew so close that they put up a tree. Running after them, the trappers were not long in dispatching the two fugitives. Thus, with two old bears, and three cubs, the huntsmen felt that they had done a good day's work. With great difficulty the booty was carried home by means of two horses, and enough meat was thus secured to last for the entire winter. Besides this, the hides of the young cubs made an excellent carpet for the cabin of the pioneers.

Soon afterwards Meshack purchased some cattle, and, as there were scores of wolves about, on the same night that he took his stock to his home he missed one yearling, which he found had been killed by a wolf. This made him very angry.

" Mr. Wolf shall pay me for my calf," said he, " and with interest."

Taking a shoulder of the calf, he laid it in a steel trap and placed the bait in a running branch of water, taking care to hide it very securely. On the third morning after putting out this snare he went to the spot and found that the trap had disappeared.

Rain had fallen during the night and every trace of the wolf's footprints was destroyed. Nothing daunted, Meshack returned home, called to both of his dogs, and endeavored to lay them on the trail. But they could not scent it on account of the great rain.

The trapper knew that the wolf would go to the nearest laurel swamp, to do which he had to cross a creek. Into this the pioneer waded and walked down it for some distance. Finally he saw where the trap had struck the bank as the wolf was crossing the stream. Wading back to the dogs, he carried them to the other shore, and harked them on the track of the wolf. At first the trail was very indistinct, but as they went forward it became fresher and fresher.

In about half an hour the dogs began to give tongue and soon were hot on the scent of the wary old fellow, who could not run very far because the trap was fast to his hind legs. Finally there was a terrible hullabaloo, and, running to the sound of the noise, Meshack saw that the wolf had taken to a hollow tree. His head was sticking out, and every time a dog approached, he bit at him and howled dismally.

The dogs were not afraid of the beast, and kept springing at him. Every time a dog would come near enough the animal would snap viciously at him, and, if possible, would sink every tooth in that part of his body which he could reach. He was a terrible fellow, — black and shaggy. Meshack encouraged his pets to do all in their power, crying:

" Hark on, boys! Lay on to him! Fetch the old varmint! Bite the old calf-killer. Hit him, boys! Hit him! "

Finally the strongest dog took a deep hold on one of the wolf's ears, while the other seized the remaining one. The wolf came out of the tree in a second, but the now energetic attackers threw him to the ground. Again and again he endeavored to recover his feet, but they pulled him over and over. They were all growing exhausted.

At this moment Meshack seized a club and took part in the battle. Again and again he beat the old fellow over the head. Again and again the dogs rolled him about. At length the fierce and ferocious beast gave a great, despairing kick, and it was all over.

The trapper was delighted. Taking off the scalp and hide, he returned to his cabin, and subsequently sold both for nine dollars, — the price of two calves.

"My good wife," said he, "I told you that I would make Mr. Wolf pay me well, with interest, for his incursions upon my cattle. I have done it."

And his wife answered:

"Meshack, you are a man of your word — God bless you!"

One other adventure of this famous trapper of the Alleghanies is interesting, for he had another startling experience. This time he was accompanied by his good friend, Hugh, who was often his companion in bear and wolf hunting.

Deciding to go after bear at the Big Gap, Hugh and Meshack went into camp within three miles of some rocks where many of these animals had previously been seen in abundance. They arrived at the hunting-grounds quite early, having one of their best dogs along, a fellow who could handle almost any bear, whatever his size. The animal grew very lively when near some rocks, and soon ran into a hole, where his yelping was intermingled with loud growls, showing that some large animal was inside. Again and again the trappers called to their faithful hound, but he would not come out. There were three holes out of which Mr. Bear might come bounding forth at any moment.

Meshack had given Hugh a bayonet, fixed on a handle like a pitchfork, with directions to run it through the bear if he rushed by him. He, himself, guarded the hole at which the animal was most likely to appear. The dog was making a terrific noise, as he struggled with the infuriated beast. The fight continued for half an hour, at the end of which time Meshack espied a part of the bear, when peering through a small crack in the rock. Putting his musket to the opening he fired. With a roar and rush the wounded beast dashed into the open.

"Run your bayonet through him, Hugh!" yelled the trapper. "Run your bayonet through him before he gets away!"

But Hugh was too timid to make the attempt. The enraged animal passed him with an evil snarl, and as he scampered to a tree Meshack vainly endeavored to ram another ball home in his rifle. The animal climbed slowly up to a limb and lay there growling evilly.

"Now is your chance, Meshack!" shouted Hugh. "Get after him! Give him a dose of lead!"

The trapper approached in order to secure a bead upon his victim, and, standing beneath the tree, was just raising his rifle so as to take good aim, when, with a mighty rush, Bruin came at him, through the air. It was an unexpected attack, and quite out of the ordinary, so you can well imagine what must the feelings of the trapper have been, as the bear whirled above his head. Stepping aside, he fired at the brown mass just as it reached the ground.

The fighting beast made a savage stroke at the trapper's legs with his right paw, but Meshack was too quick for him and jumped swiftly aside. Again and again the monster endeavored to get a blow in upon the pioneer, but each time the trapper dodged. Just then his dog appeared, seized Bruin by the hind leg, causing the old fellow to turn about, and snap at his antagonist. This gave the trapper a chance to load, and, quickly ramming home another ball, he pointed his flintlock at the struggling beast, pulled the trigger, and planted a bullet in his body near the heart. With a savage growl of despair the bear dropped to the ground, where the faithful dog soon terminated his career.

"Hugh, where were you all this time?" asked the smiling Meshack.

His companion approached; much abashed at the small part he had taken in the fray.

"R-e-ally," said he, "I feared that my weapon was not sufficiently strong in order to dispatch this monster. It might have bent, you know. Then, where would I have been?"

Meshack laughed loudly.

"Well, I reckon, you would have been bent, too," said he. "For this fellow was surely a scrapper. Here, help me swing him on a pole and we will take him home for the winter's supply of food."

This they did, and Bruin increased very materially the slender larder for the winter months, when snow covered the trackless forests and it was impossible to hunt, to fish, or to secure venison or bear-meat in the deep and sombre woodland.

The early settlers, you see, being but few in numbers, had a hard time to maintain themselves; if they had not been extremely economical they could not have lived in the wilderness at all. They fashioned their own clothes, they raised flax and wool, which the women spun and wove into linen and linsey for the men; and made flannel for their own wear. If any man wished to hire help there would be an understanding beforehand as to what the wages were to be paid in. Sometimes pork, beef, honey, or corn was used as a substitute for money. Sometimes a calf, pig, deer-skin, bear-skin, coon-skin, or a wolf's scalp would suffice. The settlers all lived in cabins, and fed their children on bread, meat, butter, honey, and milk. Coffee and tea were almost out of the question. A few of the older ladies, who had been raised in other parts of the country, alone could use these staples of diet. Meat was plentiful, for, if the farmers could keep the wild animals away from their hogs, the nuts and acorns would make them very fat. Pork, beef, bear-meat, and venison were easily obtained. Wild meat was not thought very much of, because it was most plentiful at all times.

Politics were little understood among the men in buckskin. Most of them were Federalists. An election was usually held on the first Monday in October, when all the settlers would gather at the polling booths, arrayed in hunting-shirt and moccasins, almost every one of them with a big knife stuck in his belt. A stranger would have thought this some military party going to war, and, if a quarrel occurred, the two contestants would rip off both coat and shirt, and fight until one or the other acknowledged that he was the beaten individual. Then their friends would take the bleeding combatants to the nearest stream and give them both a good washing. This would usually end the quarrel. The people were generous to strangers travelling through the country, and if a wayfarer lost his path a hunter would pilot him five, six, or even ten miles, until he was out of danger of being lost. They would refuse all compensation for their services.

In such a community Meshack Browning continued his life, and, in spite of numerous hairbreadth escapes from wounded bears and panthers, successfully escaped from any serious injuries, and he did not kill merely for the sake of killing. Honest and warm sentiments stirred his bosom, as the following story will show.

One day he was following a large buck, which ran into a crevice in some high rocks and there lay down. The trapper hurried after him, and, mounting a large boulder, eagerly searched for a view of the cunning animal. He stood on the rock and looked about him with the utmost care, but could see nothing of the buck, until casting his eyes down at the base of the rock directly below where he stood, there lay the fine fellow contentedly chewing his cud, apparently considering himself perfectly secure. He was watching the ground in front, not thinking that an enemy could approach on the side which the rocks so completely covered. Let me here quote the old trapper:

"The rock being fully twenty feet high, I was obliged to shoot nearly straight down, but when I saw what a complete advantage I had, it greatly marred my pleasure to think that such a noble animal, possessing all the beauty bestowed by a pair of fine, large horns, a well formed body, and tapering limbs; whose life had been innocently spent (never having committed an injury against either man or beast) should be thus sacrificed. My desire of killing him was so weakened, that I really had thought of letting him escape the death that was then hanging over him, but again it occurred to me that he was one of the creatures placed here for the use of man, that, if I let him go, probably the next hunter who caught him in his power would surely kill him, and that it would be as well for me to take him as to let any other person have him.

" So, taking a good aim, I fired at this monarch of the forest, when the poor fellow gave a few jumps, and fell dead. I declare the death of that deer gave me more real pain than pleasure. He was a large, old fellow, his head and his face being quite gray with age. I took his skin and returned to my cabin, having the river to wade and at least a mile to travel before I could reach home. The winter being then near, I believe that the death of this buck ended the fall hunt."

The seasoned trapper was not always accustomed to shoot bears. Sometimes he would trap them in large log traps, hewn out of the forest timber by means of the axe. To entice the animals into this box, he used to roast the leg of a deer, and, while the meat was cooking, he would rub honey over it, so that it would smell very strongly of the latter. Then he would cut off pieces of this sweetened meat, would tie them beneath his moccasins, would walk through the grounds which the bears frequented and would return to the trap. Every bear which smelled his tracks would follow the trail to the trap and would get caught in it.

Shooting wolves was also varied by trapping wolves, and for this he used to take a carcass of a cow or a horse, and lay it in a small stream of water. Then he would go off some distance, so that the wolf could not see where, and would cut bushes. He would stick the ends in the mud so thickly that the wolf could get at the meat only in one place, which was left open and clear. The carcass was so laid that the wolf could eat at either side.

A wolf will never jump over the bait, but will hunt the stream for a place to cross, in order to go around the other side, and eat. Therefore, the wise trapper would leave a passage for the animal to cross the water, and would set bushes about so thickly that they could not get through in any other place. The stream would then be widened where the wolves would pass, so that they could not step over it, and a flat stone be placed in the centre with green moss laid on top, so that it would look as if it had never been moved. Then meat would be cut into small pieces, and strewn on both sides of these crossing-places, both above and below the carcass.

When a gang of wolves would come to the meat the larger ones would drive the smaller ones off.

These would run about seeking food, and, soon finding the small pieces strewn about the crossing-places, they would run across, stepping upon the moss-covered stone as they did so. Every time they returned they would be sure to go over the place, setting their feet precisely in the same position on the stone.

The trapper would carefully watch the marks of the presence of the wolves. When he found that they made tracks on the stone by wearing away the moss with their feet he would remove the stone and put a steel trap in its place, covering it over with green moss just as he had covered the stone. When the animals came back, in order to seek food, they would cross as before, place their feet in the trap, and would be securely caught. The old ones, being at the meat when a young one would be caught in the trap, would not be afraid to return, — as there was nothing to scare them. After a while, however, all would become afraid of the crossing-places. Then wise Meshack would place his trap in the mud where they would stand to eat the meat. But after one was caught in this place, all would desert, and trapping would be over with this particular gang of wolves.

After capturing them in this manner for several years they became so cunning that they would not touch any bait which was offered them. The trapper therefore adopted another plan, which was as follows:

He found that they would pick up any fragments of old bones that lay upon the ground, but if they lay in water, or close to it, they would not touch them. He therefore saved all the large bones from the table, particularly the joint ends of beef bones. He would beat them to pieces, mount his horse, so that his tracks would not be scented, and would scatter the stuff over a considerable area of land. Around this space he would then stick some bushes; so that the wolves, in order to get at the mess, would have to pass through an opening in the brush.

The wolves would soon find the bones and eat them up. Then they would be given a second meal. But, meanwhile, a trap would be placed at the opening of the bushes and would be stuck in a hole of its own size. All the extra dirt would be carried away. The trap would be pressed down an inch below the surface. Old leaves would then be laid over it, and it would also be covered with an inch of buckwheat bran, which would keep the wolves from smelling the iron. Then the skillful trapper would take some of the grass, which grew around the spot, and lay it carefully over the trap, so that no eye would discern the difference between that particular place and the surrounding earth. When this was done early in the morning, or before a shower of rain which would destroy all smell, a wolf would be always caught as he came up in search of the little bones. The pioneer was most successful in this method of defeating the cunning of the shy and treacherous animals, who were so destructive to the live stock of the settlers that a considerable sum was paid for their scalps.

That the wolves were fearless the following story will bear full witness:

A friend of the trapper's called Mr. Calmes, was

travelling from Virginia to Kentucky with a number
of others, at a time when the Indians were very
troublesome. In passing through the wilderness they
saw so many trails of the red men that they were
afraid to keep a fire burning at night for fear that
the prowling savages might see their light and attack
them by surprise. They would therefore let their
wood burn until their supper was cooked, then they
would smother the embers and lie down in the dark.

One night they heard an animal moving around
them, and seizing their guns, made ready to shoot it.
But the animal, whatever it was, made off in the
woodland. By its tracks they could see that it was
a huge wolf. After the excitement had subsided they
all lay down again to sleep, and one of them so
stretched himself upon the ground that his head was
exposed outside of the camp. When he was asleep
the wolf returned, and, creeping upon him stealthily,
bit him so severely about the head that he died before
daybreak, without speaking a word to his anxious
companions. Mr. Calmes often said that had this
ferocious animal found a man in the woods by himself, and if it was at a time when he was particularly
hungry, he would have fallen upon him and would
have killed him at once. He wound up this grewsome
yarn with the sage advice to the trapper to kill all the
wolves that he could.

" Browning," said he, " your hunting is really a
great service to this country, for, if you come upon
one of these sneaking wolves, you must spare no pain
to kill him. There is no knowing how many cattle,

sheep, and hogs you will thus save to the inhabitants. I was going to tell you to be prepared for them, but I know that you understand the rascals and will take care of yourself. Whatever you do, do not let one of these bad fellows escape if you can help it."

Meshack Browning did not do so. His long and active life was one of constant battling with the wild animals of the Blue Ridge, and at the close of his career all could justly say that nowhere had a more famous huntsman ever lived in the eastern portion of the then half-settled United States. Now little game is to be found where once deer, wolves, bears, and wild cats were plentiful, and, although sturdy and honest men still reside in the Alleghanies, seldom does one meet with a character like this bluff old trapper and pioneer.

"HAD KILLED INNUMERABLE BRAVES IN OPEN CONFLICT."

"BILL" BENT:

HERO OF THE OLD SANTA FÉ TRAIL

WHAT one of the plainsmen did not know "Bill" Bent; "Bill," the fellow who had battled so often with the Comanches, Kiowas, and other Indians that they called him "The Red Panther:" "Bill," who had killed innumerable braves in open conflict; and "Bill" who had often just escaped the scalping-knife by a mere hair's breadth? The old fellow was a true plains' hero, and after you have heard some of the stories about his escapades with the redskins I'll warrant that you will agree that he was a marvellously lucky scout.

In 1829 the brother of this fellow — Charles Bent — was upon an expedition to the mountains near Santa Fé, New Mexico. With him were numerous others, well armed and well mounted. It was lucky that this was the case, for every day a cloud of Comanches and Kiowas hung upon the flanks of the moving line of trappers and kept up a continuous and rapid fire. Every night the trappers slept upon their arms, certain that an assault would come before the dawn. Bill Bent was several miles away — at a little frontier post — and, hearing of the peril of his brother and his friends, determined to ride to the rescue.

Old Bill rode a large black mule with split ears, which showed that he had once been owned by a Comanche brave. The Comanches soon sighted him, and about fifty of them made after him at full tilt. Arrows and bullets whistled about the head of the gallant scout, but he paid no more attention to these missiles than if they were flies. Occasionally he would turn in his saddle and drop some too eager buck whose zeal had outstripped discretion, and who had galloped within easy range of Bill's deadly Hawken rifle.

"Here he comes, boys!" shouted one of the band of plainsmen. "A brave fellow is after us, sure."

Bent came dashing up and reached two plainsmen called Coates and Waldo, who fired at the pursuing redskins, bringing down three of the foremost. Seeing this, the other Comanches retreated and left the little band to plod on alone. A force of one hundred and twenty Mexicans joined the party shortly afterwards, in order to be protected by them against the overwhelming numbers of the redskins.

The frontiersmen kept on their way across the lava dust and sage brush, but the Indians — although drawing off at a distance — still pursued. A famous scout called Ewing Young was travelling about twenty miles off, and from a fleeing Mexican heard that his brother trappers were sorely pressed. This particular scout was one of the bravest and most generous of men. As a trapper, hunter, and Indian fighter, he had few superiors. He had learned from a friendly redskin that the mountain canyon towards which the scouts were journeying was occupied by two thousand warriors, who lay in ambush waiting to entrap and annihilate the whites. Gathering forty trusty men-of-the-plains around him he rode to warn the fleeing plainsmen of their danger.

" By George, boys, there they are! "

One of the advance trappers spoke thus, as — from a summit of a high hill — he saw below him the vast horde of redskins surrounding and following the re-treating scouts with whom Bill Bent was associated. The redskins set up a wild whooping as soon as they viewed the oncoming whites. " Crack! crack! " the rifles began to spit and spatter at the advancing plains-men.

The scouts were courageous, but the odds were too great even for such valor as theirs. Swarms of In-dians enveloped them, shouting:

" Ki yi! ki yi! The palefaces will soon all be dead! "

At this juncture young Kit Carson first showed the material that he was made of. Riding out in front, he swung himself under his horse, — and shooting at a redskin from below its neck, brought him to the ground.

" Bully for you, Kit! " shouted Scout Young. " But these infernal redskins are too thick for me. I must break loose and retreat to Tavo."

This the plainsman speedily did, and, although pur-sued for some distance, finally got safely away. At Tavo a crowd of trappers were assembled for their yearly rendezvous. Ninety-five of them joined

Young, crying: " To the rescue of Bill Bent! To the fore! We'll clean up all the Comanches in the state! "

" Hurrah, boys! " shouted Young. " That's the kind of talk I like to hear. We'll get right after them."

The Indians, meanwhile, still pursued Bill Bent and his party.

The trappers under Young were not long in riding to the rescue of their comrades. As they came in sight the redskins gave whoops of disgust, for they saw that they were outnumbered and outclassed.

" Back to the woods! " shouted young Kit Carson, as he galloped his steed in the direction of the braves. " Back to the plains, for we'll get you now! "

As the party came on, Bill Bent's followers set up a wild whooping. " We're saved! " cried several. " Old Scout Young, we knew, would not let us be annihilated."

The Indians now became dispirited. Seeing the reinforcements coming up in battle array they quickly retired, chanting a death song, for they had lost fully fifty men in killed and wounded.

Bill Bent's followers were now free, and Bill, himself, was overjoyed to have saved his scalp. But he soon came near losing it again.

In the winter of 1830-1831, the tried and seasoned trapper, together with Robert Isaacs and a comrade whose name is unknown, made his way to Arizona, on a trapping expedition. For a time they met with fair success and saw nothing of the redskins. But one day they were surrounded by a body of Mescalero

Apaches, who were the fiercest of the savage tribes
upon the frontier. The Indians were one hundred and
fifty strong. There were but three trappers. What
chance had they, you ask. They had no hope of freedom, but, as Bill Bent expressed it: " We will sell
our lives as dearly as possible and we will make as
many redskins go under as we can before we, ourselves, will give up! "

The trappers threw up a rude stone breast-work
when first surrounded. They were working hard on
this, when, with terrific whoops, the Apaches were
after them on the charge.

" Go easy, boys! " shouted Bill Bent. " Make every
shot count! "

Two of the trappers fired as he spoke and two of
the chiefs fell to the sod. Before they could get out
of range the third man shot off his rifle, and another
one of the braves dropped to the ground. The
Apaches were not disconcerted and again returned to
the charge, but they were met by the deadly fire of the
reloaded rifles and the pistols of the trappers, also.

" Ugh! Ugh! " said they, " we've had enough!
We must go back! "

Conducting the siege now at long range, the
Apaches kept up a desultory fire for two days. Then
they retired in disgust, for they could not dislodge the
trappers.

" Hurrah! " cried Bill Bent, as he saw them going
away. " Boys, we can now get some water! "

The scouts, in fact, were nearly dead with thirst,
but they soon found a spring and refreshed themselves.

Leaving Arizona soon afterwards, they avoided any further trouble with the terrible Apaches, who, remembering the drubbing which they had received, were glad to allow them to retreat unmolested.

The old Santa Fé trail in New Mexico was much used by emigrants at this time and was well watched by the redskins. Should a train be slightly guarded it would be unsafe for men, women and children, for the Indians would make short work of them. This deterred all except the boldest spirits from venturing where was certain peril and probable death. But among the heroes who were still willing to encounter the fearful odds of Indian combat were to be found Bill Bent, his brother Charles, the Waldos, and a few others whom no danger ever daunted, and who saw a splendid field for trade in this country. In 1839 a party of these men applied to Andrew Jackson, who had just taken his seat as President. They asked for a military escort to accompany them to the Arkansas River, which — at that time — formed the boundary between Mexico and the United States.

This request was speedily granted, and Major Bennett Riley was detailed, with two hundred men, to meet the emigrants at Fort Leavenworth and to accompany them to the Arkansas River. The traders met at Round Grove, Missouri, where Charles Bent was chosen Captain and where Bill Bent also joined. With thirty-six wagons, fully freighted with valuable goods, they set out for Santa Fé, New Mexico.

In due time they reached the Arkansas River at Chateau's Island, and here the traders bade farewell to the gallant Major and his brave soldiers. Plunging into the shallow waters of the stream they were soon on Mexican soil. But their troubles now commenced. The dry sand engulfed their wagon wheels almost to the hubs, stalling the teams, and utterly preventing an orderly march.

"Close up! Close up!" Bill Bent kept shouting.

But in spite of these orders, the wagons were soon strung over a half a mile of road. Advance and rear detachments had been thrown out to guard against surprise, but either through the negligence of the videttes, or from the completeness with which the Indians had concealed themselves, they had only gone nine miles when the savages seemed to spring out of the very bowels of the earth. Their rifles spat a deadly fire.

"My stars, look at the redskins!" cried Bill Bent. "They're after us, for sure, this time!"

The surprise had been complete, but Charles Bent — mounted upon a large, black horse — with his long, dark hair floating upon the wind, dashed up and down the line, forming his men. Every ravine swarmed with the redskins, and, although they yelled fiercely, above their loud calls could be heard the voice of Charles Bent.

"Close up, men! Close up!" he kept shouting. "It's our only chance! And keep cool! Keep cool!"

Two of the men had been lagging in the rear of the train, and, at the first fire, one fell dead, while the other — with fifty Indians in pursuit — dashed for the wagons. Escape seemed to be impossible, but

Bent saw the situation at a glance and charged towards the advancing savages with twenty scouts. The Indians drew off at this show of force, and the fleeing trapper was thus able to join his comrades.

Crash! Crash! sounded the rifles, and the battle continued to rage with fury. Nothing but Bent's coolness and the desperate bravery of his men prevented a charge by the red men, who numbered at least a thousand. Luckily a small, brass cannon was in the train — the first that ever crossed the Arkansas — and, as it spat its fire, the Comanches withdrew.

The trappers now dug rifle-pits, but Bent soon saw that without water his men would be unable to hold their own.

" Who will creep through the hostile redskins and go after Major Riley and his men? " he asked. " Unless we get his aid we will have to give in to these frightfully bloodthirsty savages! "

" I will go! I will go! " came from the throats of many. In fact all seemed to wish to undertake the hazardous journey.

Captain Bent could not help laughing. Nine were finally selected for the trip. They knew that their only salvation lay in their rifles, for their mules were so worn down by fatigue that flight was out of the question.

They rode out expecting to have a tough time of it, but the redskins allowed them to pass through their lines without firing a single shot at them. Spurring on their broken-down beasts they hastened towards

the Arkansas River, where they still hoped to find
Major Riley with his troops.

The Major was surely there. He saw them coming
away off on the plains, and, striking his tents, was
all prepared to meet them when they arrived.

" Gentlemen," said he, when he heard their story,
" it is a breach of national etiquette for me to cross
the boundary line into Mexico — a friendly power —
but blood is thicker than water, and I cannot see my
countrymen suffer. I will be with you as soon as my
troops can pack up."

The soldiers were soon on their way. So rapid and
silent was the approach of the force that they even
penetrated between the pickets of the traders and their
camp before they were discovered. Cheer after cheer
welled from the throats of the beleaguered plainsmen,
as they approached. The savages heard them, and,
seeing that they now would have to assume the defensive, quietly slipped away.

" Ow! Ow!" said one brave. " We get those
palefaces yet."

Much overjoyed, Bent and his traders again started
on their journey, turning their course from Santa Fé,
which point they at first intended to reach, to Taos,
some eighty miles further to the North. By this
détour they not only avoided many canyons, in which
were sure to be lurking savages, but were also able
to obtain a military escort of Mexicans. A General
Viscarro — with a goodly number of Mexican ran-
cheros — accompanied them. But there was still to
be trouble.

They reached the rippling courses of the river Cimarron. There a party of savages approached the Mexicans, who rode on in front. One of them bore an arrow tied transversely across a spear, it being the symbol of the cross. Viscarro was a Catholic, and, honoring this novel flag with true devotion, he was spoken to by one of the braves.

" If the Americans will move aside to some distance," said he, " we will lay down our arms and will surrender."

Viscarro smiled.

" Certainly, red brother," said he.

The Americans retired beyond a ridge, and no sooner were they out of the way than the treacherous savages poured a destructive fire into the Mexican ranks. Many men and officers were wounded. But luckily the two Bents heard the firing, and suspecting treachery, gathered a number of mounted soldiers and went to the relief of the men who lived south of the Rio Grande.

Now was a desperate affair. Bent and his men burst upon the savages with fierce cries and delivered a deadly volley right in their faces. Their rifles were then discarded, and, having next emptied their pistols, they followed up the attack with tomahawks and clubbed rifles. Soon the Comanches were in full flight and the field was strewn thickly with their dead and wounded.

A gallant action was performed by a Pueblo (or Village) Indian. He was near the Mexican General, Viscarro, and understanding the language of the hostiles, heard one of the latter exclaim in his native tongue: " Now for the General! " As he spoke he aimed a bullet at the body of the Mexican commander. The Indian threw himself in front of him — at this juncture — and fell to the ground; as noble a hero as the lists of chivalry tell of. Viscarro was much affected by this show of devotion.

Thanks to Bill Bent and his brother Charles, the caravan had been saved from the hostiles. It was well. From this time on nothing exciting occurred and the Americans and Mexicans reached their respective homes in safety, meeting with no more serious annoyance than the nightly serenade of coyotes. The disheartened Comanches had given up their attempt to crush out the travel along the Arkansas trail, and fortunately for the white traders entered into no more military combinations, — preferring the safer and more natural warfare of the small, predatory bands. They could then move quickly and could cut off small unguarded bodies of men.

Bill Bent had done well. Now he did even better, for a fort was named after him. This was situated on the Arkansas River; was first called Fort William, and was the property of Lieutenant Vrain and himself. Built in 1833, here the celebrated Kit Carson was the post hunter from 1834 to 1842. Could the walls of the old fort speak, they would tell many tales of thrilling battles with the red men.

On one occasion it was besieged by many thousands of plains Indians. All of the tribes had determined to lay aside their mutual dislike for one another for once, and to league together for the extermination of the "palefaces." They saw that the white traders would soon have all of this country and they did not like the idea. Bill Bent was approaching the fort with a wagon-train about this time. Knowing that two or three hundred raw recruits of the United States garrison formed its only defense, he hastened rapidly to its relief. On his way he met several deserters, who (in the night) had scaled the walls of what they regarded to be a place of doom, and stealing cautiously through the savage lines, had fled with all speed towards the rising sun, — for they knew that help was there.

Bill Bent was somewhat alarmed at this. When he arrived in sight of the fort he saw that it was menaced by a great and awful danger. There were thousands of hostile Indians dancing their war and scalp dances around it, and endeavoring to work themselves up to the proper frenzy in order to make the attack. Bent's blood began to boil.

"Here!" he cried to one of his best men, "you take charge of the train! I have to move forward!"

His hat came off as he rode on, but he galloped straight at the fort. His long hair — meanwhile — trailed out behind like a banner from its staff. It was a trophy which any of the savages would have been very proud to wear in his belt.

The Indians were too surprised to fire at him. As he dashed along, he uttered a fierce war-whoop, and fired his revolver at a savage who was unwise enough to approach. Behind him came thundering his friend and ally, — Yellow Bear. He was a great Apache chief, but a friend of the whites and their staunch supporter. Strung out in the rear were a few Apache braves, who would have cheerfully sacrificed their lives for either Bent or Yellow Bear.

Bill Bent reached the fort in safety. So did Yellow Bear and his braves. The wagon-train came steadily on, its men marching alongside, fully armed. It, too, reached the doorway of the fort without a mishap. Here the pioneers found Bent getting everything in proper shape to give a warm reception to the braves, who from their actions were apparently ready for the assault. They were met with a hot reception.

Now an unforeseen event occurred.

Upon the morning after Bent's arrival the lookout beheld a slight cloud of dust far to the Eastward. After a while, a few black specks could be seen. They came nearer and were seen to be Indian videttes with their ponies on a dead run.

The videttes dashed into the Indian encampment, said a few hasty words to some of the chiefs, and then consternation seemed to take possession of the redskins. The squaws began at once to take down the lodges. The travois poles were slung with the tents and equipment. Soon the entire Indian camp was in full retreat. Amidst the yelping of the dogs, squalling of the babies, the rattle of pots and kettles piled up on the travois, and the insulting yells of the warriors, the savage host of besiegers crossed the Arkansas River and disappeared from view.

"Why, now," said Bill Bent. "Boys! Seems they're afraid of us!"

But the mystery was soon explained. Late on the evening of the next day those in the fort beheld the approach of a regiment of United States cavalry, which had been sent to its relief. The redskins had an admirable picket system. By means of this their pony express had told them of the approach of the cavalry, and, fearing that vengeance might be taken upon them for their hostile attitude and war-like threats, they prudently decamped.

Bill Bent had many another adventure upon the plains which was as thrilling as this. He was known for his courage and was never badly wounded, although he took a thousand chances. Sad to relate, he married a Cheyenne wife, and his children — suffering from this taint of redskin blood — never attained the prominence upon the plains which their fond parent had held. At last the good old fellow passed to the Happy Hunting Grounds. He had indeed seen the wild and woolly West in its palmiest days. Good-by to old Bill, hardy frontiersman and scout, whose reputation was spotless! Good-by and good luck, Bill Bent!

THOMAS EDDIE:

THE LAST OF THE OLD SCHOOL TRAPPERS

"YOU will do, boy, I will need you!"

The man who spoke — a grizzled old plainsman — nodded to a strong-looking young Scotchman who was standing before him, rifle in hand, and motioned to him to take a position among a number of trappers who stood near by. The fellow who thus spoke was John Ashley (a famous trader and explorer) who had just organized the Rocky Mountain Fur Company. As he was in need of vigorous young men his heart naturally warmed towards the stalwart youth before him, who was yearning for adventure in the Far West.

This athletic frontiersman was none other than Thomas Eddie, who was now twenty-four years of age, and whose aim with the rifle was steady and sure. Born on August 29th, 1799, he had naturally drifted to the plains, where he was as quick to volunteer upon a dangerous mission as were "Old Bill" Williams, Bill Gordon, or any of the other valiant pioneers. He was a fellow of iron will, and the older members of this expedition soon found that the canny young Scot would do and dare as much as any of them. As ready and willing to go to the relief of a stricken comrade as the most experienced man on the plains, he had not an enemy on the border, except among the redskins, whose hand was against every white man. As wiry as steel, as keen as a sword blade: such was the youthful Thomas Eddie, soon to be the hero of many a startling adventure.

The trappers under Ashley made their way up the waters of the Missouri in keel-boats. The muddy current of the turbid stream raged furiously against them, but by vigorous rowing they managed to thread their way among the numerous snags and sand-bars. At length they reached the vicinity of an Arickara village, filled with several hundred savages, and here they intended to trade, before passing up the Yellowstone River, where was splendid trapping. They rowed on with confidence, little suspecting that the redskins were in a terrible state of agitation and anger against all of the white men of the West. In fact, not many weeks before, an adventurous trapper, who had been travelling near by, had caught the son of the head chief of this nation, as he was stealing his horse. He had shot him down as he was in the act of throwing his leg over his mount. The Arickaras had soon heard of this, and, in spite of the fact that the white man had been perfectly justified in killing the horse-thief, determined to avenge the death of their comrade.

Ashley and his companions did not know of this adventure. Therefore they rowed onward with confidence, and soon sighted the tepees of the red men on the right bank of the stream.

" There they are! " cried Eddie, who was in the

bow of one of the boats. "We will have good trade, for I know that they are greatly in need of arms and of ammunition."

"Look out for them!" spoke a fellow named Rose, in one of the other vessels. "From certain signs I know that the red vermin mean mischief."

This fellow was a Kentuckian who, for some misdemeanor, had been outlawed in his own state and had then lived among the Crow Indians, who had made him a chief. Ashley did not like him and believed him to be a villain. Eddie, however, knew that he spoke with keen knowledge of the redskins. He, therefore, turned around and cried loudly:

"Ashley, look out for the Indians! They mean mischief!"

To this, the head of the expedition paid not the slightest attention. Instead, he pushed forward, anchored his boat close in shore, near a long strip of small cottonwood trees, and pulled out his pipe, smoking it complacently.

"Be ready for an ambush," said Rose, "I know that the Arickaras are in an ugly mood."

"Oh, pshaw!" answered Ashley. "The red men are over anxious to trade. It has been ten years since they have been on the war-path against the whites and I know that they will treat us well. Why, man, these Indians love me like a brother."

Rose frowned.

"I have lived among these redskins for many moons," said he. "And I know them like a book. Look out. They mean trouble!"

Ashley again pooh-poohed the idea, and rowed to the bank, where he deposited his articles of trade upon several gaudy blankets. The Arickaras crowded around him, crying:

"Oh, palefaced brother, you have brought us fine things. Oh, good brother! Oh, kind brother!"

They showed feverish anxiety to obtain guns and ammunition, saying that they were soon going against their old enemies, the Sioux. The trade went on, many of the trappers coming ashore in order to better bargain with the redskins; a few, however, remaining in the boats. Ashley seemed to be well satisfied with the manner in which everything was going. He suspected nothing until one of his men came to him and whispered in his ear:

"Three of our trappers have secretly disappeared, and I fear that they have been murdered."

The leader of the Rocky Mountain Fur Company was at last alarmed. He made preparations for defense and gathered his men about him in a hollow square. But the Indians, finding that they no longer could conceal their enmity, now set up a loud whooping and yelling. A shot was fired. Another and another followed in quick succession, and the cottonwood thickets swarmed with the savages, who poured a rain of bullets at the trappers upon the bank and upon those in the boats.

"Drop to the ground, boys!" shouted Ashley, "and we will fight for our lives."

A desperate encounter ensued. Although surrounded in the rear, the trappers fought their way to the bank, jumped into the river, and attempted to swim to their boats. Many were drowned, others were killed by bullets as they splashed towards their craft, but the majority clambered aboard in safety.

"Cut the ropes," shouted Ashley, "and get away from here as quickly as you are able!"

Under a terrific fire the boats began to slowly drift down the river. Oars were soon run out and the trappers were well beyond range of the murderous Arickara rifles. Of one hundred and forty-nine men they had lost sixty killed and drowned, and scarcely one of them did not bear marks of bullet or arrow wounds. It had been a desperate affair. Had the confident Ashley but listened to the sage advice of the Crow renegade there would have been no such slaughter. Thus ended the famous stampede of the Rocky Mountain Fur Company, on the ninth day of March, 1828.

But how about the stalwart young Eddie? This lucky plainsman escaped with only one arrow wound in his forearm. He was heroic in the defense of the boats, and, taking charge of one of them, managed to get her safely to Council Bluffs, where the Fur Company retreated in good order. Poor, old trappers! They had met with a warmer reception than they had bargained for!

As luck would have it, a Colonel Leavenworth was then at Council Bluffs with a detachment of United States troopers. Ashley soon told him his story, and wound up his sad tale with the request that he help him to chastise the savages.

" That I will do right willingly," answered the gallant soldier. " White Bear, with his band of Sioux warriors, will go with me, I know. He says that he is just itching for a little brush with the Arickaras. He will be of great assistance to us."

Eddie joined the detachment as it departed, and, marching speedily towards the village, the soldiers and allied Sioux found the Arickaras abandoning it. A sharp skirmish took place; the soldiers and trappers fell upon the rear guard, and, routing it speedily, dashed among the tepees, which were set on fire and quickly consumed. The Arickaras fled across the prairie. As the skirmish was in progress White Bear, .he Sioux leader, was the hero of a desperate affair, whicn made him always well known among the whites, and greatly respected by all of the valiant men of the frontier.

While the fight was at its hottest this Sioux chieftain singled out a giant Arickara warrior, rushed upon him, tomahawk in hand, and cried out:

" If you are a man, halt and struggle with me. We will see which is the better."

The Arickara had a bow in his hand, and, turning upon the Bear, sent a shower of arrows whistling around him. One of them pierced his thigh, but the Sioux stopped and pulled the missile from the wound. Then, with tomahawk upraised, he charged upon his enemy.

The Arickara chief had discharged his last arrow, and, seeing that it was too late to fly, wheeled and faced his antagonist. He was a large and powerful man, but the Sioux warrior was more agile. Uttering a loud and discordant yell, White Bear rushed at his foe. All the other combatants stopped for a moment, in order to view this strange and startling contest.

The sun gleamed upon the tomahawks of the two braves as they danced around each other. Again and again each endeavored to strike a blow, but, by skillful dodging, the weapon was evaded, and the warriors continued to prance about in a circle. Suddenly the Sioux bent over and struck the Arickara warrior a fierce stroke upon the knee; so fierce, indeed, that he nearly severed his leg from his body. White Bear leaped forward, dodged sideways, and evaded the descending tomahawk of the Arickara chieftain. The latter tottered and then fell to the ground.

Before he could recover, the Sioux had dealt a death-blow, and, amidst the wild yelling and screeching of the spectators, deftly scalped his enemy, holding the top-knot aloft, and himself uttering the wild yelp of triumph. "Um-Yah! Um-Yah! Uh-Yah!"

The Arickaras were dispersed and well punished for their attack upon Ashley and his men. The troops returned in triumph to Council Bluffs, and Eddie was congratulated by the head trapper for his part in the affair.

"But now, my boy," said the veteran plainsman, "I want you to go up the Yellowstone, cross the mountains, and, with fourteen others, bring back a whole lot of peltries."

"I'm your man," said Eddie. "I'm off as soon as you say the word."

The fourteen trappers moved to the Yellowstone, where they hunted and trapped with great success, until winter. Then they made their way to the village of some friendly Crows. They were treated with kindness and hospitality, and had great good luck in procuring beaver peltries. When spring came they travelled towards the Rocky Mountains, after making appropriate speeches of friendship to their hosts, and giving them many presents.

In the mountains their old enemies — the Black-feet — were very mischievous. They often stole their traps, attempted to stampede their ponies, and fired at them from ambush. Nearly every night the alarm would sound: "Indians! Indians! Look to your horses!" And, during the day, the Blackfoot senti-nels could be seen upon the skyline, perched upon the summit of some high hill. They would signal to their friends in the valleys below and tell them of the prog-ress of the trappers. The pioneers were repeatedly ambushed, but they marched valiantly on, fighting as they went. At last they left the mountains, pressed onward towards the Pacific slope, and, almost perish-ing from hunger, were rescued by some trappers of the Hudson Bay Company, who took them to their post on the Columbia River. They spent the winter in this place.

When spring approached, the pioneers again set out for the Yellowstone. As they approached the Bear River, an Indian runner came bounding down the trail. He was of the Snake tribe and held up his right hand in token of friendship.

" I come from the people of the great chief, Pim,"
said he. " The Great Spirit has taken our beloved
ruler to the land of the hereafter. It is requested by
his people that our white brothers read over him their
medicine book (the Bible) and sing one of their songs.
Then lay our great chief to rest upon the banks of
the Bear River. Here he can ever hear the wonderful
music of the stream, and here his spirit can make the
beaver plenty for our white brothers."

It was a strange request.

" Boys," said Thomas Eddie, " we will do as our
red brother wishes. We will bury our good friend
Pim in a Christian manner, for he was always kindly
disposed to all the trappers and pioneers who came
in contact with him."

Turning back upon their trail, the trappers travelled
forty miles to the camp of the Snakes. In relays of
four, they carried the dead chieftain slowly and ten-
derly to the banks of the roaring Bear River, and
there laid him to rest, reading over him the burial
service and singing a hymn. A volley was fired over
the open grave, then, turning sadly towards the mountains, the men in buckskin left the red men to perform
their own last rites over the dead chieftain.

As they neared the hills, the pugnacious Blackfeet again began to harass them. Every day they
made an attack, but as they were principally armed
with arrows they did little damage. A few had rifles,
but they rarely used them. When the trappers had
been fighting with these fellows, the year before, numbers of them had fallen beneath the steady aim of the

whites, but not a single trapper had been killed or even dangerously wounded. This shows you what poor marksmen the Indians were.

Not long afterwards the little band of adventurers was passing through a narrow and lonely valley. As they reached a passage-way through high and precipitous cliffs, a shot rang out, and a wild Indian yell told them the Blackfeet were again on their trail.

"We're ambushed, boys!" cried Eddie. "Take to cover and ward off these skulkers, for from the sound of their fire it is apparent that they have plenty of guns and ammunition."

He had scarcely spoken when he uttered a sharp cry of pain, for a rifle ball struck him in the thigh and penetrated well into his flesh. It was cut out by a trapper called Will Sublette, with a beaver knife, but our hero was in a serious condition for some time thereafter. Fortunately the members of the party were near water, so they threw up a rough barricade, by means of digging with their hunting-knives, and adding brush and tree trunks to the fortification. Several were unable to proceed, five had been killed, and twenty were severely wounded.

The Blackfeet could be easily seen as they circled about, some on foot, some on their ponies. They continuously yelped, howled like coyotes, and kept up a fusillade against the earth and brush fortification. Fortune favored the trappers, however, as there was an abundance of beaver in the stream which ran through the valley and these were easily captured. Trout were also plentiful and the wanderers managed to put up a fortification behind which they could catch the speckled beauties without molestation by the painted and bloodthirsty Blackfeet. The wounded made a rapid recovery, and in ten days were able to travel.

"Now, boys," said Eddie, at this time, "it is important that we get away. Let us take our old clothes, stuff them with grass in order to deceive the red men, and light our camp-fires as usual. The Blackfeet will see the dark bodies near the flames and will not suspect that we have gotten away. We will move off towards the North, but you must make no noise."

The trappers were eager to be off. That night they lighted their fires, placed the dummy figures so that they could be readily seen, and crept away from their little fortification. The Blackfeet did not suspect this departure, and, although it was a hazardous march over a rough path, allowed the men under Eddie to get safely away. By forced marches, and travelling over a crooked trail, the pioneers at length reached the Yellowstone. But their troubles were not yet at an end.

Trapper Eddie had left camp one day in order to look for game, and was returning to the place where the horses were tethered, when he saw a small band of Crow Indians who were endeavoring to drive off the stock. Firing at the leader of the expedition he knocked him to the ground. One of the braves jumped to the earth, lifted the dead chieftain upon his horse, and rode off with him. Eddie's comrades heard the shooting and galloped to meet their leader.

Eddie knew the valley well. It doubled almost upon itself, making a horse-shoe curve, and he was aware that should he ascend the mountain on the right he would be able to head off the redskins.

"Boys!" cried he. "Follow me over that mountain. We will meet the red men, recapture our bronchos, and pay them well for their dastardly attempt to run off our steeds."

His men gave a cheer, and, putting spurs to their horses, galloped up the steep slope of the mountain. Sure enough, as they reached the top, there were the redskins just below them. Uttering a wild cow-boy yell, the trappers dashed to the assault.

A narrow pass in the mountains lay before them and for this the Indians hastened, yelping fiercely as they went. The trappers were as experienced men at shooting on horseback as Buffalo Bill, and they soon dropped most of the Crows as they vainly endeavored to escape. The fellow who was carrying the leader was badly wounded, and as he endeavored to ride his heavily burdened horse across a stream, which flowed through the valley, the animal stumbled and fell, throwing both the live and the dead man into the water. The trappers were close upon them as they went down, but what became of the dead chieftain and his attendant was never known. They disappeared from view. Whether the live Crow was killed by the fall, or was stunned and perished in the swift current, is still a question. Perhaps he made his way back to his own tribe. At any rate, a careful search failed to discover the whereabouts of either of them.

"By George!" cried "Old Bill" Williams, who was one of Eddie's party, "I reckon that the dead one has carried the live fellow to Heaven with him."

The horses were soon re-taken, and with smiles of satisfaction upon their faces the trappers returned to their camp on the Yellowstone. Here, seated around the blazing camp-fire, they again fought over their battles, compared notes of the country, made rude maps of their routes, with the various rivers, mountains, and plains; and those who had seen the waters of the Great Salt Lake told their comrades of this vast inland sea, whose waters were bitterly salt, and into whose depths nothing could sink because of the great buoyancy of the waves.

There was an abundance of game in the Yellowstone country. The fourteen scouts spent the entire season, and part of the next, in trapping for mink, beaver, otter, and bear. They set their beaver traps in all the suitable streams between the head of the Missouri River and the upper waters of the Platte, meeting with great success. Indians were plentiful, but seemed to leave them alone, for they had undoubtedly heard of the summary vengeance which the trappers had taken upon the thieving Crows.

"Boys," said Eddie, one day, "we are about all through with our ammunition and I would like to send seven of our number to Santa Fé, New Mexico, in order to get a supply. Who will be willing to undertake the trip?"

"I will," came from the throats of many, and it was plainly evident that there would be little difficulty in getting volunteers for this hazardous duty.

Seven were chosen for the journey — seven of the strongest and most hardy — but the seven were never seen again. Cheerfully they set out across the sandy plains of Colorado. When they were just about to disappear from view, they turned and waved their hands to those left behind.

"So long, boys," cried one. "We will meet again in a few months."

But they never met again. From the time that they disappeared upon the horizon all trace of them was lost. Perhaps they fell before the arrows and bullets of the Sioux, Kiowa, Apache, Comanche, Navajo, or other red men. Perhaps the lounging and lazy Spanish banditti captured them and carried them across the Mexican line. At any rate, their fate is enveloped in impenetrable mystery.

Eddie and his companions waited for many months for some sign of their comrades. At length they gave up hopes of their return, and leaving a note to direct them where to go should they ever come back, made their way to the Yellowstone. Hostile red men hovered about them and endeavored to cut off their ponies, but these were dispersed in several smart skirmishes. Finally they reached a camp some forty miles above Boulder, Colorado, where Eddie and Bill Gordon had a rather serious encounter with some Arapahoes, when returning from an antelope hunt.

"By gracious!" cried Bill, the trapper, as he saw

the redskins swooping down upon them. "I believe that we are about to lose our scalps, Eddie. '*Never say die*,' must be our motto."

"Let's break for that canyon," answered the lion-hearted Eddie. "If we get into those rocks the yelping redskins can shoot all they want to but they can't hurt us. We'll crawl over there by the water so that they cannot starve us out. We have food enough to last us for some time."

Crack! Crack! sounded the rifles of the red men, and both Eddie and Gordon were struck. Nothing daunted, they ran to the shelter of the ravine, where they returned the fire with so much accuracy that two of the redskins fell to the ground. The Indians numbered about twelve, but only five were detached to follow the two scouts, while the rest rode away, carrying the two dead men with them. As they went in the direction of the camp of the plainsmen Eddie feared that they would surprise his comrades and would annihilate them.

"Gordon," said he, "you must remain here, while I run back to camp and warn our companions of the approach of these murderers. You have only five to deal with, and I know that you can handle them."

Eddie ran swiftly up the canyon, and then, back-tracking, hid himself behind a huge boulder. The redskins saw him and made after his retreating form with great speed, but failed to see him in his hiding-place. They were soon out of sight.

The scout darted down the canyon as rapidly as possible and dashed out upon the open prairie as hard as he could go. Before him was an Arapaho who was watching the Indian ponies. He was mounted upon a buckskin pinto and was armed with a rifle, tomahawk, and knife. As Eddie approached, he raised his rifle. The scout did likewise and both fired at about the same moment.

The trapper was struck in the shoulder, but the injury was not severe, while his own ball passed through the red man's thigh, breaking the leg of the horse upon which he was riding. This brought him to the earth and pinned the warrior beneath him, but the savage frantically struggled to escape, and, as the white man approached, drew his knife. His tomahawk had dropped some distance away as he fell.

Now was a thrilling encounter. Notwithstanding the pain in his wound and his weakness from loss of blood, the Indian made a desperate fight. He hoped, no doubt, that the shots which both he and his antagonist had fired would bring his companions to his assistance. No such luck was in store for him. Eddie was a small and wiry man, while the Arapaho was a veritable giant in stature. The scout was armed with a tomahawk and endeavored to get in a thrust, but with ill success, for the redskin parried his every attempt. Just as Eddie had succeeded in making a sweeping blow, which, had it reached the red man, would have cut him down, the savage caught his arm, and the tomahawk flew from his grasp. The Indian's knife was in his left hand and the scout made a desperate lunge in order to seize it.

It was a hazardous moment for Thomas Eddie.

As he struggled for the possession of the coveted knife he saw four Arapahoes emerge from the mouth of the canyon and dash towards them. It was touch and go with the famous man of the frontier. The savage made a thrust at this moment. Eddie caught the blade in his right hand, but the knife cut him through and through, inflicting a desperate and gaping wound. In spite of the pain it caused him, the trapper held on. With his other hand he seized the Arapaho by the throat and pushed him to the earth.

A new complication arose. A shot rang out from the mouth of the canyon and the foremost Indian fell to the ground. The other three halted and faced the new enemy, while the big fellow with whom he was struggling turned his head for a moment, in order to see who was approaching. On the short moment hung his life, for Eddie wrested the long knife from him, and, as he looked around, buried the blade in his side. The Arapaho fell to the ground, with a long, gasping cry. The three savages, who were approaching, were now about fifty yards away and they fired upon the victorious scout, but did not hit him. Instead of this they wounded another one of their horses.

Hurrah for Eddie! He had certainly done well, and was in the same class with Adam Poe, who, if you remember, had such a desperate battle with Big Foot, the celebrated Shawnee warrior and athlete.[1] The nervy fellow was not to be caught napping. Dashing to the nearest pony, he set off at full speed for the mouth of the canyon, circling as he did so,

[1] See " Famous Scouts."

in order to avoid the three savages. To his surprise,
he met Bill Gordon, who told him that from the top
of a low mountain he had seen the Arapahoes engaged
in a battle with a band of Crows, way off upon the
plain, and that therefore he had returned to his assistance, as he knew that their companions in camp would
not be molested.

"Well, let's finish up these Arapahoes," cried Eddie.
"And punish them for their interference with honest
men. Are you with me, Bill?"

Old Bill uttered a wild yell.

"Of course I'm with you, son," said he. "Lay
on! Lay on!"

Spurring their mustangs, the two scouts dashed
madly after the fleeing redskins. They caught up
with them, and by excellent shooting succeeded in
killing them all. At once they returned to their own
camp with the arms and ponies of the savages, and,
upon narrating their adventures to the other scouts,
it was decided to move as rapidly as possible from
such a dangerous locality. Turning towards the turbid waters of the Yellowstone, they soon reached this
wonderful stream, where no other bands of Indians
molested them. Their battles were over.

Upon their return to the settlement at Council
Bluffs all welcomed them uproariously, for many
thought that the nervy fellows had perished in the
wilderness. Their furs and peltries netted them a
snug figure; so snug, in fact, that plainsman Eddie
purchased a tavern of his own called the Green Tree.
Here he dispensed a lavish hospitality and here he

brought his bride in 1833. She was a Miss Clarke, a reigning belle of St. Louis, and, although the mother of eleven sturdy children (five boys and six girls) always remained a woman of remarkable beauty. Many were the tales which the trapper used to tell his children of his early experiences on the plains, and, although the frost of old age gradually touched his auburn hair with snow, the fire and imagination of youth always kept the spirit of the old pioneer as fresh as when, as a young man, he made that dangerous trip to the wild region of the West as a member of the Rocky Mountain Fur Company. Thus in peace and comfort passed the declining years of the last of the trappers of the Great Frontier.

JIM BRIDGER:

FOUNDER OF BRIDGER, WYOMING, AND FAMOUS INDIAN FIGHTER

IN the lower corner of the mighty state of Wyoming is a town named after one of the most noted of the trappers of the West — Jim Bridger — who not only fought Indians but also traded and trapped in many an unexplored portion of the once unknown regions near the Rocky Mountains. Fort Bridger — a strong stockade near by — received its name from this famous plainsman, who hailed from Illinois, and who was not only of humble, but also of somewhat unrespectable parentage. Young Jim ran away, when quite young, in order to escape the hard usage which was his lot at home. On the border he soon made his mark, for he was not only a great rifle shot but also a man of unusual strength and agility.

One day the scout was in a block-house, with a number of other frontiersmen who had recently been attacked by a band of Blackfoot warriors. These were encamped at no great distance, and a truce had been declared whereby neither side should molest the other. Jim Bridger wandered into the camp of the red men, and walked down the main street, looking,

Courtesy of the Century Company.

JIM BRIDGER.

with an interested eye, at their tepees, their squaws, and the little papooses.

" Ugh! Ugh! " grunted some young bucks. " Paleface he look like pig. Ugh! Ugh! He no fight. He run away."

Bridger grew crimson, but said nothing.

" Paleface waddle like duck," continued one of the Blackfeet. " Paleface have nose like black dog."

This was too much for the usually calm and collected Jim Bridger. Spinning upon his heel he rushed up to the nearest redskin, hit him a blow between the eyes and sent him reeling to the ground. Immediately the whole camp was in an uproar. The trapper was surrounded by a yelling, screeching mob of savages — was made a prisoner — and was carried, struggling, to a lodge upon the outskirts of the village. Then the Indians gathered in a dense throng in order to decide upon the fate of their captive.

There was much discussion as to what was to be done with the scout. Some were for a light punishment, as the trappers in the block-house were numerous, and their rifles were accurate shooters when held by the steady hands of the frontiersmen. " No! No! " shouted many others. " He should be carried to the mountains and there tortured. He has struck one of our braves. The paleface must suffer death! "

Three older chiefs listened to all of this wild talk and then gave their decision.

" The Paleface shall suffer death and torture! Let some of the young men go to his lodge and bring him to us."

With a wild whoop, a number of the youthful warriors rushed to the tepee in which they had shoved
the trapper, stoutly bound with deer thongs. As they
threw open the flap which hung over the doorway
surprise and dismay marked their features, for the
bird had flown. All were chagrined and angered at
the loss of their quarry. Whooping savagely, they
dashed back to their companions, many of whom
favored an immediate attack upon the block-house;
but the counsel of the older chiefs prevailed.

" The paleface warriors have sticks which shoot
very straight," said they. " We must go away, or
they may attack us."

Packing up their goods, and loading their travois,
they fled to the mountains.

But how had the daring plainsman escaped? Hush!
It was a dusky-hued maiden who had set him free,
and love will always find a way.

Jim Bridger, in fact, had met a young Indian girl
in the village who had returned the sudden affection
of the young trapper with much interest. With sadness and dismay she watched his capture, and, when
she saw him thrown into the lodge, at first she determined to run to the block-house in order to notify his
comrades of his predicament. She knew that they
would then demand his release, but, fearing an attack
in which some of her relatives would be killed and
her lover would be doubtless assassinated, she decided
to say nothing to the trappers. Instead, she determined to set him free by her own hand. While the
savages wrangled over what was to be his fate she

determined to creep to his tent, cut the deer thongs, and point out the way to freedom.

Two sentinels watched the lodge where Jim Bridger lay, and, as the Indian maid approached, one of them moved towards her. She stooped almost to the earth, darted behind a neighboring tepee, and crept stealthily towards the rear of the tent. As luck would have it, there was no sentinel at this point, and she cut a long slit in the buffalo-skin curtain. Bridger was lying upon a robe endeavoring to snap his bonds, and as he saw her uttered an exclamation of surprise. At this, the girl clapped one hand over his mouth. With the other she cut the raw-hide thongs, and beckoned to him to follow her.

The scout wormed his way out of the side of the tent, crept upon all fours to a safe distance, then rose and faced the Indian maiden.

"Dearest," said he, "you have saved my life, and Jim Bridger never forgets the kindness of such a one as you. You shall be my wife."

The Blackfoot maiden blushed, and answered that whether there was peace or war between her people and his, she would meet him in a certain grove of pine trees, at the base of a distant mountain peak, after two full moons. She counselled him how to avoid the sentinels, how to elude any pursuers by darting through a certain canyon, and then, as he pressed her to his heart, their lips met. A moment more and she had torn herself away, and had vanished down the steep cliffs upon which they had clambered.

The scout did not tell his comrades how he had escaped, for he feared that they would laugh at him. And as the days passed by his brother trappers noticed that he was cutting notches in a stick in order to mark the time elapsing before some important event. At length the stick was almost filled with little triangular marks, and Bridger, saddling his horse, led another by a long lariat, and set off for a certain towering peak in the mountains. His companions little guessed what was his real destination. Five days elapsed before they again laid eyes upon him, but all were startled and much surprised to see him ride into the camp, one brilliant morning, with a dusky, Indian maiden by his side. A broad smile was upon his face, while the bride looked radiantly happy. As they rode up, the joyous trappers gave three times three for Mr. and Mrs. Jim Bridger.

From now on the pioneer had an adventurous career, and, although away from his home for months at a time, was always devoted to his Blackfoot bride, although he often had passages at arms with her kinsmen. Not long after his marriage he was in the Medicine Bow Mountains, with a party of trappers, when they were surrounded by hundreds of the Blackfeet. Crying to them to surrender, the savage warriors circled about upon their ponies, screeching like so many devils, for they were sure that they had the white men cornered. It looked dark for the adventurous trappers.

"We must fight desperately, men," cried out the gallant Jim. "And must make our way towards the mountains near the Yellowstone. There we can stand these pesky varmints off from behind the boulders. But now we must break through their circle. Are you all ready? Then — come on."

The trappers cheered as Bridger led a charge against the wild riders of the plains, who scattered before the resolute attack. By alternately fighting and retreating, the frontiersmen gradually made their way towards the distant hills, and — although a few were badly wounded — at length they reached the protection of some giant boulders which afforded them excellent protection against the bullets and arrows of the red men. Seeing that it was now impossible to get them, the savages fired a parting volley and retired. The last shot proved to be an unlucky one for Jim Bridger's best friend — a man named Milton Sublette — as a ball from an Indian rifle struck him in the ankle and tore through both flesh and bone.

Stanching the flow of blood as best they could, the trappers carried their wounded companion away with them upon a Mackinaw blanket, slung between two of the pack-animals. His leg was amputated with the aid of a beaver knife hacked into a saw, and in spite of the fact that they possessed no chloroform, ether, or other anesthetic, the patient bore everything with stoical indifference. His life was saved, and — strange as it may seem — upon his arrival at Saint Louis he submitted to a second operation in order to obtain a better-looking stump, and was back again in his old haunts within six months: trapping, fishing, and travelling with as much joy in living as before. Such was the spirit and energy of these old men of the mountains.

Bridger was later engaged in piloting emigrant trains across the prairie, in the vicinity of the Republican River, where Sandy Forsyth had his great battle with Roman Nose some years later. With him was a scout called Jim Beckwith, who has left the following account of a tight, little brush which was indulged in by two bands of Sioux and Pawnee warriors, just after the trappers had driven away a force of about fifty Pawnees who had attempted to run off their horses.

" I seen that the Pawnees would soon be after us again," said the gallant Beckwith, " and I knowed that the Sioux would do the same thing. So I saw that we'd have about a thousand redskins after us, and we wouldn't be a taste for them. I seen that this wouldn't do, so I says to Jim Bridger, says I, ' Jim, what are we goin' ter do? ' ' Give it up,' said Jim, says he, ' Fight till the reds down us, I reckon, and then turn up our toes like men.' All this time — bless your soul — them pilgrims what we wuz a-guidin', wuz in the wagons cryin'. It wuz awful.

" Wall, I jest made up my mind, sir, that I didn't intend tew give my heart tew no Injun jest then, so I callates about whar th' two parties of red devils would meet. When we got thar, we drove over a raise in th' plain and jes' waited fur 'em. In about two hours I seen th' dust raisin' in th' East in er gret, big cloud. ' Them's Pawnees,' says I, ' by th' tarnal prophet.' Then I looked intew th' West, and thar th'

dust wuz raisin', too. ' Them's Sioux,' says I, ' an' th'
Devil take 'em. I hev seen pleasanter sights.' Wall,
after waitin' some time th' Injuns seen each other, an'
of all th' cussed yellin' you ever heard, it wuz thar.
I jes' laid back an' laughed, while Bridger done some
tall chucklin' too, when them two bands got together.
It was lively times, yew bet.

"Th' Injuns didn't have many guns in them days,
but you kin jest rest assured that they used their arrers fur what wuz in 'em. Thar they went circlin'
aroun' each other, bendin' under their hosses' necks,
an' lettin' th' arrers fly. At one time th' air wuz near
so full uv arrers thet it made a cloud, shettin' out th'
sun. Their ponies got stuck full uv 'em. Their dogs
wuz full uv 'em, an' every Injun in th' gang had er
lot uv 'em stickin' inter him. I seed a big, fat feller
ridin' off with two uv 'em stickin' into th' seat uv his
buckskins, an' it reminded me so uv er big pincushion,
thet I near died uv laughin'. Then they begun tew
run. They run this way, an' they run that, and — by
Gravy — I believe thet some uv them Injuns be still
runnin' from one another. By Gum, they wuz so busy
fightin' each other, thet they left us plum aione."

This was certainly a laughable incident, but a bit
later occurred another episode which was not quite
so amusing for the daring and adventurous Jim
Bridger.

About six months after the fight upon the Republican, with five companions, the trapper was travelling
near the Platte River. The plainsmen were in search
of buffalo and had seen a fair sized herd when a band

of Sioux Indians appeared upon one of the rolling
bluffs. The trappers sought cover, for they expected
an attack, and they were not far from being wrong,
for the red men immediately made after them; circled
about them upon their ponies, and fired their rifles at
long range.

"Dig a trench with your knives," shouted Bridger.
"These fellows are out for our blood and they are
going to come pretty near getting us. Move over
near that water hole so that they can't make us die
of thirst, and we'll see who can last the longest."

Scrambling to their knees, the plainsmen quickly
threw up a barricade near the water hole, and, hob-
bling their ponies behind them, began to take careful
aim at the Sioux — one of whom was soon sent to the
Happy Hunting Grounds. This enraged the remainder, and wild, blood-curdling yells echoed across the
prairie as they drew nearer, hoping to make a rush
and annihilate the five white trappers.

"Get ready, boys!" again shouted Bridger.
"They're going to rush us!"

All prepared for the advance by laying out additional ammunition and placing long hunting-knives
near at hand. In a few moments the Sioux came on,
whipping their ponies to their utmost speed, and
yelping madly.

A ringing volley knocked over four of the leaders,
but still on they came. Another shot sent a fifth
chieftain to the Great Beyond, and, as the trappers
reloaded, the Sioux seemed to lose heart. They
swerved aside from the breastwork, offering excellent

targets to the plainsmen, and, with a dull thud, still another red warrior fell from his galloping pinto. Two of the trappers, meanwhile, were wounded by bullets, while an arrow stuck into the coat sleeve of Jim Bridger, himself.

Now retiring beyond range, the redskins kept up a perpetual fusillade with rifles and with arrows. The trappers held their fire, threw up still higher entrenchments, and waited for the next onslaught, but this did not come. Instead, the Sioux lighted the long, dry prairie grass, and a sheet of flame and smoke curled surely and steadily towards the band of plainsmen, for the wind was blowing directly upon them. What were they to do now?

Necessity is the mother of invention. Quick as a flash, Jim Bridger leaped across the embankment, touched the grass off immediately in front of them, and burnt off quite a small alley-way before the roaring crackling flames came to their place of refuge. The force of the flames thus spent itself before the embankment was reached, and the wily savages renewed their whooping and yelling. Again they charged, but again they were driven off; while night closed over both besieger and besieged, bringing a lull to the unequal battle.

Next day the fight was renewed, and all five of the trappers were wounded. Towards evening it was decided that one of the party should creep through the lines and bring aid from a camp of fifty trappers, who were some miles down the river. The choice fell upon Jim Bridger, and it found him ready to undertake the hazardous expedition.   At twelve o'clock he crawled over the side of the little fortification and wormed his way towards the fringe of red warriors who lay about them in a circle.

The scout kept on as quietly as he could and crawled for fully two hundred yards before he saw, or heard, anything of the redskins.   Then he got to his feet (as he considered himself through their lines) and prepared to run.   But before him was an Indian pony, its master sound asleep by its side.   The horse had been feeding in a deep ravine, and — suddenly scenting the trapper — gave a snort which roused its master.   The Sioux warrior gazed stupidly at the frontiersman.

But Bridger did not take long to make up his mind what to do.   He dashed towards the Indian, intending to strangle him before he could give the alarm.   The redskin uttered a loud whoop, and his companions immediately ran in his direction.   The scout realized that nothing was now to be gained by silence, and, pulling out his pistol, shot the red man dead.   Then, leaping upon his mustang, he urged him upon the gallop.   The Sioux were all around him on their pintos, but he had the good fortune to be upon one of their fastest horses, which seemed to outdistance any of the pursuers.

It was a hot chase.   The red men fired again and again at the fleeing trapper but they could not hit him. His mustang leaped over the deep crevasses, dodged badger and prairie-dog holes, and brought him safely to the camp of his companions by two o'clock in the afternoon. The Sioux had given up the chase, and, little suspecting that other trappers were camped near by, had returned to the siege of the four, hoping now to make one sudden rush and gain their scalps. Their blood was up, for twenty-five of their number had fallen before the accurate fire of the besieged.

" Come at once! " cried the panting Bridger, as he reached the camp of the plainsmen. " If you do not hurry, my four companions will all be massacred by the red men. To horse! To horse! "

It did not take the trappers long to catch their ponies and jump into their saddles.

" Show us where your friends are! " cried they, " and we'll fix th' redskins before another sun."

Bridger turned and piloted the band of plainsmen back to the place where he had left his beleaguered companions. They went on the run, but, making a wide détour in order to gain the sand-hills in the rear of the besiegers, waited until morning. Then they heard rifle shots in the distance and knew that the battle was on again.

Creeping towards the sound of firing, they soon saw the Sioux preparing for a final charge upon the valorous four, and opened upon them. They had clustered together for a rush, and this weltering volley fairly took the heart out of those of small courage. Many fell dead, — the rest made all haste to get out of range, — while the four trappers in the embankment came running towards their deliverers like wild men. With yells of joy they hugged the burly form of Jim

Bridger, to whose nerve and courage they owed their lives.

The scout and plainsman soon moved from the upper waters of the Missouri — after the fur trade had ceased to be prosperous — and founded a trading post in the southwestern part of the State of Wyoming — named Fort Bridger. Here he dealt in skins, furs, and peltries, accumulating a large amount of property, as the Fort was a stopping-place for all the emigrant trains bound for Salt Lake City and for California. He remained true to his Blackfoot wife, and several half-breed children made life merry in the long, low log-hut which the scout had erected as his abode. The famous plainsman lived to a ripe, old age — like most of the early trappers — and was ever ready to tell of his battle with the Sioux, when he rescued his four companions from their clutches. This was the most thrilling of all his many adventures upon the frontier.

"OLD BILL" WILLIAMS:

THE FAMOUS LOG RIDER OF COLORADO

"I HATE every Indian that I ever saw and would just as lief take a shot at one as eat!"

So spoke a raw-boned trapper, with a tangled mat of brown hair hanging across his shoulders, and, as he said this, he gazed vindictively toward some Indian warriors who were riding slowly past the wagon-train with which the plainsman was travelling. His comrades looked at him and laughed, for this was the favorite theme of Bill Williams, familiarly known as "Old Bill," although this was a term of endearment and not because of his years, for he was as young as any of them.

The Indians rode on, and from their own glances, which they threw at the gaunt and ungainly trapper, it was plainly evident that they fully reciprocated the feeling which the plainsman held for them. "Ugh! He one bad man!" a gaudy warrior was heard to remark.

"Old Bill" Williams was born in Tennessee, his father being one of the Virginian pioneers who crossed the Blue Ridge and settled in the state when it was swarming with Indians, — all eager to have the land for themselves alone — and not willing to allow the whites to get possession of it without a severe struggle. His son grew up in surroundings of savagery and warfare. He took part in many of the Ohio campaigns against the red men in that state, and was invariably used as a scout, for his knowledge of woodcraft was excellent. After the red men were partially subdued, he moved further west to the Rockies, where his scouting habits still clung to him. He would often be absent for many weeks upon his solitary expeditions, and would as frequently return with scalps as with the furs of wild animals.

The Crows and the Blackfeet were continually at war with each other, with the advantage upon the side of the latter, for the Crows were more cowardly than their warlike enemies. They had the advantage, however, of having a white renegade to lead them. His name was Rose: formerly one of the land pirates who lived near and upon the treacherous waters of the Mississippi. This desperate man taught the redskins how to fight like the whites and continually advised them in their councils of war, so that they often defeated the Blackfeet in their sanguinary encounters.

One day " Old Bill " Williams was off on a scout with Bill Gordon, and, becoming separated from him, was endeavoring to reach camp by water, so as to leave no trail for the eye of some lurking Blackfoot warrior. He was therefore floating down stream on a log. As he reached a shallow part of the creek the muddied water and footprints upon the bank showed where a big grizzly had just gone by.

" By Gravy," said the scout to himself, " here's the

chance to make a hundred dollars from that old fellow's hide. I'm after him."

Wading to the shore, he started off through the brush, and followed Bruin with his head down, for the bushes kept slapping him in the eyes. As he was thus proceeding, he suddenly debouched from the brush into a cleared space. Before him was no grizzly, but a band of ten Blackfoot warriors. They stopped in amazement, and so did Williams, who said in loud tones: "Gee-hos-i-phat!"

The Indians, on the other hand, set up a loud yelping, and, seeing them preparing to fire, "Old Bill" raised his trusty flint-lock, pulled the trigger, and knocked over a big, fine-looking savage who had on the war-bonnet of a chieftain. Not stopping to make closer acquaintance, the wiry Bill then dashed into a neighboring canyon. As he glanced over his shoulder he saw that only four of the Blackfeet were coming after him.

The scout raced along for about a quarter of a mile; then, seeing that the redskins were far behind, stopped in order to load his rifle. He had just rammed home a ball when the Blackfeet began to draw near, so he dropped behind the stump of a moss-grown tree and waited for them to come on. They approached quite hurriedly, gazing at the ground for tracks, and eagerly pointing out the traces of the trapper's footprints. When they came within good range "Old Bill" pressed the trigger and a Blackfoot brave fell to the earth, shot through the heart.

"I reckon that this will stop 'em fer er minute er

two," said the man of the plains as he continued his
flight up the canyon. He raced ahead for about a half
a mile, then halted again in order to load his gun.

The Indians were soon upon him, but they had
learned caution, and spread out on either side of him,
in order to get in his rear. " Old Bill " was not to be
caught napping, and ran like a deer still further up
the divide. He was much swifter of foot than the
red men, and soon left them far behind. The scout
sat down upon a fallen tree trunk, and said to himself :

" Now, I'll back track like a grizzly, and will get
another shot at these painted hyenas."

Suiting the action to the words, he put on a furious
burst of speed for about a half a mile, then doubled
back for about two hundred yards. To the right was
some fallen timber, and into this the trapper skipped
like a molly cotton-tail. " Ah ha! " said he. " I
think this will get 'em! "

In a few moments the red warriors hastened by on
the run: one of them about a hundred yards astern
of the rest. As he came opposite the hiding-place of
the scout, " Old Bill " leaped into view, and knocking
him down with a well directed bullet, seized his victim's gun just as another started to come back to
where he was standing. This one was dispatched by
the Blackfoot rifle, and " Old Bill " had the satisfaction of seeing the fourth (and last) savage run up
the canyon in terror, screaming:

" The Great Spirit is with him! The Great Spirit
is with him! "

As he disappeared a broad smile came to the face of the trapper, while he wiped the beads of perspiration from his brow.

" By Crickets! " said he. " A tight squeeze, Bill. A tight squeeze! "

I regret to state that the old fellow *scalped* the dead redskins, for he was apparently as much of an Indian as were his enemies. He also took the precaution to plunge into a mountain stream which gurgled and rushed down a side of the canyon. He followed the water until he reached the mouth of the canyon, then, as he heard voices, dashed into a crevasse in the rocks. A number of Blackfeet soon went by.

" Where has the old wolf gone? " he heard one of them ask. " He runs like a rabbit."

" You are right," said another, " but he has an eye like a hawk, and can hold the shooting-stick without flinching. Go carefully! Go carefully! He may be hidden near by! "

They went on up the canyon, and not long afterwards a wailing and screeching came from their direction, showing that they had discovered their dead.

" This is no place for me," mused the old scout. " I must get away quickly."

Darting up a neighboring gully, he had just stowed himself away in a fissure of the rocky wall when he heard the Blackfeet returning. They were carrying their dead companions and were wailing dismally. " Old Bill " knew that there would be small chance for him should he fall into their clutches. The cold shivers ran up and down his spine as he contemplated such a happening.

For two days the trapper remained in the canyon. He was afraid to venture forth, because the Blackfeet were undoubtedly near by, and he knew that, once they again saw him, it would be all up with " Old Bill." He had a tough, dried piece of buffalo meat with him, which kept up his strength, although he suffered terribly from thirst during the day, for he was afraid to venture to the stream until nightfall. Far off, in the valley, he could hear the death chant of the red men.

Three days passed and " Old Bill " was feeling faint from lack of food. Climbing the wall of the canyon, behind his place of refuge, he saw the Blackfeet far below him in the valley. They were moving camp. Hurrah! Their tepee poles were coming down and they were walking away. They gradually faded from view. Again Hurrah! The old scout was smiling now.

Luck was still with him, for he shot an antelope soon afterwards, cooked the stringy meat and felt stronger. Then he rolled a stout log loose from some fallen timber, pushed it into the river and paddled down stream upon this flimsy boat.

" I reckon I'll dodge the redskins, now," he said to himself. " A feller walkin' leaves too good er trail."

No savage eye detected him in his journey upon this log, and, about a week later, he arrived, smiling, at a frontier trading post. " Old Bill " was royally

welcomed by his brother trappers, who slapped him
on the back, drank his health, not once, but twenty
times, and gave him a new rifle which they had just
captured from some half-breeds.

"Old Bill" took this with good humor, for it was
all in the day's work of a scout upon the frontier. In a
week he left upon another excursion into the wilds,
and alone, for he was like a "solitary," or buffalo
bull, who roams the prairie away from the rest of
the herd. He preferred to be without associates
in his work. "Two men," said he, "leave a
broader trail than one, and there are many Indians
in the country. Two men make more noise. I go
alone."

"He was a great hunter," said an old Indian. "He
was a great trapper — took many beaver — and a
great warrior, for his belt was full of scalps. But he
have no friend: no squaw. Always by himself. He
like the eagle in the heavens, or the panther in the
mountains. He one strange man."

Yes, "Old Bill" was a strange man, but he lived
his life upon the frontier for many years without a
mishap, although his body bore the marks of many
an encounter. Silent and taciturn, those who were
associated with him knew only of his deeds by the
fresh scalps at his girdle, the notches upon the stock
of his gun, and the scars upon the exposed portion
of his body. His traps yielded him a small living,
and with this he seemed to be content.

The trapper lived to be an old man. Although in
innumerable skirmishes and hand-to-hand encounters

with the Blackfeet, Crows, Sioux, and other wild
riders of the plains, he came off scott free until he
met a band of Blackfeet when trapping near the headwaters of the Missouri River.   Here he was surrounded by twenty or thirty braves, but, by skillfully
climbing his pony down the shelving sides of a canyon, made his escape.   They found his tracks, however, and followed him like a pack of hounds after
a fox.

"Old Bill" still was lithe and active, although
sixty years, and more, of age.   Again and again he
hid himself, and, with two or three shots, laid out
as many of the advancing redskins.   He was fortunate in being able to keep away from the vindictive
warriors for four full days, although wounded twice:
an arrow point in his thigh and a bullet through the
fleshy part of his leg.   Finally, he reached a series of
canyons   near   the   Yellowstone,   where   numerous
streams   made   it   possible   for   him   to   leave   little
trace   of   his   trail,   and   great   boulders   of   rock   hid
his   retreating   form.   The   red   men   here   gave   up
the chase, for their quarry defied both fatigue and
wounds.

"The Great Spirit is still with the Lone Wolf,"
said they.   "We will let him go, for here he can kill
many of us before we can reach him."

It was November.   A bleak wind blew gusts of
snow across the sandy plain as the red warriors retreated.   "Old Bill" continued on his way into the
advancing storm.   The white flakes now covered the
earth.   A bitter wind assailed him, and great piles of

drifting snow whirled and eddied about his gaunt and emaciated form. Dismounting under the side of a projecting cliff, he made a fire by means of rubbing two dried sticks together, ate some *biltong,* which he fortunately had stowed away in a saddle-bag, and lay down to rest. His poor, shivering pony cropped the dry bunches of grass in silent misery.

Two weeks later a party of trappers were crossing the stream near the place where the old fellow had lain down, and saw a pony nibbling the bark from a cotton-wood tree. He was gaunt, famished, and his ribs were fairly sticking through his flesh. They rode up to him and were much distressed to see the form of a man lying beneath the white mantle of newly fallen snow. They brushed this away and found " Old Bill; " his grizzled head bent forward upon his breast, and his clothing stained with the wounds which had sapped his very life-blood. He had gone to the Great Beyond.

With tears in their eyes the trappers hollowed out a grave for the lone refugee. Here they buried him, and finding his faithful steed unwilling to leave the place where he had carried his master, shot the emaciated animal. They placed both in the same grave, and over their forms erected a huge pile of stones, not only to mark the last resting-place of " Old Bill," but also to keep the wolves and coyotes from digging up the remains.

Thus, in a wild canyon perished the aged solitary, and in the peace and quiet of that wilderness in which he loved to wander, hovers the spirit of the lonely

man of the plains.   His last resting-place well suited
the career of " Old Bill: " trapper, scout, and fearless
adventurer among the savage men, wild beasts, and
inhospitable wastes of the then unpeopled West.

"BIG FOOT" WALLACE:

NOTED RANGER ON THE TEXAN FRONTIER

ABOUT the year 1839, a Waco Indian chieftain lived in the State of Texas, whose feet were of such giant proportions that he was called "Big Foot." He was a bold and daring fellow. Often, when darkness hid his movement, he would sneak into the frontier town of Austin, would kill whom he could, and would carry off horses and other property. In vain the settlers tried to dispatch him, for he was a veritable scourge to the settlements.

The fellow was a physical giant, being six feet seven inches in height, of muscular build, and weighing about three hundred pounds. His tracks measured fourteen inches, from heel to toe, so you can readily see that the name that was applied to him was not ill chosen. Often these footprints would be seen in the sandy soil, after he had committed one of his thieving expeditions, and the settlers used to cry out:

"Good-by to our horses! Old 'Big Foot' is around again. Good-by!"

One evening the big Indian came into Austin, and, after prowling around for a time, committed some theft upon the property of a settler named Gravis.

223

He then went to the cabin occupied by a huge, lanky ranger called Wallace. Next morning Gravis trailed the Indian to the doorstep of the pioneer, and, without trying to trace it any further, aroused the owner of the cabin.

"See here, Wallace," said he, "you've been stealing from my place and I intend to get even with you. No one has as big feet as you have around here, and I have found your tracks leading from my hut to your very door."

The accused man grew angry and prepared to whip the other.

"Look here," said Gravis, at this juncture, "if you prove to me that these are not your foot-prints you can go clear and I will apologize."

He stepped aside, as he spoke, and Wallace immediately went to the Indian's track. He placed his foot in it, exclaiming:

"By Gravy, Gravis, this is old 'Big Foot,' the Injin's, track. Can't you see that it's mor'n two inches longer than my own!"

The first speaker bent over the marks with an exclamation of astonishment.

"You're right," said he. "Wallace, old man, I beg your pardon." And, shaking him warmly by the hand, he walked away.

While this was going on, a man named Fox came to the doorway of Wallace's hut. He had been spending the night there, for he was a business partner of the frontiersman. As his friend turned towards the cabin, he cried out gleefully:

"BIG FOOT" WALLACE.

"Well, well, old scout.   When 'Big Foot' — the Indian — is not around we will all call *you* 'Big Foot.'   Ha! Ha! That's a good one, I swan.   'Big Foot' you'll be from henceforth."

And that is the way that William Alexander Anderson Wallace came to be called "Big Foot" Wallace.

Born in Lexington, Virginia, in 1817, this intrepid frontiersman came of good, old Scottish stock, and stock that was of fighting spirit, for two of his uncles were killed in the battle of Guilford Court House. The Wallaces were all of powerful build, and the hero of our sketch was six feet two inches in height (in his moccasins) and weighed two hundred and forty pounds.   He had long arms, large hands, and thick, curly, black hair.   One of his uncles was nearly seven feet tall and his brother was six feet five inches in height.

As a young fellow, "Big Foot" Wallace had little of the excitement which was to come to him in later years.   When about twenty years of age war commenced between the American colonists and Mexicans for the possession of Texas.   Many young men went from Virginia to assist the Texans in driving out the soldiers under Santa Anna, among them Samuel Wallace, the older brother of William with the big feet.   Samuel was killed in the massacre of Colonel Fannin's men at Goliad, which has been described in "Famous Scouts," and with him were also dispatched three cousins of our hero.   When the news of this affair reached Lexington, Virginia, great was the grief

among the relatives of these brave and valiant frontiersmen, and William was much upset by it.

"I am going to Texas," he cried out. "And I
intend to spend my life in killing Mexicans. Those
men who could massacre my brother after he had surrendered and had been disarmed, can expect no quarter from me. I intend to have revenge!"

He had splendid opportunities in later years to make
good this threat.

Taking ship from New Orleans to Galveston, William soon set foot on Texan soil. The war was over.
Santa Anna had been defeated and captured the year
before, at the famous battle of San Jacinto, and Texas
was now an independent republic. So the young
ranger drifted to Colorado, where he was soon surrounded by a large party of Indians and was captured.
They carried him to their camp, but he only remained
there a week, before he slipped away, eluded his pursuers, and got back to the settlement of San Antonio.
His restless spirit could not be confined to the streets
of a city and he soon went far to the southwest, where
he camped and hunted along the Medina River.
Finally he built a cabin there and lived the life of a
lone huntsman and trapper in a region which was
infested by Indians, horse-thieves, and fugitives from
justice.

"Big Foot" Wallace had not been long in the
country before he realized that something had to be
done in order to keep law and order in this unsettled
land. Besides the numerous raids of hostile bands of
Indians — who roamed at will from New Mexico to

the coast region of Texas — desperadoes and gamblers swarmed around all the border towns, and more particularly around San Antonio. No one was safe who opposed these wild fellows, and it was almost impossible to keep horses. The thieves would even dig through the adobe walls of the stables in order to steal them. A strong hand was needed to awe these desperate men and keep the Indians in check. There was one man in western Texas at this time who was quite equal to the emergency. His name was "Captain" Jack Hays.

The Governor of Texas sent for him.

"I hereby commission you to raise a company of Rangers," said he to the gallant Captain Jack. "You will make San Antonio your headquarters and you must hold both Indians and horse-thieves in check. You can follow the redskins anywhere that you wish, and, if necessary, you can shoot any horse-thief upon the spot."

"Big Foot" Wallace soon heard of the Rangers, and applied for admission at once. He was accepted, for he was strong, fearless, a good rider, and an excellent shot. Captain Hays was very particular as to the kind of men that he enlisted, and that is why he had the best set of Indian fighters that Texas ever produced. Each man had to have a good horse, valued at one hundred dollars, and also a rifle of the best make. The desperadoes and horse-thieves soon began to disappear from the neighborhood of San Antonio.

In the numerous affrays which now took place "Big Foot" Wallace had a prominent part. Several battles were fought with the Indians. In 1842 the Mexicans made a sudden descent from Mexico and captured San Antonio. At the quarters used by the Texan Rangers they found a pair of pantaloons belonging to " Big Foot " Wallace, and this they appropriated as their own.

" By the eternal prophet," shouted the scout, when he hear of the theft. " I will sure get even with the Greasers for this, and I will kill a Señor and get another pair of breeches, or bust."

Not long afterwards Jack Hays and his men rode near the town and gave the Mexicans such " a dare " that their whole force of cavalry and infantry came out to chase them. There were four hundred Mexicans and but a small squad of Rangers, yet the Texans kept up a stiff firing and retreated slowly across the plains. During the battle, " Big Foot " Wallace was continually upon the lookout to kill a big Mexican and get another pair of trousers to replace his own. He had not long to wait.

The Mexicans soon charged, and in the mix-up that ensued one daring fellow approached Wallace, and pointing his carbine at him, cried out: " Take that, you accursed cow-thief! " Whereupon he discharged his piece in his face. The large ounce ball from the clumsy musket just grazed the nose of the scout and nearly blinded him with smoke. " Big Foot " fired his own piece, but missed. As this occurred, another Ranger cried out: " My, my, what awful bad shooting," and — aiming his rifle — quickly sent a ball through the Mexican's body. The man from the south of the Rio Grande fell against a mesquite tree and soon died.

" Big Foot " breathed more easily, and during the next charge heard one of his companions call out:

" ' Big Foot,' yonder is a Mexican who has on a pair of pants large enough to fit you. Go get 'em, boy! Go get 'em! "

The Mexican in question was assisting some of the wounded back to the rear. Wallace kept his eye on him and said:

" If I can get him, I will. But th' critter moves about so fast that I can't draw a bead on him."

As he spoke, he attracted the attention of General Caldwell, who commanded some infantrymen who had come to the assistance of the Rangers. The dress of the giant Texan, his massive frame, and his actions, were sufficient to mark him as a man born to leadership.

" What command do you hold, sir? " inquired Caldwell, as he rode up to the fighting Ranger.

" None," answered " Big Foot," saluting. " I am one of Jack Hays' Rangers and I want that fellow's breeches over there, as the Greasers have stolen mine from me." He pointed, as he spoke, to his intended victim.

The general laughed and rode on, determined to advance " Big Foot " to a Lieutenancy, if the opportunity presented itself. The Ranger, meanwhile, crept nearer to the fellow with the big pantaloons, and before many moments laid him low by a well directed shot. Making a dash for the fallen man, he seized

him by the shoulders, dragged him into the American
lines, and soon was wearing a new pair of yellow
trousers.

" Hurrah for ' Big Foot,' " shouted his companions.
" He has, at last, made good his threat of vengeance.
Hurrah for ' Big Foot!' "

The Mexicans were defeated, driven from San Antonio, and were followed by Captain Jack Hays and
his Rangers as far as the Hondo River, where the
rear guard was attacked by a detachment under " Big
Foot," and some cannon were captured. The mule
which the leader was riding was slightly wounded,
but this was the only mishap to the Americans. The
Mexicans withdrew in safety to their own territory.

The blood of the Texans was now up. " Revenge
for the taking of San Antonio!" was heard on every
side. " Vengeance upon the Mexicans! Revenge!"

Thus, in retaliation for the invasion of Texas under
Wall, an expedition started for Mexico in 1843, commanded by General Somervell. Captain Jack Hays
was there with his Rangers, but the expedition went
to pieces on the Rio Grande and most of the men came
back, among them Captain Jack and many of his followers. Five captains, however, determined to go on,
in the invasion of Mexico, — that is, if they could
get men enough. Three hundred Texans immediately
decided to fight: among this number, " Big Foot "
Wallace and several other Rangers. Electing a certain Captain Fisher to the chief command, they crossed
the Rio Grande and encamped opposite the town of
Mier. Its streets were soon to run red with blood.

The chief man of a Mexican town is called an alcade, and, on the following morning, the Americans
marched into the town and told the alcade that he
must furnish them with provisions and with clothing.

" Yes, yes, Señors," said the Mexican official, bow-
ing. " To-morrow the articles will be delivered to
you, two miles below your camp."

But the Texans did not believe in taking any
chances. They brought the alcade along with them
when they went back to their camp, so as to be sure
that the provisions would really be delivered. They
waited two full days and no goods were to be seen.
They grew anxious and soon their spies made them
more so, for these reported that General Ampudia had
arrived in Mier with a large force of Mexican troops.

" We will proceed to the town and give them battle!" cried out the Texan commander.

By four o'clock in the afternoon the Americans had
all crossed and were on their way to the little Mexican
post. The spies were in front and first met the Mexicans as they sallied out from Mier. But the Rangers
knew how to shoot and Ampudia retreated before the
Texan bullets. At dark the Mexicans again entered
their stronghold and barricaded themselves.

The Texans had their fighting blood up, and, in
spite of the darkness, advanced to Alcantra Creek, east
of the little town, where they halted for some time.
The stream ran rapidly, so that it was difficult to find
a crossing, but at last they all got over. As they
scrambled up the bank, they were met by a hot fire,

and the Mexican cavalry advanced against them. Five of the Rangers were cut off and captured. Others made narrow escapes, for the Mexicans now came in close enough for hand to hand fighting, and surrounded many of the more daring. Several of the invaders were compelled to abandon their horses and make a run for it across fences and ditches. A Ranger called Sam Walker was caught by a powerful Mexican and was held down, while others tied him. One man named McMullins was seized by the legs as he was getting over a fence, but his boots pulled off and he made his escape. This was fortunate.

"Big Foot" Wallace was not among those first over the creek, and advanced with the main body, which now came on, driving the Mexicans into the town. The troops soon entered Mier and passed down a street leading to the public square, where the Mexicans had planted cannon. While advancing rapidly, they were repeatedly fired upon, and a Ranger named Jones was killed. As he fell, he lurched against "Big Foot" Wallace, who had felt the wind from the bullet that laid him low. The Texans pressed on and soon arrived at a point near the cannon, where they received a charge of grape-shot, which made them seek shelter behind some buildings. It was now dark. It was also Christmas evening, but there were no peaceful revels in Mier that winter's day.

The Texans had but one way to advance: by opening a passageway through the buildings so that they could get in the rear of the deadly cannon. They worked all night in digging a hole through the adobe

walls. When daylight came, they were within fifty
yards of the death-dealing artillery.

" Big Foot " Wallace was among those in the very
forefront of battle. While engaged in tunnelling
through the building he discovered a Mexican baby
which had been abandoned during the hasty retreat
of the occupants of the house upon the approach of
the Texans. It set up a terrific squalling when the
Americans approached it, so " Big Foot " carefully
took it up, and, advancing to a wall enclosing a yard,
climbed up and dropped it over. At the same time, he
shouted out in Spanish:

" Come and get the muchacho. Quick! "

He soon heard a woman's voice and supposed that
the poor infant was being taken care of.

Daylight dawned upon a scene of great activity.
Port-holes had been opened in the various rooms into
which the men had clambered, and the deadly crack
of the rifles was soon heard, as the Texans began to
fire at the artillerymen. The cannon were quickly
silenced, for it was death for a Mexican to venture
near them. Three attempts were made by the " Greasers " to storm and carry the Texan position, but each
failed with fearful loss. The Mexicans, in fact, came
on so thickly packed together that it was impossible
to miss them. The bravest of all were the town
guards, who wore black hats with white bands around
them. They were nearly all killed.

The Texans were fighting gamely and the Mexicans were soon forced to abandon all of their artillery.
Ropes were thrown around these instruments of war,

from the corners of buildings, and the men from the South succeeded in dragging some of them away. " Big Foot " Wallace was doing a great deal of shooting. He says that he loaded and fired his rifle fifteen times, always waited for a good chance, and had a bead upon a Mexican every time that he pulled the trigger.

During the battle bugles sounded constantly, and it was reported that the Mexicans were being largely reinforced. The Texans, however, were undismayed at this report, and continued to load and fire their rifles with such deadly effect that great confusion prevailed among their foes, who continually uttered cries of rage and pain, amidst a constant blast of bugles. They occupied the house tops, where they kept their bodies well hid, and fired from the gutters and from behind the chimneys. The American leader, himself, was severely wounded, while many of the gallant Texans lay bleeding in the narrow streets of the quaint, little Mexican town.

A small guard had been left by the Rangers upon the other side of the creek. Just after daylight, upon the twenty-sixth of December, these attacked about sixty of the Mexican cavalry and routed them, but, seeing a large reinforcement approaching, they desperately endeavored to join their comrades in the little town. Out of the nine men who made this desperate charge, two succeeded; four were killed; and three were captured.

The fortune of war was apparently going badly with the Mexicans, but a sudden turn of events placed victory in their very hands. Captain Cameron had fortified himself and his men in the rear of a building occupied by Fisher and his support, where he had been exposed to a fearful fire. Upon the morning after Christmas day he entered the room occupied by his superior officer.

" Send me reinforcements," he said, " for the bugles are blowing the charge and I am afraid that I will be annihilated."

" I have no reinforcements," Fisher replied. " You will have to fight on as you are."

As he ceased speaking a white flag was seen approaching from the Mexican lines. With it was a Doctor Sinnickson — a Texan who had been recently captured by the Mexican troops. He had been ordered to tell the Rangers that there were one thousand seven hundred Mexican troops in the city, and that three hundred more were approaching from Monterey.

" Ampudia says that it will be useless for you to resist," said the Doctor. " If you surrender, you will be treated like prisoners of war. If you resist, no quarter will be given!"

The Texan leader looked gloomily before him. He was on foreign soil. He was hemmed in on every side by his enemies. His men were nearly all worn out. The streets of Mier had run red with Mexican blood; and there was no chance to win. He was in favor of an honorable surrender. But some thought that they could make a sally from their barricaded position, and, by keeping together, could fight their way out of town and to the borders of the Rio Grande.

These gathered around Cameron and begged him to take command; to make a rush; and to fight a way out. Great confusion prevailed. Some began to leave their positions and give their guns up to their enemies. Every few moments barricades would be torn away and men would march out and surrender.

Cameron held on to his position until many had given themselves up. Then he saw that all hope was gone, and therefore turned to his men.

"Boys," said he, "it is useless for us to continue the fight any longer. They are all gone except ourselves."

His followers stood for a few moments watching the crowds of Mexicans, who were making a great demonstration. Their cavalry was charging up and down the streets, while many were carrying away the guns of the Texans who were collected upon the plaza. The citizens of the town were cheering for victory.

"I'll never give up," said "Big Foot" Wallace. "My relatives were massacred after they had surrendered at Goliad, and that is what the Mexicans will do to us."

But Cameron wished to save the lives of his men and so took the lead. As he marched towards the Mexican line, his soldiers followed. When they emerged from their position into the street they were met by a strong detachment of Mexicans. The painful work of surrendering their arms now commenced. "Big Foot" Wallace was the last man to give up his gun, his knife, and his pistol.

The bloody battle of Mier was over. The Mexican
loss had been heavy. With two thousand in the field,
five hundred had been killed. The Texans had two
hundred and sixty in the town, sixteen of whom were
killed and thirty of whom were wounded. The Mexicans lost forty artillerymen. The bodies of the slain
Texans were dragged through the streets by the cavalry, and were followed by crowds of yelling towns-
folk. Four rows of dead Mexicans were laid out upon
the plaza, where the priests said mass among them.
It had been a fierce little battle.

Now the troubles of the Texan Rangers really commenced. The wounded were left at the blood-bespat-
tered Mier in charge of the good Doctor Sinnickson,
while the able-bodied Americans were marched
towards Mexico City, in charge of General Ampudia.
Everywhere they were met by jubilant Mexicans, who
made grand demonstrations as they passed through
the towns, blowing bugles, hallooing, and charging
around upon their horses. The Texans were so
starved that they became thin and haggard, while
their shoes were worn completely through. The Mexican women pitied the half-fed Americans, some of
whom were mere boys. At Monterey they came in
with provisions and fed them. " Big Foot " Wallace
— still wearing the trousers which he had captured —
was thin but game. " Just give me a chance to escape," he muttered to a companion. " Then, — watch
me go! "

Finally the Texans were placed in prison at the
Hacienda Salado. Their numbers were increased by

a few ranchers who had been captured in other raids.
All were anxious to make the attempt to escape, and
a plan was set on foot to rush the guards at sunrise
on the eleventh day of February, 1843. At Monterey
a similar plot had been hatched, but one of the Texan
officers had disclosed it to the Mexicans, so the attempt had not been made.

All was soon ready for the struggle for freedom.
Captain Cameron gave the signal by throwing up his
hat, and two scouts named Lyons and Brennan led
the charge upon the guards. The Mexicans were
taken completely by surprise, were disarmed at the
door of the prison, and saw the Texans dash into the
outer court of the building where about one hundred
and fifty infantrymen were guarding the arms and
boxes of cartridges. The Texans numbered two
hundred.

The frontiersmen rushed immediately upon the regular soldiers, who levelled their muskets at them and
fired in their very faces. The Texans were not armed
but they pressed onward, received the fire, and closed
in upon the yellow-skinned custodians of the jail. It
was too bold a dash for the Mexicans. They surrendered or fled after the first fire, but the Texans
had other soldiers to face.

A second company of infantry was stationed at the
gate and a force of cavalry was outside. The gallant
Texans did not hesitate for an instant. The desperate
fellows rushed upon them, and a terrible fight ensued.
Most of them had secured guns by now, and, when the
second hand-to-hand fight took place, they were better

prepared to force their way. "Big Foot" Wallace did not have a gun, so he rushed at a Mexican who had discharged his piece, and tried to disarm him. The fellow had a bayonet upon the end of his musket. He made a vicious thrust at the gaunt and lanky man from Texas.

"Big Foot" seized the bayonet with his bare hands, and a hard struggle took place for the possession of it. As they bent to and fro, an unarmed prisoner came up behind, and, seizing the gun in the centre, wrested it from the Mexican. The soldier fell upon his knees, held up his hands, and called out loudly: "Señors, have mercy! Have mercy!"

"You can go," shouted "Big Foot" Wallace.

The fight was now raging fiercely and the scout went into the thick of it, brandishing the musket which he had just captured, and doing awful execution with the bayonet. The Texans were getting nearer and nearer to the gate which opened upon the streets of the town. The Mexicans were uttering screams and yells of terror and surprise. The Rangers were among them with clubbed guns and were delivering blows to the right and left. The cavalry became terror-stricken and fled. The infantrymen at the gate began to throw down their arms and try to surrender.

One Mexican lieutenant showed extraordinary bravery. His name was Barragan, — a son of the commander of the Mexican force. Backing against a wall, he brandished his sword aloft, and refused to surrender except to an officer. Six Texans surrounded him and thrust bayonets at his breast, but he kept his arm in motion and successfully parried every thrust. His sabre was moved about with such rapidity that it could hardly be seen.

At this time " Big Foot " Wallace came up. " Here," cried a Texan, " you shoot this fellow, ' Big Foot.' He deserves death."

But the lanky Texan shook his head. " No," said he. " This man deserves better treatment, for he is a brave soldier. I refuse to shoot him."

" Let me see your Captain," cried the Mexican. " To him I will surrender my sword."

Captain Cameron came up at once and the blade was turned over to him. With a proud look the Mexican stepped back and folded his arms.

" You are a brave man," said Cameron. " You must be our prisoner, but you will not be injured."

The Texans were now masters of the situation. They dictated terms to their enemies, one of which was that the wounded should be well taken care of. Meanwhile they prepared for instant flight, for they knew that a large force would soon be on their trail. Some of the Mexicans had tied their horses near by, and these were at once seized.

By ten o'clock in the morning the Texans were all mounted and set out for the Rio Grande. It was touch and go with them. The chances for their getting away were very slight, for they did not know the country.

" Big Foot " Wallace had secured a fine dun-colored mule which had belonged to a Mexican officer. The other Texans had good mounts, and by midnight were fifty miles from the scene of their battle. A short halt was made and the horses were fed. The men slept two hours, and, early in the morning, left the main road so as to go around the city of Saltillo. They soon abandoned the road for the mountains. This was a fatal mistake, for it was a barren waste with no water and no food.

For six days the gallant Texans pressed onward. They were soon perishing with thirst and starvation. So hungry were they that horses were killed and eaten. The Texans drank the blood of their mounts, and, leaving the remains of their slaughtered beasts for the coyotes and buzzards, they plunged into the arid, brown mountains in a vain endeavor to reach the Rio Grande. Many were on foot. Some became delirious and wandered away to die in lonely ravines. The party became badly scattered. " Big Foot " Wallace dried some mule meat in the sun and carried it along in a haversack. The frontiersmen toiled onward in the direction of the Rio Grande, but the Mexican cavalry was hot upon their trail.

Finally the yellow-skinned soldiers of the country began to come up with the half-dead Texans and to capture them. The majority of the invaders formed a hollow square and refused to surrender unless they could do so as prisoners of war. They were hollow-cheeked, sunken-eyed and half alive, yet they cried out that they would fight unless granted an honorable surrender. The Mexicans were well mounted and well fed. They had the Rangers at their mercy, yet they granted them what they asked for. Of one hundred and ninety-three Texans who had made their escape, five died of thirst and starvation, four got through to Texas, and three were never heard of again.

The Texans were tied together with ropes and were marched in a single line to Saltillo. When they were brought into the city an order was received from Santa Anna to have them shot. The Mexican officer in charge of the prisoners refused to comply, and said that he would resign his commission before he would do so. The British consul also interfered, so the poor Texans were allowed to go on to Solado, where they had had their fierce battle for freedom. They were placed in irons. As they reached the town an order came from Santa Anna to have every tenth man shot.

When the prisoners arrived at the jail from which they had so gloriously escaped, some Mexicans were seen digging a ditch. " Big Foot " Wallace nudged a companion. " That ditch is for us! " said he. He was quite right.

The Mexican officers now decided to let the prisoners draw lots in order to see who should, and who should not be, shot. A large jar was filled with beans: as many beans as Texans. White and black beans were there. The white ones meant life; the black, — death. There were nine white beans to one black.

The Texans were now marched out from their jail and were formed in a long line. An officer soon approached with the jar in his hand, in which were one hundred and fifty-nine white beans and seventeen black ones. The poor Texans were to pass through a fearful ordeal, but they were all gamblers with life, so they took it philosophically. Soldiers will rush to almost certain death in the excitement of battle, but to stand and decide one's fate by the drawing of a bean is worse than charging upon a spitting cannon.

The Mexican officers were very anxious to kill Captain Cameron, the gallant leader of the gaunt and half-starved Texans. They were therefore in great hopes that he would draw a black bean, and, for this reason, placed black beans on top, within the jar. He was also requested to draw first.

But one of the captives — a fellow named "Bill" Wilson — saw the trick, and, as Cameron placed his hand in the jar, the Ranger called out: "Dip deep, Captain! Dip deep!"

Cameron followed his advice, ran his fingers to the bottom, and pulled out a white bean. A look of satisfaction passed over the faces of the Texans, for they all loved the brave and unselfish Captain. The Mexicans scowled as the drawing went rapidly on.

All "dipped deep" and it was thus some time before a black bean was pulled forth. The Texans knew that some of them would be compelled to draw the black beans, but they grinned with delight as friend after friend extracted a white bean from the fateful jar. Most of the scouts showed the utmost coolness. One noted gambler from Austin, Texas, stepped up to the jar with a smile, saying: "Boys, this is the largest stake that I ever played for!" When he drew out his hand a black bean was between thumb and fore-finger. Without changing the smile on his face, he muttered: "Just my luck! Good-by to dear, old Texas!"

One young fellow, almost a boy, drew a black bean, and giving one appealing look at his comrades, cried out:

"Boys, avenge my death on these hounds!"

As the drawing progressed, some of the petty Mexican officers did all in their power to annoy the prisoners. When one would draw a black bean they would express great sorrow, and would say: "Cheer up! Better luck next time!" although they knew that this was the last chance which the poor fellow would ever have.

One witty Texan cried out, when his time came to draw:

"Boys, I had rather draw for a Spanish horse and lose him!" He drew a white bean.

The time approached for "Big Foot" Wallace to have his turn, for the men drew in alphabetical order, and W was well down upon the list. The boys were "dipping deep" and nearly all of the white beans had been dipped out. As "Big Foot" reached into the jar there were about an equal number of black beans and white. His hand was so large that he had difficulty in squeezing it down to the beans.

The wily Ranger was under the impression that the black beans were a little larger than the white ones, so he scooped up two against the side of the vessel, and, getting them between his fingers, felt them with great care. The Mexicans were watching him very closely. " Hurry up! " cried one. " If you pull out two beans and one of them is a black one, you will have to take the black."

" Big Foot " paid no attention to this remark. Life was now at stake. He deliberately felt the beans for some time and one seemed to be larger than the other. He let it go, drew out his hand, and breathed easier. He had drawn out a white bean. The next two men drew black.

The black beans had now all been extracted, and the last three Texans did not draw. An officer turned up the jar and three white beans fell to the ground. The condemned men were then placed in a row and the firing squad was detailed and counted off.

The irons were now taken from the unfortunate Texans and they were led away to execution, bidding their more fortunate companions good-by, as they moved off. Tears were running down the cheeks of the emaciated Texans as they bade their comrades a last adieu A man named Whaling asked not to be blindfolded, saying that he wished to look the man in the face that shot him, and show them how a Texan could die. His request was refused.

The bold and intrepid Texan Rangers were now ready for execution. All were blindfolded, a sharp order rang out, and the crash of muskets woke the echoes of the high adobe walls of the quaint, rambling prison. Without a sound the condemned Texans fell to the ground, all of them dead save one. This man — a fellow named Shephard — was wounded in the shoulder, although a Mexican musket was within a few feet of him when it had been fired. He feigned death, so that he was able to crawl off and escape to the mountains after the Mexicans had gone away. But the men of the south discovered that one of their victims had disappeared when they came to remove the bodies to the ditch which had been prepared for them. Scouts were sent out in every direction to hunt for the missing corpse. In ten days the Ranger was retaken and was shot.

The survivors — in irons — were started on foot for the City of Mexico. They were half starved. They were derided, hooted at, and beaten by the populace. "Big Foot" Wallace suffered terribly, for the shackles were too small and cut deep into the flesh. His arms became badly swollen.

When the poor prisoners arrived at San Louis Potosi, the Governor's wife came to look at the half-fed men and particularly noted the condition of Wallace. Her sympathies were at once aroused and she ordered the chains to be taken off. The officer who commanded the Mexican troops refused to do so, saying that only the Governor had authority to give such an order.

"I am the Governor's wife," replied the woman. "I command you — in his name — to take off these terrible bands."

To this the soldier consented. Sending for a blacksmith, he had the shackles removed. The Governor's wife bathed the swollen arms of "Big Foot" Wallace with her own hands.

" You should be President of Mexico," said the half-dead Ranger.

The prisoners were marched onward and soon arrived at an Indian village about eighteen miles from the City of Mexico. Here an order came from Santa Anna to shoot Captain Ewing Cameron. He had drawn a white bean, but the Mexican leader did not respect his former decision. The order was kept a secret from the balance of the prisoners out of fear that they would make a demonstration. That night Cameron was put in a room alone, with a separate guard. The rest of the prisoners suspected some treachery and were fearful of the fate of their brave leader.

Next morning, when they were all marched out, each Texan filled his shirt full of rocks, determined to die for their captain if need be.

" Why are you getting those rocks?" asked the guards.

" It is for ballast," replied " Big Foot " Wallace. " We want to walk better."

The Mexican soldiers made no attempt to take the stones away. They were probably afraid to do so, as they saw a desperate look upon the faces of the Rangers. As they marched on, the prisoners frequently inquired about Cameron and wanted to know if he were going to be shot.

" No! No!" replied the Mexicans. " Go on! Your Captain will soon be with you!"

Somewhat reassured, the Rangers went forward, but, when they were about a mile from the town, they heard a platoon of soldiers fire their muskets in their rear. Some one cried out: " Brave Cameron has been massacred, boys! A finer man never breathed!"

It was only too true. The patriotic Texan had met his death unflinchingly, — a victim of the treachery of the wily Santa Anna.

Texas was then an independent Republic, for it had not yet been admitted into the Union. The United States had nothing to do with protecting the citizens of Texas, and the young Republic did not have forces enough to invade Mexico with an army, so as to rescue these unfortunate men. The British consul, however, had a good deal to say about the killing of Cameron, and had a personal interview with Santa Anna regarding it. He severely condemned this cruel procedure.

The Rangers were now closely confined in a miserable dungeon. Many went insane and died. Twenty-four succeeded in digging their way out, underneath the wall. Four scaled over the high enclosure and made their way back to Texas in safety. " Big Foot " Wallace, himself, had a fit of temporary insanity, but he recovered and managed to live through the months of terrible imprisonment. The Texans were so badly fed that they caught the rats which ran across the dungeon floor and ate them. Meanwhile Santa Anna's wife was continually pleading with her husband to liberate the miserable men. The stern dictator was greatly attached to her, and would grant almost anything that she asked.

Friends of the Texans were using their best en-

deavors to have the prisoners released. Through the
influence of his father and Governor McDowell of
Virginia, " Big Foot " Wallace was finally set free.
Upon the fifth day of August, 1844, he and four
others were allowed to go, after an imprisonment of
twenty-two months. Upon the same day the good
wife of Santa Anna died, — regretted and beloved by
every Texan who had worn the chains of Mexico.
Soon afterwards an order came to set free the remainder of the Texans, for Santa Anna had promised his wife — on her death-bed — that he would
release them. To his honor be it said that he kept
his promise.

The intrepid " Big Foot " was, of course, delighted
with his freedom. Taking ship at Vera Cruz, he soon
reached New Orleans, and from there found his way
back to his old cabin upon the Medina River. Many
settlers had taken up ranches near by, so he was no
longer alone. Still the Indians were very thick, and
there were frequent brushes with the wild riders of
the plains.

One day — near Fort Inge — the pioneer discovered the track of the famous Big Foot Indian, where
he and six followers had crossed the road. The old
fellow's footprint was fourteen inches in length, and,
as he had seen it several times before, the plainsman
knew that there was trouble in the wind. When he
reached the fort, he found a friend of his named Westfall.

" That Big Foot redskin is around," said he. " This
means horse stealing. If the old cuss does get your

stock, just let me know and I will join you in a little Injun round-up."

" All right," Westfall replied. " If I need you, I will let you know."

As Wallace expected, in three or four days a Ranger came after him with the information that all of Westfall's horses had been stolen and that he was needed — very badly needed — to assist in their recapture. The Indians had ridden up the Nueces Canyon to its source, and then had crossed over to the headwaters of the South Llano, where they had gone into camp in a dense cedar grove. They thought that they had captured all of the white men's horses, and so would not be followed. As they had shot a small bear, they proceeded to cook it over a glowing fire.

But the redskins did not remember that the white settlers had some very good mules, which they had not captured. On these the Texans followed the Indian trail, and soon located the redskin encampment by the smoke from the fire. Westfall rested, but did not cook anything. He was waiting for morning, before making the attack.

As day dawned, the plainsman crept towards the Indian camp; accompanied by a youth named Preston Polly. The other men — four in number — were told to come on when they heard his gun. At first the two whites descended into the bed of a gorge to a point opposite the camp of the famous Big Foot Indian. When nearing the smoke from the fire, a trail was discovered, which led down the hill to a pool of water fed by two deep springs. Below the pool was some rank, coarse grass. Westfall and the boy halted in this.

Suddenly, as he peered beneath some bushes, Westfall saw an Indian coming towards the pool of water. He was mounted upon a pie-bald pony, and was a tall, well-formed brave. The plainsman lay still, scarcely daring to breathe. Silently he cocked his rifle and kept his eyes upon the savage.

In a few moments the Indian came into full view. The heart of the plainsman beat quickly, for before him was the terrible Big Foot: his face all daubed up with vermilion paint, and eagle feathers in his scalp-lock. Motioning to the boy to remain absolutely quiet, Westfall slowly raised his rifle. At this moment the horse discovered the ambushed marksman and snorted. Big Foot turned quickly in order to see what was the matter and was for a moment stationary. Bang! The burly chieftain — the scourge and terror of the border — pitched forward upon his face. He had been shot clean through the heart.

True to their orders to approach when they heard the discharge of a rifle, the other men came up quickly, on the run. They charged up the hill, past the body of the dead chief, and into the camp of the red men. The Indians had gone, but the stolen horses were all in camp, except those ridden away by the redskins. The pioneers ate a good portion of the bear meat, which was fat, juicy, and well roasted.

When they examined the big chief, they found that he was indeed the giant of a man, for he was seven

feet tall and weighed about three hundred pounds.
His hand clutched the bridle-reins so firmly that his
pony was unable to pull away from him. His hair
was fully a yard in length and he had strong arms and
legs. Upon his right knee was the mark of a bullet
where he had been wounded some years before. The
white men took his moccasins in order to prove that
it was the real Big Foot; rounded up their horses;
and were soon travelling back to their ranches. The
great chief was buried without ceremony.

"Big Foot" Wallace was shortly afterwards commissioned by the Governor of Texas to raise a company of Rangers for frontier defense. He was made
Captain and appointed his friend Westfall a Lieutenant. They were soon to see plenty of stiff fighting.

The hardest battle which they engaged in was on
Todos Santos (All Saints) Creek, at a place called
the Black Hills, sixteen miles from the town of Co-
tulla. Eighty redskins were near this spot, and had
camped near a waterhole, which the whites wished to
get to, as they had been three days without water.
The plainsmen had come through prickly pear and
catclaw bushes only to find the Indians in their path.
A stiff fight ensued. The Rangers circled around the
savages for over an hour, and, after they had wounded
a good many, charged the remainder. There was
hand-to-hand fighting, but the red men were finally
driven away, leaving twenty-two of their number dead
upon the ground, among whom was their chief. "Big
Foot" Wallace had dispatched him with a rifle, which

had been presented to him by Colonel James Bowie, from whom the bowie knife took its name.

The redoubtable Wallace was one of the first to enlist in the Mexican War of 1846, and served under the famous Texan Jack Hays. The war, as you know, was brought on by a dispute over the boundary-line between Mexico and the United States, and, as many of the Rangers had old scores to settle with the Mexicans, they did good service in the campaign which ended in the capture of the City of Mexico. " Big Foot" Wallace was a second Lieutenant and acquitted himself nobly, particularly in the storming of Monterey, where he captured the very officer who had held the fatal bean-pot when the Texans were drawing for their lives at Solado. To his credit be it said that he let the fellow go.

The famous plainsman never married, although he was once engaged to a belle of Austin, Texas. He was taken ill, shortly after pledging his troth, and had the misfortune to lose all of his hair. As soon as he was able to travel, he left town and hid himself in a cave in the mountains. Here he resided until his hair grew out again. Meanwhile his sweetheart had grown tired of waiting for him and had married another man. As she turned out to be a terrible scold, he was lucky.

The old scout was the proud possessor of four dogs —half-bred specimens—which he prized very highly. He called them Rock, Ring, Speck and Blas, and was particularly fond of Rock, who was so well trained that he could follow an Indian by his scent. Wallace could always tell by the dog's actions when Indians

were around, and, when night came, would feel perfectly secure when his pets were on guard near by.
The faithful animals would lie near him and would
make no noise unless some wild man, or still wilder
animal, approached.

One morning Rock gave unmistakable signs that
Indians were near by, so the scout took his gun in
order to watch for the redskins. As none put in an
appearance, he told his dogs to "go on and find."
They rushed forward, yelping, and he soon heard
them baying loudly. Coming to the spot, he saw an
Indian down in a gully with the dogs around him.
They were endeavoring to bite him, but he kept them
from seizing him by throwing his blanket over their
heads. Wallace raised his gun to fire, but, seeing that
the poor redskin was afraid, he lowered his piece.
Then, calling his pets to his side, he made signs to
the Indian to come towards him.

When the redskin approached, "Big Foot" saw
that he was unarmed, save for a small knife which
he held in his right hand. This was broken in two.

"I have been a captive among the Comanches,"
said the red man. "I have had nothing to kill game
with and am nearly starved. Pray give me something
to eat, Señor. I broke my knife while trying to open
a terrapin."

The old scout's heart was touched by the sad spec-
tacle before him. He took pity on the poor savage,
and, leading him to his cabin, there gave him all that
he could eat. He then turned him over to the Indian
agent at San Antonio. This shows that, although

keen in pursuing hostile redskins, the famous Ranger could be also kind and gentle to the unfortunate.

The fame of " Big Foot " Wallace was great among the pioneers of Texas; so great, in fact, that when he appeared at the Dallas fair in 1898, hundreds crowded around him in order to take his hand and talk with the famous scout. All had heard of the giant plainsman and wanted to see him. Shortly after Christmas, of this year, he caught a heavy cold, and died on the seventh of January, 1899, in his eighty-third year. To the very end his eyesight was so keen that he had no need of glasses, and he was apparently hale and hearty up to the last. Thus peacefully closed the career of one of the most adventurous men who ever hunted, fished, and fought the red men and Mexicans upon the wide plains of Texas.

Although buried in Medina County, where he had built his first log cabin, shortly after his death, a bill was passed in the legislature, so that his remains were taken up and were deposited in the State cemetery at Austin. This was a city which he had helped to build. He had also assisted in the construction of the first well which had been sunk there. He had been among those who had killed the last herd of buffalo on the plains near by.

Here — in the peace of the rolling plain — lies the last of the Great Captains of those gallant Rangers of the Texan prairie. His spirit slumbers where the coyote and Indian once followed the dun-colored herds of buffalo, and where — in the blue azure of the cloudless sky — the wheeling vulture watched the canvas-covered wagons of the emigrant trains, which brought a people who were to construct great and populous cities, where was then only dust and desolation.

CAPTAIN JACK HAYS:

FAMOUS TEXAN RANGER AND COMMANDER OF VALIANT BORDER FIGHTERS

IT was the year 1840. Texas was still a wild country, but the white settlers were pressing forward to farm and to raise cattle and horses. The redskins did not like it. The Comanches were particularly troublesome: they had been severely chastised by General Burleson and a Colonel John H. More, so they had sworn to revenge themselves upon the white-skinned invaders. With a large body of painted warriors they made a raid upon the defenseless settlers of Texas. They sacked and burned the town of Linnville, partly destroyed Victoria, and commenced their retreat back to the mountains with a great deal of plunder. There were six hundred warriors and many squaws in the party of invasion.

In going down from the mountains the Indians had kept between the rivers, where there were no settlements, and consequently they were not discovered until a short time before the attack upon Linnville. Runners were immediately sent to the various settlements, and men began to cut across the country in small squads from the valleys of the Colorado, the Guadalupe, and San Marcos. All of them were excited and eager for revenge, none more so than General Burleson, who — at the head of a large company — was just starting for the scene of action. When about one hundred and fifty men had arrived — among them settlers from Guadalupe and San Marcos — they started for the Indians.

Among those who came riding to the defense of the Texan frontier was a splendid looking, young fellow, who was the perfect picture of manly vigor. Clad in blue shirt, buckskin chaparejos (large trousers slipping over those usually worn) and high-heeled boots, the youthful Texan was a noble example of health and agility. A broad sombrero was upon his head, while a cartridge-belt hung about his supple waist. His name was John Coffee Hays; better known as Jack Hays: the Ranger.

This celebrated scout and Indian fighter had been named after General Coffee, who commanded a brigade in the army of General Jackson, at the battle of New Orleans. He had been born in Wilson County, Tennessee, in 1818, but had come to Texas in 1837, when but nineteen years of age. A surveyor by profession, he had taken up a residence at San Antonio, where he was employed to measure lands upon the frontier. His life in the open had given him a hardy constitution, and no one could endure more hardships or privations than he. His talent as a commander and director of rough-and-ready fighters early developed, and he was soon among the leaders of the borderers in Southwest Texas.

With a wild hurrah, which spelled REVENGE, in

large letters, the Texans started after the Indians, and, after travelling for nine miles upon their broad trail, caught up with them near a winding stream called Plum Creek. Two redskins had been left by the invaders as spies. They were upon a ridge and sat quietly upon their horses, watching the approach of the white men, until the Texans were almost within gunshot. Both of these Indians had on tall hats which they had obtained at the looting of Linnville. You can well imagine how comical they looked, for a black, stovepipe hat hardly becomes a wild rider of the plains. With his thick, long hair it never quite fits, and it certainly gives the red man a most grotesque appearance.

One of the Texan Rangers had a long-range gun. Dismounting, he cried out:

" Boys! Just watch me make the redskins hump!"

At the crack of his rifle, the Indians wheeled their horses in order to run away. As they did so, both lost their plug hats. They moved swiftly to their comrades, warning them of the approach of the Rangers, who spread out in a fan-shaped line, and kept on after the retreating braves.

Now began a hot fight. The redskins were well armed and made a good showing, but nothing could withstand the terrible fire of the Texan rifles. After an hour of rapid shooting the Rangers charged with a wild, ear-splitting whoop. Jack Hays was well up in front of the line as they did so. The Indians broke and galloped away in a disorganized mass.

Many of the redskins had on fine coats and boots

which they had stolen during the raid. Some of
them even carried umbrellas. Their spare horses and
mules were packed with stolen goods, and these were
driven ahead by the squaws, while the warriors fought
the battle. After about a mile of fighting, the Comanches rallied in large force and a sharp contest ensued. But they could not stand the accurate rifle-fire
from the Texans, and again fled in a scattered mass.

The pursuit continued in hot haste, for some high
mountains were in front, and the Rangers knew that
if the red men once reached them it would be quite
possible for them to get away. Many of the pack-
animals now gave out, were abandoned, and fell into
the hands of the Texans. A boggy branch was in the
path of the retreating braves. Several of the Indian
ponies stuck fast in the mire: all of the pack-animals
which had not yet been captured, became hard aground
in the mud. The hindmost Indians used some of the
poor, bogged animals as pontoons, and passed over
the marsh by jumping from body to body. The Texans saw the predicament which the redskins were in
and ran around the branch to the other side, where
they cut off some of the Indians who were on foot,
and killed them. The rest got away to the foot of
the mountains, where the pursuit ended.

The Rangers collected at the spot where the fight
had been most severe and where most of the Indians
had been dispatched. Here they camped for the
night. Some of the Texans had been wounded, but
none had been killed. Thus the battle of Plum Creek
came to a glorious end.

Jack Hays had certainly distinguished himself in this affair. He distinguished himself still more in 1842, when San Antonio was captured by the Mexicans. Shortly after the battle of Plum Creek, Jack had been commissioned by General Houston to raise a force for protection of the frontier. He had no difficulty in doing this and was soon in command of several hundred Texan Rangers. They were wild fellows; ready for any emergency that might arise.

The Mexicans had about fifteen hundred men in San Antonio. They were commanded by a General Wall. Jack Hays and his Rangers rode up near the town and "dared" the Mexicans to come out and fight. This they were quite willing to do, and soon marched from the adobe huts of San Antonio, crossed a creek in order to face the Texans, planted cannon, and the battle commenced. The Rangers acted upon the defensive, dodged the limbs of the pecan trees which the whistling bullets began to cut off, and prepared to meet the Mexicans when they should charge.

General Wall, the Mexican leader, thought to rout the Texans with his artillery fire, but, as he failed to do this, he made preparations to charge them. Cavalry was dispatched across the creek in order to cut off retreat upon this side, and a band of Cherokee Indians were posted upon a branch below. The Mexicans believed that they would have an easy time of it, but they little thought with what kind of men they had to deal. Before them were expert riflemen: all keen shots and frontier fighters. They made a good account of themselves.

The bugles sounded the charge and the Mexicans came on in fine style. They were massed together densely, and, for a time, it looked as if the Rangers would be annihilated by mere force of numbers. But the Texans lay down behind the creek bank, and poured such a volley of death and destruction into the ranks of the oncoming foe that their formation was broken up and they retreated in confusion and disorder to their batteries, posted upon elevated ground. A company of their cavalry also charged, but the horses would not come on before the sheet of lead which the Rangers pumped into them. Many lost their riders and ran among the infantrymen, knocking them down as they galloped wildly about. The Rangers cheered loudly, and Captain Jack Hays grinned from ear to ear.

As the Mexicans gathered behind their cannon, about fifty Texans, under Captain Nicholas Dawson, came up on the right flank. They heard the sound of firing and hurried towards it, only to find that they had run into Wall's entire army. The Mexicans surrounded them immediately, and poured a destructive fire into their ranks. What could fifty do against one thousand? Two Texans made their escape. About twelve were captured. The rest fell before the bullets of the invaders. Dawson, himself, was one of the last to go down.

After this, the Mexicans seemed to think that they had had sufficient fighting. They retired towards

San Antonio, followed by the exultant Texans. Captain Jack Hays with his Rangers fought the rearguard near Hondo, but the pursuit was soon abandoned and the frontiersmen returned to their homes. They had lost less than one hundred in killed and wounded.

The Rangers retreated to a place called Somervell, and, not long afterwards, were ordered out to look for Indians, which were then pretty thick in the neighborhood, and were doing considerable damage. There were between thirty and forty men in this expedition, some of whom had just returned from Mexico, where they had participated in the battle of Mier. They moved off towards the northwest, struck the Medina River, and kept on up the stream towards the place where now stands the town of Bandera. Here they made camp, and next morning turned north towards the Bandera Pass, which they entered at about ten o'clock in the morning.

The Comanches were waiting for them. They had discovered the approach of the Rangers as they came through the open country, and laid an ambush for them in the Pass. The famous Bandera Pass is some five hundred yards in length by one hundred and twenty-five in breadth. The red men were concealed among the rocks and gullies on both sides of the gorge, and they allowed Captain Jack Hays with his Texan Rangers to get about one-third of the way through before they commenced firing from both sides at once. The Rangers were riding three abreast, and, when this fusillade commenced, were thrown into momentary confusion, because of the frightened and wounded horses, which endeavored to wheel and run back.

"Steady, boys, steady!" exclaimed Captain Jack Hays. "Get down from your horses and tie them to the brush. We can whip these infernal redskins if you will only keep cool."

The Comanches greatly outnumbered the Rangers. They were armed with rifles and with bows and arrows. Many came down the Pass and rode up to close quarters with the Rangers. Pistols were freely used and many hand-to-hand conflicts took place. The Comanche chief was struck down by a ball from the rifle of "Kit" Ackland, who, himself, was wounded a moment later. It was a furious affair, — one of the most desperate Indian battles of the frontier.

One of the scouts — a fellow named Galbreath — was wounded by an arrow which struck him above the pistol-belt, on the left side. It penetrated as far as the hip bone. The hardy frontiersman made no complaint, but drew the missile out at once, loaded his gun, and continued to fight on as if nothing had happened. No one knew that he had been wounded until the worst part of the battle was over.

The Indians fought with great fury, but they soon saw that they could not drive the Rangers back, and so withdrew to the north end of the Pass. Here they buried their dead chieftain; killed all of their crippled horses, and held a scalp dance over the remains of their fallen comrades. Five Rangers had been killed and six had been wounded. The men under

Jack Hays retreated to the south end of the Pass, where they buried those who had met their end, and attended to the wounded. Next morning they jogged along to San Antonio. The Indians did not pursue.

The battle of Bandera Pass had taught the red men that the Rangers were not to be trifled with. Captain Jack was continually on the lookout for them, and soon had another experience which he had no occasion to forget. It happened about a year after the famous battle at the Pass.

Fourteen Rangers — under Captain Jack — went upon a scout up the Neuces Canyon, with the expectation of meeting the Indians, who were then upon the war-path. After a long trip to the head of the river, without seeing any fresh Indian sign, Hays turned back down the canyon and camped. Next day the little party travelled onward, and — about noon — some one discovered a bee tree.

" Hold on, Captain! " said a Ranger. " Just wait a minute and I'll chop all the honey out of that tree-top."

" All right," replied Hays. " Sail in and let's see what you can do. Pull your bridles off, men. Let your ropes down and allow your horses to graze. We will rest here awhile and get some honey."

The Ranger secured a small axe that was in the luggage on a pack-mule, and ascended the tree, for the purpose of chopping into the honey without cutting down this stout piece of timber.

About this time a large band of Comanches were coming down the canyon on a raid, and, seeing the trail of the Rangers, they followed it. The fellow in the tree had a good view of the valley, and, to his startled vision appeared a great body of redskins.

"Jerusalem, the Golden, Captain!" he sang out. "Yonder come a thousand Indians! Jerusalem!"

The Comanches were riding rapidly down the trail and made a good deal of dust. Hays sprang to his feet, as quick as a cat, and sang out his orders promptly, and to the point.

"Come out of that tree, there! Men, put on your bridles! Take up your ropes! Be ready for them! Be ready for them!"

All sprang to their horses, and were soon prepared to meet the onrush of the red men.

The Rangers were armed with Colt's five-shooters, besides their rifles and a brace of holster single-shot pistols. Thus each man could fire nine shots. The Indians had never before come in conflict with scouts armed with the five-shooter, and they rode on exultingly, for they greatly outnumbered the whites. Jack Hays never ran from Indians, and had never yet been defeated by them.

The Comanches came forward, yelling loudly. They thought that it would be an easy matter to ride over the small squad of white men, who were drawn up around the old bee tree. Some of the scouts began to raise their guns, but Captain Jack cried out:

"Now, boys, do not shoot too quickly. Let the redskins come closer. Hit something when you do shoot. Stand your ground. We can whip them when we shoot. There is no doubt about that."

The redskins thundered down upon the Rangers. When they were quite close, Captain Jack called:

" Fire, and let every shot tell! "

A sheet of flame burst from the rifles of the scouts, and so many ponies went down that the redskins divided to the right and left, discharging their arrows as they swept by.

At this moment Captain Jack sprang into his saddle.

" After them, men," he cried. " Give them no chance to turn on us! Crowd them! Powder-burn them! "

Never was a band of redskins more surprised; for they expected the Rangers to remain near the tree, and upon the defensive. With a wild whoop, the followers of Jack Hays galloped after the running braves, keeping up a perfect fusillade with their pistols. The Comanches were thunderstruck at this turn of affairs. Some tried in vain to turn their horses and make a stand, but such was the wild confusion of running horses, popping pistols, and yelling Rangers, that they abandoned the idea of a rally, and sought safety in furious flight. In endeavoring to dodge the terrible five-shooters, some dropped their bows and round shields. Some kept off the Rangers by thrusting at them with their long lances.

The Indians ran for three miles before they could get away. The Rangers now rode back, well satisfied with the day's work, and were surprised to see the result of their charge. The ground was fairly black with dead redskins. Many years afterwards a

friendly Delaware Indian, called "Bob," met the
Comanche chieftain who led his warriors in this
fight.

"Who did you battle with upon this occasion?" he
asked.

"Ugh! Jack Hays and his Rangers," gloomily replied the Comanche chief, shaking his head. "I
never want to fight him again. Ugh! Ugh! His
soldiers had a shot for every finger on their hands.
I lost half of all my warriors. Ugh! Me never fight
with him again."

The Rangers soon afterwards had another tough
little scrimmage with the Comanches. Fifteen of the
Rangers were together at this time and they met an
almost equal number of Indians, who were discovered
at the foot of the mountains near the Frio River. The
Indians were riding very tired horses, and the scouts
thus gained upon them rapidly. The red men kept
under cover, as much as possible, riding in ravines
which had brushes and prickly pears around them,
wherever they could do so.

Captain Jack and his men arrived at a little dried-up
creek called Ci Bolo (buffalo creek) where they came
close to the Indians, who were travelling in a ravine
which hid them from view. The Rangers heard their
leggings scraping against the brush, so, for some distance, they rode parallel with the savages, waiting
for a chance to make a charge. The redskins could
be heard talking to each other.

Suddenly the Comanches left the ravine and rode
out in open view, not more than thirty yards away.

They apparently were not aware of the presence of the scouts until a sharp crack warned them of their danger. At the first discharge, a redskin fell from his horse. The others attempted to run back to cover, yelling and shooting at the Rangers as they did so. But the scouts were too speedy for them and cut them off. One, however, seemed determined to get into the ravine. He disappeared into a thicket, at the edge of the gully, but a Ranger called Tom Galbraith dismounted, and, running to the edge of the thicket after the Indian had reached it, fired, and killed him.

The rest of the savages endeavored to make their escape across the open country, which was filled with scattered bunches of the prickly pear, cactus, and catclaw bushes. Some were on mules, and others on jaded horses. The Rangers rode hard after them and fired with deadly effect. The Indians had no guns — only bows and arrows — so they did but little damage.

As the chase continued, one young Ranger called Stoke Holmes, who rode a fast little pony, singled out an Indian and cried out:

" Watch me, Boys! I'm going to rope him!"

While he was running along and was swinging his lariat, the pony attempted to jump a large bunch of prickly pears. He reared so high that his rider lost his seat in the saddle and fell backwards into the terrible cactus. Some of his comrades saw the mishap. They quickly shot the redskin and then came rapidly to his rescue, as he was unable to get up. The valiant

scout was in a sad plight. His body had thousands
of pear thorns in it, and his clothing was pinned to
him on all sides. He was in agonies of pain. Pulling
him away from the grip of the cactus, the Rangers
stripped off all of his clothing, extracted all of the
large thorns, and endeavored to pull out the small
ones. But this was an impossibility, as there were
thousands of small needle-like prickers in his flesh.
With a sharp knife the Ranger shaved them close to
the skin so that his clothing would not irritate his
body by rubbing against them. The bold young
fellow was hardly able to ride for several days thereafter. As for the rest of the redskins, — only three
escaped.

Not many months later Captain Hays and his men
were close upon a band of Indians, who had been
located by his scouts in a bunch of cedars. The Rangers had not eaten all day, because they had been hot
in pursuit.

" Dismount, men," cried the captain. " Stay here a
few minutes and partake of the cold bread and beef
in your saddle-bags. But, boys, by no means raise
any smoke, or the redskins will surely see it, and will
know that the Rangers are upon their trail."

" You're right, Captain!" cried many. " We
are half famished."

Captain Hays always had a few Mexicans with him,
as they were good guides and trailers, but, upon this
occasion, they lighted their cigarettes after eating and
dropped the hot ashes into a pile of leaves. Smoke
was soon curling above the tree-tops.

"Curse it, boys!" cried Captain Hays. "Did I not tell you not to set fire to anything. Put that out, immediately!"

Some of the Rangers began to stamp upon the glowing fire. Hays was so angry that he struck the Mexicans with his quirt.

"Mount! Mount!" cried he. "We must go quickly after the redskins, as I fear that they have seen the tell-tale fire and have decamped."

A furious run was now made for the tepees of the hostiles, which were a mile away. It was as the knowing Captain had anticipated. The Indians saw the smoke and knew that the Rangers were on their trail. They had fled, leaving many things in their camp, which were seized by the troopers. The Comanches had gotten safely away.

In 1844 Captain Hays and his men had a hard fight, — one of his hardest, in fact. It was near the Pedernales River. Upon this occasion he had gone out with fourteen men, about eighty miles northwest from San Antonio, for the purpose of finding out the position of the redskins and the probable location of their camp.

As the river came in view, about fifteen Indians were discovered. They soon saw the Rangers. Riding towards them, they shook their clenched fists and seemed to be desirous of having a fight. As the Rangers rode forward they retreated and endeavored to lead them towards a ridge which was covered with thick underbrush.

"Oh, no," said Captain Hays, "I am too well

acquainted with your wiles to move on. I know that
you have an ambush laid for me and my men."

It was hard to keep the Rangers from advancing to
the attack.

" Go around the redskins to the second ridge," cried
the knowing Captain. " We can thus get the Indians
in the rear."

The Rangers were posted upon a long hillock, separated from the Indian position by a deep ravine.
They were not here long before the redskins discovered who was before them, and, as they knew Captain
Jack full well, decided to give up trying to catch him
by stratagem. They now showed themselves to the
number of seventy-five and cried out, in pigeon English :

" Come on, white men! Ugh! Come on! We
get your scalps soon! "

" I'll meet you right away! " answered Captain
Hays.

He started down the hill immediately, followed by
his entire command. He moved slowly, and, when
the bottom of the ravine had been reached, turned —
raced ahead at full speed — and came up in the rear
of the Indians. While they had their eyes glued to
the front, eagerly awaiting the advance from that
direction, they were charged in the rear by the
Rangers. The first fire threw them into instant confusion.

Yells, war-whoops, and shrill screams rent the air.
The redskins scattered like quail, but, seeing the
superiority of their own force, soon rallied.

"Draw your five-shooters, men," cried the Captain of the Rangers. "We must meet the charge of the Comanches as we have always met them."

The redskins were surrounding the Texans, so the Rangers were formed in a circle, fronting outwards. They were still mounted on their horses, and, for several minutes maintained that position without firing a shot. The Indians came on, yelping, and were soon near enough to throw their lances at the Texan frontiersmen.

Crash!

A spitting volley came from the five-shooters of the scouts and many a red man fell to the sod. Again a volley rang out and the Comanches ceased to advance, for the fire of the Rangers was fearfully accurate. The redskins fell back, but they were not defeated, and — in a few moments — again came on to the attack. The fight continued for an hour. Twice the Rangers charged and retreated to their first position. Their loads were now exhausted. The Comanche chief was rallying his henchmen for one more assault. Twenty-five of his painted warriors were prostrate upon the prairie.

The situation was critical for the Rangers, as many were badly wounded. Several had been killed.

Captain Hays, who was in the centre of the circle, now saw that their only chance was to kill the Indian chief.

"Have any of you men a loaded rifle?" he asked.

"I have," answered a scout called Gillespie.

" Then dismount, my boy," said the Ranger Captain, " and make sure work of that chief."

Gillespie was a brave man. He had been badly wounded by an Indian spear which had gone clean through his body. He was hardly able to sit his horse, but, slipping to the ground, took careful aim and fired. As his rifle cracked, the chief fell headlong from his horse.

It is a strange thing, but Indians always lose heart when their leader is slain. Wailing loudly, the Comanches now left the field, pursued by a portion of the Texans. They carried their chieftain safely away, in spite of the fact that they were pressed very closely by the Rangers. Thirty Indians lay dead upon the battle-ground, while only two of the Texan frontiersmen had been killed. Five, however, were badly wounded; chief among whom was Gillespie, who had really ended the fight.

Captain Hays and his men went back to San Antonio well satisfied with the day's work. A month later he had another desperate encounter with the Comanches.

With twenty of his men the gallant Ranger was on a scout near the " Enchanted Rock." This was a depression in a hill, which was conical in shape, and was doubtless the crater of an extinct volcano. A dozen or more men could hide in this place and put up a stout defense against a great number of enemies, as the ascent was steep and rugged. Not far from the bottom of this curious hillock the Rangers were attacked by a large force of Comanches.

When the first shot was fired, Captain Hays was some distance from his men, looking about in order to see whether or not he could discover the whereabouts of the Indians. As he turned to run towards the " Enchanted Rock," he was cut off and was closely pursued by a number of red warriors.

The nervy Captain Jack dashed madly up the side of the hill and entrenched himself in the extinct crater. He was determined to make the best fight that he could, and to " sell out " as dearly as possible. The redskins arrived upon the summit shortly after he had entrenched, and, after surrounding the famous Captain of Rangers, set up a most hideous howling.

" There, Captain Jack," said one. " Ugh! We get Big Smoky Stick this time. Ugh! We get scalp this time! Ugh! Ugh!"

But Captain Jack was game. Each time that the muzzle of his rifle would appear over the rim of the crater the warriors would dodge backwards, knowing that to face his unerring aim was sure death.

The Indians grew bolder and made a charge. Hays fired his rifle, killing a redskin at the discharge, — then shot his five-shooter at the yelping braves. Each bullet found a victim, so the redskins withdrew, which gave the gallant Captain a chance to reload. Again they came on, but again they were met with the same cool bravery. Howling dismally, they again drew away and made ready for another attack.

Suddenly wild cheering sounded from below the Ranger Captain. Shots came thick and fast. Wild yells arose. His comrades were coming to his rescue.

The Rangers had heard the rifle-fire upon the top
of the hill and knew that their Captain was surrounded. So they were fighting their way up to him,
in spite of the odds. Soon they came cheering and
yelling to the edge of the crater, itself, to be greeted
by the cool remark:

" Boys, I'm sure glad to see you! I was nearly
all in! "

When the Comanches saw that the Big Chief had
been rescued they retreated down the steep sides of
the " Enchanted Rock." They met their comrades,
who had been badly cut up, and, deciding that the
Rangers were too good for them, withdrew. Wild
cheers welled from the crater of " Enchanted Rock,"
and loud were the hurrahs for Texas Jack, the gallant
and intrepid Ranger.

The war with Mexico found Captain Jack Hays
ready and willing to march against the hated " Greasers." He and his famous Rangers fought in nearly
all of the desperate battles of the campaign. Many of
his faithful friends and companions fell before the
leaden missiles of the foe. But Captain Jack had a
charmed life: he came through unscathed, returned
to his beloved Texas, and then moved to California,
where he was elected Sheriff of San Francisco County.
He was very efficient as an officer and left an excellent
record behind him.

In 1860 he had his last Indian fight. The Piute
Indians in the state of Nevada declared war upon the
whites, in that year, and committed many depreda-
tions. They massacred Major Ormsby and his men

and spread terror broadcast. At this time there were rich mines in Virginia City, and among the many men who were employed there was an old Texan Ranger, Captain Edward Storey, a man of great personal courage. He was also very popular among the people. "This Indian fighting has to stop, immediately," said the old fellow, his fighting blood again boiling. At once a company was raised, called the Virginia Rifles. Colonel Jack Hays heard of it, and immediately came over from California in order to enlist. With him were several other bold spirits who were eager for the excitement of a brush with the redskins. They marched to Pyramid Lake, not far from the present town of Reno, and there met the exultant braves, — about one thousand strong. They were flushed with their recent victory over Major Ormsby and his men, and thought that they could easily defeat the whites.

In this they were mistaken. The red men were in the hills and had the advantage of position, but the scouts attacked with vigor and a fierce battle ensued. Colonel Jack Hays was in the thick of the fight and conducted himself in a manner quite worthy of his name and fame. A complete victory was won by the Virginia Rangers, but at a fearful loss. Among those slain was brave Captain Storey, whose body was rolled up in a blanket and conveyed to Virginia City on the back of a pack-horse. Colonel Hays rode with the remains of his old friend of the wild days on the Texan plains, then returned to California.

Here the famous Indian fighter died in 1883. In

his later years he became very wealthy and owned a beautiful home near Piedmont, California. He never lived in Texas again, but occasionally went there, in order to visit old friends and relatives. He was buried with a simple ceremony, and thus ended the career of one of the most deadly shots and courageous men who ever rode a mustang upon the plains of the West. His spirit still lives in the hearts of the Texans.

From " My Sixty Years on the Plains " — Courtesy of the Forest and Stream Publishing Co.

" UNCLE BILL " HAMILTON.

BILL HAMILTON:

FAMOUS TRAPPER, TRADER, AND INDIAN FIGHTER

THE mountaineers were pushing, adventurous and fearless men who thought nothing of laying down their lives in the service of a friend. They usually carried very little with them. A few ponies transported their meagre supplies, and, with only enough provisions to last them a few days, they often set out to journey through a vast wilderness. Naturally they were very self-reliant. With only a gun or two they took desperate risks in a country filled with their red enemies. They overcame every difficulty with a dash and courage that is amazing. " Uncle Bill " Hamilton was a typical example of one of these men.

From the time that he was twenty years of age this famous old fellow spent his life on the plains. He became a sign-talker and was able to converse with all the Indian tribes which were met with. Sign-talking will soon be a lost art, but in the old days all of the red men used the same signs, although they spoke different languages. He was also a trapper, trader, and pathfinder. He blazed many a trail which was to lead the frontiersmen to rich agricultural regions. He set an example of courage and perseverance that will leave a bright memory in the hearts of all.

In the spring of 1842, when twenty years of age, young Bill was living in St. Louis, Missouri; but chills and fever were gradually undermining his constitution, so his doctor ordered a change of climate. Consequently his father made arrangements with a party of hunters and trappers, who were in St. Louis for a few days, to let his son accompany them on their next trip, which would last a year. The party consisted of eight " free " traders, with " Bill " Williams and a man named Perkins, as leaders. These two scouts had had fifteen years' experience on the plains among Indians, and had a wide reputation for fearless courage and daring exploits.

The trappers soon reached Independence, Missouri, — where they sold their wagons and rigged up a complete pack outfit, as the expedition would go through a country in which wagons could not travel. Young Bill Hamilton still had on city clothes, and when the old fur traders saw this, they began to laugh and poke fun at him.

" What be you going to do with that city cuss in th' mountains? " said one. " Why, he'll lose himself in a hour's time and walk down the throat of some grizzly bear."

Young Bill did not like this remark at all, and hurrying to a frontier store he traded his " store clothes " for two suits of the finest buckskin. When he appeared in camp with these fine togs on one of the mountaineers said:

"Williams, that boy o' yourn will make a fine old pioneer and mountaineer, if he catches on at this rate."

The youthful plainsman heard it and smiled, for he had felt very badly before.

The party pushed onward and reached Salt Creek. Camp had just been made when a small herd of buffalo appeared in the distance and made directly for the little band. Williams gave orders to corral all the stock, for he feared that this was the game of some plains Indians, and he was not far from being correct. The stock had barely been secured when the buffalo thundered by, followed by thirty painted Kiowa warriors. They were wild and savage.

The trappers had placed their packs in a triangle, and crouched behind them. This made an excellent breastwork. Each man was armed with a rifle, two pistols, a tomahawk, and a large knife, called a "tooth-picker." Two of the men had bows and arrows with which they were experts.

The redskins rode up insolently; examined the outfit, and demanded pay for passing through their country.

"You can neither touch our traps nor will we give you pay for riding through your country," said Williams. "This is Pawnee country and you are Kiowas."

The Indians seemed to be ill pleased and looked vindictively at the sturdy men of the plains. The leader was given some tobacco. He was not a chief, but a young brave with two feathers stuck in his scalplock. After receiving this gift the savages withdrew, saying: "Ugh! Ugh! We come again!"

The trapper kept close watch during the night, expecting that the Indians would attempt to steal some of the stock and attack the camp. But nothing occured. Many outfits have come to grief by putting confidence in the red man, who always covets the belongings of the paleface. Old and experienced mountain men like these left nothing to chance.

Pretty soon the trappers reached the camp of some Cheyennes and there unpacked their goods in order to trade. Young Bill accompanied the chief's son, Swift Runner, through the village, who introduced him to all the leading men.

" There will be a large hunting party starting out to-morrow after buffalo," said he, " and if you wish to go along I will furnish you with a good hunting horse."

" I shall be delighted to go," cried young Bill, so next morning found him riding across the prairie with about fifty Indians and twenty squaws.

After travelling for nearly ten miles the scouts discovered a herd and reported its location to the hunting chief. This leader was thoroughly acquainted with the topography of the country and led the redskins upon a long détour, so as to get on the leeward side of the herd. As soon as a favorable position had been reached the Indians stripped to their breechclouts and advanced, leading their running horses as they did so.

The chief now divided the hunters into two divisions, in order to get the buffalo into a small area.

AN INDIAN BUFFALO HUNT.

They rode to within a quarter of a mile of the herd and then the word was given to " Sail in! "

In an instant the wild array of naked Indians started for the herd, sending forth yell after yell, and riding like demons in their eagerness to bring down the first buffalo. For this is quite a feat and is commented upon by the whole village.

Swift Runner, himself, had the fastest horse in the party and brought down the first buffalo, much to the chagrin of many a young brave — who coveted the honor — for it would bring him smiles from his lady love. Young Bill's pony loped along with willingness, and Swift Runner pointed out a fat cow for him to dispose of. In a few jumps he was alongside of the great lumbering brute, and fired into her side. As luck would have it, he broke her back and she dropped to the sod. Swift Runner yelled hilariously at this success, but it was a very careless shot, and, had he missed, the cow might have made things ugly for him.

There was a great yelling and shooting upon every hand and several riderless ponies were mixed in with the buffalo. Many prairie-dog holes were the cause of this, for when the ponies stepped into them their riders were, of course, thrown over their heads. Ponies are usually sure-footed beasts, but when in a chase like this, where over a thousand buffalo are tearing over the prairie and kicking up a big lot of dust, it makes it impossible for the animals to see the holes.

Young Bill brought down four of the huge brown bison and received great praise from the Indians for his skill. They used arrows in their killing and shot behind the shoulder, bringing the buffalo to his knees. Another arrow would be sent deep enough to penetrate the lungs of the beast and it would then be soon over with him.

For three-quarters of a mile the prairie was dotted with the dead buffalo. They were soon butchered; the ponies were packed with three hundred pounds of the choicest meat, and the caravan started for home. Several Indians who had been thrown limped quite badly, but no one was seriously injured. At sundown the village was reached, a feast was prepared, and all joined in the affair with the greatest good will and friendship. Young Bill was warmly congratulated upon his success, and this was well, for if a white man fails to acquit himself creditably with the redskins it casts a reflection upon all the whites.

The Indians made pemmican and " dupuyer " from the buffalo. The first is manufactured in the following manner: the choicest portions of the buffalo meat are selected, sliced, and cut into flakes. They are then dried. All of the marrow, from the centre of the bones, is put into one pile with the sweetest of the tallow. These ingredients are mixed together and stirred around in a pot which is hung over a slow fire. The combination is then cooled. Some red men put berries into the mixture, which harden and give a sweetish taste. The mountaineers and trappers — when sugar was scarce — always made their pemmican in this manner. The Indian squaws pulverized the meat by beating it upon a flat rock, and then placed it in skin-bags for future use. It is estimated that one pound of pemmican is equal to about five pounds of beef.

A fat substance which lies along the buffalo's backbone, next to the hide, is known as " dupuyer." It is about as thick as the hand of a trapper and runs from the shoulder-blade to the last rib. In breadth it measures between seven to eleven inches. The Indians and mountaineers would strip away this substance — dip it in hot grease for thirty seconds — and then hang it to the inside poles of a lodge. A fire would be lighted beneath it and it would be allowed to dry and smoke for ten or twelve hours. " Dupuyer " was considered to be a great delicacy, for it was very nourishing. Besides this it was tender and sweet. The trappers loved this food and would pay a dollar a pound for it, while the Indians always took dried meat and " dupuyer " along with them upon their expeditions.

When Williams and his party moved on, Swift Runner presented young Bill with a pony which he had ridden in the hunt, and the squaws gave him a half a dozen pairs of beautifully embroidered moccasins.

A few days later the party reached the South Platte River and there found a Sioux village. Big Thunder was the chief, and he requested the trappers to camp there, as his people wanted to trade with them. The Sioux were then a friendly tribe and treated the white men in a cordial manner.

Just before dawn — upon the day following — a wild yelping awoke the entire village. The warriors ran out only to find that the Pawnees — the mortal enemies of the Sioux — had run off about one hundred head of ponies which had been turned out to graze only a short distance from camp. Among this number were two mules and three ponies belonging to the white men.

As soon as this news was received there was a great yelling and shouting, while fifty young warriors hastened to saddle their best ponies. Young Bill Hamilton was with them, and, under the leadership of Young Thunder, they started after the redskins. The trail of the fugitives was soon struck and followed at a brisk gallop, and, after going about eight miles, it was evident that the Pawnees were but a short distance in advance. Passing over a divide, a cloud of dust could be plainly seen about two miles in advance.

The Pawnees rode hard, but they were soon in view. There were twelve in the party. As Young Thunder gave a war-whoop, the ponies bounded forward and carried their owners towards the fugitives as if shot out of the mouth of a cannon. The Pawnees heard the chief's yell, and, leaving the herd of stolen stock, made for a neighboring cottonwood grove. While Bill Hamilton rode onward, a bullet whistled by his ear. The savages fired several more shots but their lead all went wide of its mark.

" Don't you intend to charge the grove and endeavor to capture the Pawnee warriors? " said Bill to the Sioux chief.

Young Thunder smiled and shook his head.

" No, no," he answered. " 'Nough to get back our ponies."

The young scout thought that the Indians were not such terrible fighters as some writers would have them appear, and this impression never changed, although he occasionally met a few that knew no fear.

Two of the Pawnee braves had been killed in this little skirmish, and the warriors rode back to their village carrying the fresh scalps tied on the end of long sticks. The whole village turned out to greet them, yelling like furies. Pandemonium reigned all night, but when old trapper Williams heard that young Bill had ridden in so close to the timber, he said:

" I shall have to keep you at home next time, if I expect to return you to your parents. You are a young fool to approach close to timber where hostile Indians are concealed."

" Three of our ponies were in the bunch of captured horses," answered the young scout. " I did not wish to return without them. As for the Sioux, I consider them a lot of cowards."

The Pawnees had not acted with good judgment in trying to drive off fully one hundred head of horses, so near daylight. For they should have known that the Sioux warriors would be after them, mounted upon their best war-ponies.

The trappers soon bade good-by to their kind hosts and continued on towards the Little Wind River, crossing a rugged and romantic country, where lofty, sky-piercing peaks ascended into the banks of drifting clouds. To the northwest were the Wind River Mountains; to the eastward was the Big Horn Range, — the home of the buffalo, elk, antelope, deer, and grizzly bear. It was a hunter's paradise, where many different tribes of Indians met on their annual hunt, and often battled for the right to the soil. Hostile war-parties were even now quite numerous in the mountains. At Little Wind River, Evans and Russell picked up a moccasin, showing that the redskins were quite near.

Beaver and otter seemed to be plentiful, so the men set their traps. At night they slept with arms at their sides, ready for instant action, and a close guard was stationed beyond camp, as it was almost certain that the Indians would discover them and would run off with their stock. This was the most dangerous country on the plains and was constantly invaded by war-parties of Blackfeet, Bloods, Piegans, and Crows. All had to be constantly upon the alert to avoid losing their horses and their scalps.

About four o'clock one morning two rifle reports brought every man to his feet. Yell after yell sounded from the darkness, and shot after shot came whistling into the camp. In an instant the trappers were up and about — their rifles replying to this fusillade. Evans and Russell (two of the most experienced scouts) killed a couple of the Indians with their first shots, for dawn was just coming, and two black bodies were seen to leap into the air and then roll down a hill upon which they had been crouching. The savages were shooting arrows and old Hudson Bay flintlocks which made a big flash when discharged. As the scouts aimed at these flaming jets, they must have done considerable damage, for the Indians fell back.

They continued to send shots into camp until day dawned.

"Let's charge the critters!" shouted young Bill Hamilton.

"Not on your life, boy!" shouted trapper Williams. "It's most dangerous to run into such a number of unknown redskins at night."

So the young man desisted.

Just before daylight the Indians attempted to recover their slain comrades, by crawling up to them in the grass. The scouts, however, were up to such tactics and added one more to keep company with two of the red men already sent to the Happy Hunting Grounds. At this, the redskins gave a yell of deep despair. Then they filed slowly away, sending a few parting shots at the trappers, just to show that they were still in good fighting order.

Five of the trappers' ponies had been badly wounded, and Williams was so enraged at the injury which had been done that he was determined to punish the Indians still further. Leaving two men in camp, he ordered the rest to follow him on the fresh trail of the early morning marauders, which led up a small stream. The scouts galloped eagerly forward, and, coming to a rise, were soon within plain view of the red men, who were hurrying along, trying to get two of their wounded comrades to the protection of a grove.

"Dash on to the right!" shouted Williams. "Head the redskins off from that bunch of trees!"

The red men saw in a moment that they would

be cut off from the grove, and they made for a patch
of willows and stunted box-elders just below them.
There were eleven of them in all and the trappers certainly had them cornered.

It was about a hundred yards to the Indians, and
a scout named Dockett tried a shot at them. The red
men returned fire, wounding him in the thigh. There
were a quantity of boulders near by, and Williams
ordered his men to roll them up to the brow of the
hill, in order to form breastworks. Four of the trappers were left behind this, while Williams told Noble
and young Bill Hamilton to follow him to the grove
without letting the Indians notice that they had decamped.

In the grove the trappers concealed themselves, and
the wisdom of their move was quite clear. The Indians realized that they would all be shot down if
they remained in their present position, for the men
behind the brow of the hill now had their range. Six
of them made a dash for the cluster of trees.

When the scurrying red men were within one hundred yards of the timber, Williams gave orders to
shoot. The trappers took careful aim, and, at the
flash of their rifles, three of the red men fell face
down. The other three gave a yell of despair and
ran up the hill. The trappers dashed after them, and
the Indians became panic-stricken when they saw the
mounted white men debouch from the thick woodland.

Williams raced onward, dashed right at the Indians,
and, although shot at, managed to bring both of the

redskins to the ground. Now all three had been slain, and the revenge which the trappers had wished for had been fully satisfied. The redskins were Blackfeet, the most thieving class of wild riders of the plains.

There were still five Indians in the willows. Many men would have let them go. But not so with Williams. He was considered the hardest man on the plains to down in a fight with the Indians, for he was never known to quit when once started. It was to be a battle to the bitter end.

" There are five Indians down there who shot at and insulted us," said he. " They shall have what they would have given us had they been successful in their attack." Here he turned to young Hamilton. " Boy," said he, " never let an Indian escape who has once attacked you! I want you to go with me. We will walk to the gulch and approach from below."

But the trappers held their leader in too high estimation to allow him to thus recklessly expose himself.

" Your orders are going to be disobeyed for once in your life," said they. " We cannot afford to lose you."

Williams smiled.

" Evans and I will undertake the job," cried scout Russell. " You cover us with your fire."

In a second — and before Williams could answer — they bounded into the gulch below. Both were quick of foot and had been in so many desperate battles that they understood the danger of approaching prostrate redskins, for a wounded Indian is an uncertain animal.

The rest of the scouts kept up a steady fire until Evans and Russell were seen to be close to the willows. Then they ceased, as the two scouts bounded forward, yelling like Indians. The other trappers also rushed down, and although one of the braves had his arrow in his bow — all ready to shoot — he never pulled it. In a very short time it was all over.

The Indians had now been annihilated, and among their effects were found two fine bridles, ammunition, knives, and other articles belonging to trappers. It was evident that some small body of white traders had been surprised by these Blackfeet and put out of the way forever. So ended this stiff little skirmish.

The trappers now kept on their way, set many beaver traps, caught a great many of these animals; and traded with several bands of friendly redskins. The men were all fine shots and often received praise from people for their expertness in fire-arms, but no more than they merited, for an American mountaineer had no equal on the globe. It was necessary that the trappers should be very expert, for they carried their lives in their hands, and were liable to come in contact with roving war-parties at any moment. To be taken prisoner meant torture and death, and it was therefore impossible for an Indian to capture either a scout or a trapper. They knew what would follow.

Young Hamilton thoroughly enjoyed the life and soon became one of the most proficient talkers in sign language on the plains. The trappers reached Fort Bridger, where were many Shoshones, who asked the youthful scout many questions by signs, all of which he answered correctly. This astonished even the older trappers, many of whom thought that he had been raised by some tribe.

Williams now left the men of the plains in order to go to Santa Fé on business, but promised to be back in the spring and organize a new party for a two-year expedition. Before he left he took young Hamilton aside and gave him advice in many matters. He looked upon him as a son, and few fathers ever gave their children better counsel. The trappers decided to trap near Salt Lake, and the Bear and Malade Rivers, during the fall.

When they had proceeded for some distance they were met by a party of Indians, who spoke the Shoshone tongue, and who informed them that they had to pay for going through their country. Perkins — who was now leader of the trappers — tried to make peace with them, but without success. He made the Indians keep away, but they continued to make signs, meaning " dogs," — which the white men well understood. The trappers held their rifles ready for any emergency.

Perkins cautioned his men to have patience, and, filling his pipe, offered it to the chief, who refused it with contempt, saying: " Big chief never smokes with white dogs."

The head trapper's patience was now almost exhausted and he told the chief in plain language to

" get out." His men prepared for action, as he spoke, so the redskins mounted their ponies and departed towards the South. As they rode off, they cast all kinds of insults at the white men, both with signs and in spoken language. It was certain that they would soon follow the trappers and then there would be a big fight.

That night every precaution was taken to guard against a surprise. Two guards were put on duty, to be relieved at midnight, and a well fortified position was chosen for camp. Perkins said that it was customary for the Utahs to attack just before daylight, for this is the time that the redskins expect to find the whites fast asleep. This is what occurred in the present instance.

A little before daylight two or three wolf howls were heard by the guards, who immediately notified Perkins. Soon all the men were up, their packs being placed in a semi-circle as a breastwork. Twenty of the best horses were saddled and tied in a thicket, to protect them from Indian bullets and arrows. Defeat meant death, so the trappers looked stolidly before them, fully prepared for the worst, if it were to come.

The first wolf howls were soon followed by others, coming from nearer points and in a semi-circle. Indians are experts in imitating the cries of owls, wolves and coyotes. So adept are they in the art that it is difficult to distinguish them from the calls of real birds and beasts. Few trappers can successfully imitate these animals, although many endeavor to do so.

It was not long before the attack commenced. Just

as day began to dawn the wolf howls ceased and the trappers knew that the crisis was at hand. The Indians had crept to within one hundred yards of camp before they gave the war-whoop. Then they came on — fully one hundred strong — yelping wildly. The trappers were all ready with their rifles and pistols. Three were armed with double-barrelled shot-guns, loaded with half-ounce balls and fine buck-shot.

The Indians raced to within fifty yards before a single trapper fired, — then all began to shoot. The redskins halted. At this the plainsmen began with their six-shooters, one in each hand, for — as a result of long continued practice — they could shoot equally well with either arm. These mountaineers had to be experts in the use of both rifle and pistol, for inability to fire with accuracy meant instant death upon many an occasion.

The red men were much surprised to receive so many shots from but twenty men. They became panic-stricken, for they had not supposed that the trappers possessed two pistols each — twelve shots apiece after their rifles had been discharged. They had expected to rush right over the breastworks, before the rifles could be re-loaded. They retreated — assisting many of their wounded. An arrow went through young Bill Hamilton's cap.

The redskins had received a repulse which they had not expected, and retreated to their villages, taking their dead and wounded with them. The chief, Old Bear, had been slain, as well as many of their bravest warriors. This tribe had frequently robbed small parties of trappers, killing them many times and always treating them with great cruelty. After this fight they usually gave well-organized bodies of trappers the " go by."

The plainsmen finished their work without being further molested, and then moved on to Bear River. In the spring, trapper Williams returned from Santa Fé, and made a proposition to the men that he should form a company of forty-three and make a two-years' trip. This was agreed upon, and the expedition soon started, on the 25th of March, 1843. The trappers were divided into four parties, which collected furs in common; that is, each man had an equal share in all furs caught by his own party. For mutual protection they always pitched their tents and lodges together.

They soon passed through the country inhabited by the Bannock Indians. These were troublesome and had many a brush with the stout men of the plains. But the trappers came through every escapade without much loss. The region in which they soon found themselves was rich with beaver and otter; large quantities of which were caught. It was a grandly beautiful country — a paradise for all kinds of game. Bear were particularly plentiful, and many a grizzly and cinnamon fell before the accurate aim of the men in buckskin.

" Young Bill " Hamilton could not be called " Young Bill " any more, because he was a seasoned trapper, and his many experiences with wild men and wild beasts had made it possible for him to hold his

own with the most experienced men of the party.
The trappers made a wide détour, first going far
North, then travelling South to the Carson River in
Nevada, where they lost one of their best and most
skilled men, — a fellow named Crawford. They were
in the Pah Ute country and could tell very readily
that the Indians were most unfriendly. In spite of
this they set their beaver traps, for they saw that these
animals were thick.

As Crawford did not return to camp one evening
it was decided to make a search for him. Dockett,
who was an outside trapper (or one who had his traps
furthest from camp), had seen the missing man setting his traps at a bend in the river, at some distance
away. To this point the trappers hurried, and, scouting in some cottonwood groves, in order to make sure
that there was no ambush, they went in and soon discovered where one of their number had been at work.
Indian tracks were thick near by.

They saw where a horse had stood, and, going to
a thick bunch of willows, found the ground saturated
with blood. The Indians had lain hidden in this wil-
low patch, knowing that the trapper would come in
the morning to look after his traps. They had thrown
Crawford into the river, which was four feet deep.
He could be easily seen and was soon pulled to dry
land. Crawford was a handsome Texan, six feet tall,
brave, kind, generous, and well-educated. Five of
his traps were found, and four dead beaver. The
Indians had stolen what was left, including his rifle,
two pistols, and a horse. The trappers were soon back

in camp with the body of their comrade, and, when
the men saw Crawford, it was plain that death would
be the penalty to any of the redskins who had way-
laid him.   A grave was dug — the trapper was laid
to rest in his blankets — and no monument was placed
above to mark the spot, for fear that some wandering
redskin would dig up the remains of this fearless man
of the plains.

The Pah Utes were soon to be encountered, for
at two in the afternoon the pickets signalled: " Indians coming on horseback."   The stock was corralled
and the scouts stood ready for action.   The pickets
now rode in and reported sixty Indians, who made
their appearance upon a ridge, about three hundred
yards from camp.

" Come out and fight!   Come out and fight! " yelled
the redskins.

Crawford's death had cut the scouts down to thirty-
eight, but that did not worry these hardy souls.   It
was impossible to keep the men back, so eager were
they to avenge the death of their comrade.   Leaving
three trappers to take care of camp, the others mounted
and started away in the direction of the Indians.

When the redskins saw them coming they gave yell
after yell, thinking, no doubt, that this would paralyze
the white men with fear.   Then they divided and
charged from two sides.   The trappers let them get
to within one hundred yards, when they halted and
brought their rifles into play.   Dropping these upon
the ground, they charged with pistols in hand.   Fully
twenty-five Indians fell before their accurate shots.

This bewildered the savages, and, before they could recover, the scouts were in their midst.

One tall redskin was mounted on Crawford's horse. He tried to get away, but delayed entirely too long. He was caught, knocked prostrate to the ground, and the horse, rifle, and pistols of the dead scout were recovered. Forty-three ponies were captured. Very few of the Pah Utes made their escape. Poor Crawford, you see, was thus revenged in full.

Two horses which the trappers rode were killed. A few of the scouts received arrow wounds, but none were serious. The secret of the frontiersmen's success was in making every shot count in the first volley. This bewildered the Indians, and, before they could collect their thoughts, the plainsmen were among them. The scouts were an effective body, and were as well drilled in the use of both rifle and pistol as the soldiers of any nation. Their horses, too, were trained to stand fire and to be quick in evolutions. The warwhoops and yells of the Indians simply made them prick up their ears and look unconcerned.

After this affair the little party received little molestation from the red men. At a council it was decided to move, as it was not known how many warriors these Indians could muster, and it was not safe for one or two men to go any distance from camp after furs. The hardy adventurers travelled to the Laramie River, where twenty-five of them determined to go back to St. Louis and to take their furs with them. The original thirteen all returned to the Far West; Williams going to Santa Fé, accompanied by

Perkins and six others. It was a sad parting for all, particularly for Bill Hamilton, who had grown to love his comrades like brothers.

Bill was now a seasoned trapper, and the rest of his career on the plains was marked by many hazardous adventures with the redskins. He went to California, during the gold excitement, was in the famous Modoc war of 1856, where he belonged to the " Buckskin Rangers," and was employed as a scout in the uprising of the Sioux in 1876, which was so disastrous to General Custer and his command. He was among those who followed Crazy Horse to his end, and finally resigned from the service of the Government to resume the free and independent life of a trapper. At eighty-two years of age he was living a peaceful and contented life at Columbus, Montana, where — as he says in his biography — " I am thankful that I can still enjoy and appreciate the wonderful beauties of nature."

A true plainsman, a great shot, a nervy fighter, — such was " Uncle Bill " Hamilton. At the present time there is no wild and adventurous West to create such characters as this, for bad Indians have passed away forever.

UNCLE JOB WITHERSPOON:

AND HIS EXCITING ADVENTURES WITH THE BLACKFEET

NO more famous plainsman ever lived upon the Wyoming prairies than Uncle Job Witherspoon: a veteran of many an Indian battle: of several tussles with grizzly bears; and of frequent brushes with desperadoes and bad men who had taken to the hills in order to escape jail. Born about 1830, the old fellow was still hale and hearty in the year 1898, when he was piloting a number of young men through the intricacies of the Rocky Mountains; a region which he had lived in for many years.

"Well, youngsters," said the veteran trapper to the party of young fellows who were upon an amateur hunting excursion, " when you've toted traps and peltries, and fit Injuns as long as I have, you'll sartainly have considerable more experience than you have now."

The old fellow was sitting with his back against a tree trunk, near the Grosventre River, and before him, in a semi-circle, lay five young men. All looked up at him eagerly, for they were in a country which had once been peopled by hostile redskins. It was now safe, for the savage tribesmen were upon reservations. Still, the air of romance lay over the beautiful land

and added a zest to their expedition, which would
have been absent had they been in a more unhistoric
country.

"Ha! Ha! boys!" continued Uncle Job. "You
think that you'll have a mighty nice time out on the
trapping grounds, and I ain't going to say as how
you won't. But, take my word for it, ye'll wish yourselves back in th' settlements many a time afore you'll
get there. What with fighting and hiding from Injuns
and them pesky grizzlies, and livin' sometimes fer
weeks together on nothin' but pine cones an' such
trash as luck happened to throw in my way to keep
body an' soul together, my time used to be anything
but 'specially agreeable, until I got used to it. Then
I found it barely endurable. It's a hard life, anyway, boys!"

"My, my, Uncle Job," said one of the youngsters,
"why, then, do you go back to the plains?"

The trapper laughed.

"Well, there, boys, yer have me, anyhow," he answered. "Ter be right down honest with yer, *I likes
it*. It's a fact, as sure as dry prairie grass will burn,
and I wouldn't live a whole month in Saint Lewy (St.
Louis) fer all th' money there if I could not be allowed to spend th' balance of my time in th' mountain
country. I'm used to it, youngsters, and city air is
rank poison to me; besides, I'd spoil fer th' want of
a fight with some of th' red varmints of Blackfeet,
Pawnees, and Poncas; for, my boys, that's the best
part of the life on th' plains. And now," continued
the old trapper, " I'll tell yer about a fight, and a long

battle it was, too, which I had with a party of them cowardly Blackfeet over on the Sweet-water River. It was something over twenty years ago, and one fall when I was trapping on the head-waters of the Columbia."

The boys drew closer and gazed at the old fellow with wide open eyes.

"We had about a dozen greenhorns at our post, just like yourselves. We were only a few months from the settlements and these fellows hadn't yet got toughened to the kind of a life we had to lead. Some of 'em was about dyin' with th' ager, and we hadn't a dose of medicine, or even a blessed drop of spirits to save 'em with. So, as I knew every inch of th' country from th' Pacific to Saint Lewy, I was ordered by th' head trader of th' post to go to Fort Laramie and bring back a supply of calomel, Queen Anne powders, an' sich truck fer our sick men."

"You had your nerve with you," interrupted one of the boys.

"Always had plenty of that," continued Uncle Job. "The distance was about six hundred miles over the mountains. We had come to the western side of the range the spring before, by way of the Sweet-water Valley Pass, and I concluded to take that route again toward Laramie.

"Wall, things went well with me for some time. Arter I got over the main ridge I kept along the south side of th' Wind River Mountain and stopped one day on th' Green River, in order to make me a new pair of moccasins. The rough travelling over th' hills had worn mine out and left me barefoot. While I was stitching away at my shoes I remembered a *cache* (a supply of provisions hidden or stowed away until it should be convenient to remove them) which a party of us had made the spring before about a day's travel out of my regular route. It was on the North Branch of the Sweet-water River. We had started from the head of the Platte on our way to the Columbia, with a small drove of pack-mules loaded with provisions for the new post, and when on the South Branch one of th' creeturs give out and we had to *cache* the cargo. It was a package of jerked venison and a sack of flour, with a small bag of rice for th' sick, when we had 'em, and a five gallon keg of hard cider. It is a common practice with us trappers to *cache* our provisions when we know they will be safe for some future journey that way.

"Wall, as I worked at my moccasins, all at once I got to be mighty thirsty, and a vision of that five gallon keg of delicious cider began to come into my head. Says I to myself, says I: 'Job, wouldn't you like to have a little taste of that sweet beverage, 'specially when nobody at the post would be either any wiser or any poorer for it?' I reckoned that I would. So I finished sewing up my buckskin, an' started next morning, bright an' early, for the *cache*. Now, as I told yew all, it was one day's journey from my route, and it would take me another day to put me on the right course again. That, you know, would use up two days that I certainly ought to give to my sick comrades at the post. But I argued this way to myself: ' Now, I'm pesky thirsty fer a drink of that sweet cider.   I'm actually feelin' bad fer th' want uv it.   If I gratify my natural longing I'll certainly feel better arter it, and I can then tread out so much faster that I shall more'n make up for th' lost time.'   And that's the way that I reconciled it to my conscience.

" Wall, I reached the South Branch in th' middle of the afternoon, and going down the stream a little ways from where I struck it, I found the cave where we had *cached* our provisions.   It was a pretty large one, too.   I crawled into the narrow mouth of it and drew my rifle in arter me;   and, as soon as my eyes got kinder used tew th' dim light, right up there in the corner I found everything all right.   There was that jolly little red keg of cider, and it seemed to actually laugh all over at the sight of an old friend. And well it might, for it had been shut up there in the dark for more'n six months with nothing but the flour, the rice, and the dried meat to keep it company.

" I pulled out my sharp-pointed bowie knife and tapped the head of th' cider barrel in no time.   But just as I raised the little fellow to get a taste of him I heard the tramping of horses' feet outside, and the howlin' of twenty or thirty infernal Blackfeet.   Gee Whillikins!   I had ter drop th' keg before a bit of th' amber liquid had wet my thirsty lips.   Well was it that I did so, for in that moment the entrance of the place was darkened by a rascally Injun who had been fool enough to follow me.   Boys!   I was plum skeered!

" What was I to do? I raised my rifle and fired at
Mr. Redskin, who dropped dead upon the ground,
uttering a wild war-whoop as he fell. His comrades
crept into the mouth of the cave, seized him by the
feet, and gave a terrible yell when they found that
he'd been wiped out of existence. While they were
tugging away at the old fellow I busied myself in re-
loading my rifle in order to get ready for the next
visitor. Although th' pesky redskins kept up a terrible
hullabaloo they didn't attempt to crawl into the cave
any more.

" Thinks I, ' Now's your time, old boy, if you ever
hope to have any refreshment.' So, raising the little
cask of cider, I took a good, long, glorious drink. I
tell you, boys, that was delicious, for my throat was
all parched and dry from alkali dust. It braced me
right up and I'd hardly had it down my throat when
I felt that I was a host in myself and could handle,
single-handed, all of the Blackfeet west of the Mississippi.

" Arter a few moments three or four rifles were
cautiously poked into the hole, and were fired at
random into the cave toward me. I ducked to one
side, and let 'em peg away. They were only using
up their ammunition, an' th' sooner they got rid of
that the better it was for me.

" Next they sent a shower of arrows through the
opening, but with no better effect than with their
bullets. In the meanwhile I had found a little hole
through the rocks just large enough for the barrel of
my gun, and, watching a good chance, when the var-

mints were thick about the mouth, I took good aim
and popped away at them. By the Jumping Jingoes!
boys, but I sent half an ounce of lead through the
bodies of no less than three of them at once. At this
th' Injuns fell back, yelling vengeance, an' I took
another refreshing pull at th' cider. 'For,' says I to
myself, 'Job, now it's *your* treat, and here's to as
good luck the next shot.' But th' varmints didn't try
th' shooting game any more, as they found that this
was a game which I could play as well as they, themselves. Boys! I held all the trump cards! They kept
losing their hands, while I continued to hold my
own.

"Arter they had been quiet fer a considerable time
I poked my head out of the cave and peeped down the
stream, where I could see the cowardly wolves gathering armsful of dry sticks and grass, which I at once
knew that they intended to bring up to the cavern
and smoke me out. I hadn't thought of this before,
and, thinks I, the rascals have got me now, sure. I
can fight Injuns so long as my ammunition holds out,
but when it comes to a fire and smoke I ain't a match
nohow for them fellers, shut up as I be in these here
limestone rocks.

"Presently th' savages came back again to th'
mouth of th' cave in such a direction that I couldn't
bring old Kill-Deer to bear upon 'em, and piling up
their combustibles they set fire to 'em. The wind
happened to be blowing directly into th' cave, and,
in a few moments, a nasty smudge began to suffocate
me. I had to crawl farther and farther into the place

as the smoke followed me; and I could hear the Injuns pilin' on the grass and wood all the time. They found that they couldn't get me out by any other means, and were now endeavorin' to choke me to death by their horrid smoke. Fortunately, as I shrank away from it, I saw a little streak of daylight ahead of me. It was a crevice in the rock through which the rays of the setting sun were streaming, as much as to say: ' Be of good heart, Job; they cannot smoke you out as long as you choose to breathe through this nice little air hole.'

" I ran to the crevice, and laid down, breathing the pure air, and laughing at the redskins, who were yelling and dancing for joy at the cute trick they thought that they were playing upon me. Luck was certainly with me, boys, for through the crevice that admitted the light and the air I discovered a nice little stream trickling away, while a tiny pool of fresh water had formed upon the floor of the cavern. Now, thought I, if I only had the provisions with me, I could last until the Injuns got tired and had to go away. So, holding my breath, I crawled back again into the smoke, and catching hold of the little keg of cider in one hand, and a package of jerked meat in the other, I went back to my breathing-hole and had a comfortable supper. The red fiends outside were screeching and yelling like mad men.

" Arter I had satisfied my hunger, and had taken another pull at the delicious apple juice, I laid down for a nap, for I knew that the Injuns wouldn't trouble me while they kept up their smoke.

"Wall, boys, I tell you that I had a pretty good night's rest, considerin' that I had tew keep one eye open. In the morning, after the smoke had settled, I sat quietly at the side of the opening, expectin' Mr. Injun to creep through arter my scalp. They thought that I had given up the ghost, and were all ready to make a speedy end of me. But they had reckoned without their host, for no sooner did a Blackfoot show his head than pop! a little slug of lead from Mister Kill-Deer made him remember that I was still breathing.

"Them Injuns, I reckon, thought that they had holed Old Nick himself, for they was plum surprised when they heard the bark of my trusty old rifle. When they saw another of their number fall, they even forgot to yell. They found that smoke couldn't kill the old man, and so they tried another plan. Their game was to starve me out. But here, boys, I held the trump cards again. The fact was, they hadn't the least idea that the cave had been used as a *cache;* and when they saw me take to it they thought that I had discovered them and was hiding away from them there. The old boys didn't realize that I had a store of good things piled up and ready for use.

"I could understand their gibberish well enough to learn that they had determined to stand guard over me until I should be forced to yield to starvation, at least. But I had fully two months' provisions in the cave and that would hold out for some time. I determined, therefore, to pass the time as agreeably as possible.

"I could hear that parties of Injuns rode away from the place every morning, and others came to take their place. They stood guard over me by turns. At length, after four days, when they supposed that I was about starved out to such a degree that I was no longer dangerous to approach, a redskin poked his head into the opening and began to crawl cautiously into the cave. I was waiting for the fellow.

"Boys! I made a spring like a panther. It was his life or mine, and my long knife did the work. Presently another followed, and him I served as I had the first one. Arter about a half an hour another Injun put his head down into the hole and called to his comrades. At this moment, I levelled my rifle at him and let him have it. That morning, my friends, I had wiped out three more of my persecutors.

"They did not trouble me any for some days. I think it must have been nigh onter a week, when, making sure that I was dead from starvation, another attempt was made to enter the cavern. I kept at a distance until two of them had come in, when I sprang upon them, and with old Kill-Deer and my knife, made a finish of them also.

"Boys, th' Injuns was now plum skeered. They were sure that they had none but the Evil One to deal with. In fact I blackened my face and looked out of the cave at one fellow who had ventured near. He gave an awful cry and ran away, howling. About an hour afterwards, filling the air with their yells of disappointed vengeance, the whole outfit mounted their mustangs, and I could hear them riding away down the banks of the river.

"'O-o-o-e-e! O-o-o-e-e!' they wailed; and, boys, I sure did do some tall chuckling.

"Arter a while I felt sure that the coast was clear of th' red vermin. So I ventured into th' open air, and, mounting upon the top of a river bank, I could see them spurring away across the prairie as if the Evil Spirit were arter them. Boys! I had been pent up in that dark hole for more than three weeks, as near as I could guess; so the strong light of the sun nearly blinded me at first. Arter a while I got used to it. I tell you what, boys! if this green earth and th' blue skies ever looked beautiful to my eyes, they did on that blessed morning when I crept outen that living grave, for yer must remember that there wuz dead Blackfeet all around me."

"But, Uncle Job," interrupted one of his hearers. "How did your sick men at the post get along without the medicine?"

The old trapper looked sad.

"Poorly! Poorly!" said he. "Two of them had died before I returned. They waited for ten days for me to come back, and, finding that I didn't, they sent another man to Fort Laramie for the medicine. The others were saved.

"Arter an absence of about a month I reached the post again. As I didn't want to acknowledge that I had turned out of my way merely for the sake of a taste of some excellent cider while my comrades were suffering for the want of what I had been sent for, I said nothing about it, beyond the fact that I had been a prisoner among the Injuns and had managed to make my escape arter a hard fight.

"Some months arterwards, when a party of us were trappin' out on th' Medicine Bow Range, we concluded that we would make a visit to our *cache*. We rode long and hard to reach there. Finally we came in sight of the cave, and I recognized the place where I had had a desperate battle for my life. We entered the cavern and found it just as I had left it, with the exception that the dead Blackfeet warriors had been removed. The sack of flour and bag of rice were just as the other party had *cached* them, and — not greatly to my surprise — the gallant little cask of cider had disappeared. The dried venison had also vanished."

The old trapper smiled benignly upon his listeners. " The fact is, boys," said he, " although I had a pretty onlikely time of it with them cussed Blackfeet I felt so awful ashamed of th' hull affair that I didn't let on a single word about it. Th' truth is, I wuz plum angry with myself fer gettin' caught in that ar cave simply because I hankered after some sparkling cider."

At this all the boys burst into loud laughter, and the old trapper retired to the fire in order to broil some antelope steaks for supper.

" Fellers, he's the real thing," said one. " Too bad that those good days aren't with us now, for then, we, too, might have some adventures of our own."

But the old times of roving Blackfeet, and desperate battles for life and for liberty, had long passed away.

HENRY SHANE:

HEROIC SCOUT OF THE PLAINS
OF TEXAS

ONE day a young fellow was hunting deer near Pinto Creek, twelve miles from Fort Clark in Texas. His name was Henry Shane, and, although a German by birth, he had early emigrated to the Lone Star State, where he had joined the United States army and had fought in the more important battles of the Mexican War. Deer were plentiful, and it was not long before he had killed a fat buck. Laying his gun down upon the ground, the youthful hunter took out his long knife and prepared to skin the game.

Suddenly the sharp crack of a twig made him look up. He shrank back with a cry, for before him were six large and gaudily painted redskins. One had seized his rifle, another pointed a gun at his breast. It was useless to run.

"How! How! I surrender!" said the young Texan. "You no hurt me."

"Ugh! Ugh!" grunted one of the foremost red men — evidently a chief. "We want you, paleface."

The Indians now seized the unfortunate ranchman, tied his arms behind his back, and — after whipping

314

him severely with a pair of rope-hobbles, which they used to confine their ponies — rode off with him.

"Oh, my," thought poor Henry Shane, "they'll fix me now, sure. I'm afraid that it's all up with me!"

The redskins moved off quickly towards the northwest, and had not gone very far before they were joined by nine more Indians, making fifteen in all. They travelled all that day and part of the night. Then they stopped to rest and eat. Here they again rained blows upon the back of poor Henry, but for what reason he was at a loss to know, as he had done nothing to warrant such treatment. For dinner they presented him with a small piece of burned deer meat with the hair still on it. The prisoner made a pretty poor meal of such provender.

The braves took a good rest, and did not break camp until dawn. Then they bundled up their goods and were off. They travelled rapidly until about nine o'clock in the morning, when they again made a halt near a crystal spring. They had hurried along, for they feared pursuit, and in this they were quite right, for some Mexican herders had heard Shane's gun when he killed the deer. As he did not return, later, they went in search of him, finding the slain deer and a fresh Indian trail. "He is either killed or captured," they thought. "Probably the latter, as we cannot find his body." News was at once carried to the fort, and a squad of soldiers was ordered to follow the Indians. They were guided by an excellent Mexican called "Old Roka," who had lived with the savages for many years and knew their methods of fighting.

The Indians were camped near a cedar-brake, and the blue-coats rode up, just as they had finished breakfast. " Old Roka " led the soldiers into their very midst, before they knew it. Even young Henry Shane did not suspect the presence of the troops until they were right among the redskins. The latter picked up their own rifles and other arms. For a few moments they had a lively fight with the blue-coats. Bullets and arrows were flying thick and fast, when young Henry decided to skip into the neighboring cane-brake. He knew that it was a custom of the Indians to kill their captives, when they were attacked, so he decided to get away before they could harm him.

As Henry dashed away, an Indian fired an arrow after him, which went through his arm and remained fixed there. This did not stop the young pioneer. He raced onward, and breaking off the handle of the arrow, pulled it out, — then stopped and listened. The fight was still going on, the Indians were yelling and the carbines in the hands of the soldiers still continued to pop. Some of the Indians seemed to be endeavoring to make their escape into the cane-brake, so the terrified Henry continued his flight, determined to make his way back to the fort, without waiting for the soldiers.

As young Shane made off, he saw four redskins fall before the bullets of the troops. He pressed forward and came to a wide creek which it was impossible to cross. He followed it all day and, when night came, climbed into a tree to spend the evening. A mountain lion began to screech and call near by and this kept him awake for some time. Finally he fell into deep slumber.

When daylight came, the fleeing pioneer dropped down from his perch and continued towards the fort. This he eventually reached. He had been forty-eight hours without food, except for the little piece of burnt meat which the savages had given him. He was very weak, and was welcomed like a long lost brother. The soldiers had completely annihilated the redskins, and, after the fight, had looked everywhere for the young pioneer. As they could not find him they had given him up for lost and had returned to the fort. When they saw the lost frontiersman, they gave three long cheers for the " young cuss who got away. Hurrah! Hurrah! Hurrah!"

Not long after this exciting affair Henry Shane settled upon a broad creek, called Chicon Creek, which ran near the Anna Catchi Mountains. A few settlers were near him and the Indians were quite numerous. They were also very hostile to the whites, and the young pioneer soon had a very serious affair with them.

One day he was riding by the San Miguel ranch, which was an old-time Mexican ranch with a rock wall around it and an entrance through a gate. When he arrived at this place he could see no one stirring. The gate was open, so he dismounted and went in. He saw no signs of life. A little dog barked at him, — that was all.

Upon a smooth piece of sheet-iron, which lay near two rocks, were several cakes of bread. They had been turned and were burned upon the under side. As the fire still gleamed beneath them, the pioneer was sure that something was wrong. He could see no one, — so continued upon his way.

His horse trotted slowly along, and Henry soon crossed a creek where he found a dead Mexican. It was evident that the " Greaser " had been killed by Indians, for his body was full of arrows, and near by was his horse, lying motionless upon the ground. The Mexican had been endeavoring to get to the ranch when the Indians caught up with him. They first killed his horse and then killed him.

Shane rode onward. As he came upon the top of a ridge he saw a broncho tied some distance off. He knew enough about Indians to keep well away from the animal. So — riding around him — he continued upon his journey. He soon saw the wisdom of his move, for as he rode onward he beheld an Indian crouching near his pony. Soon five others came into view and started after him at a hard gallop.

The plainsman pushed rapidly along and came to a ranch where there was a crowd of excited Mexicans, some of whom were from the place where the dead Mexican had been employed. The murdered vaquero, they said, had been away from the ranch when it was attacked. The Indians had headed him off and had killed him, after he had made a run to get inside the walls of the adobe house.

" We outnumber the infernal redskins," cried

Henry. "Come on, boys, let's go back and clean 'em up!"

"We're with you!" cried the others, and, quickly mounting their mustangs, they were soon started towards the place where the Indians had last been seen. As they rode over a small hillock, the murderous redskins could be sighted far below on the plain. They were intent upon setting fire to the ranch buildings and did not notice the approach of Shane and his companions.

"Spread out, boys!" cried the now excited plainsman. "Spread out and try to surround the red devils!"

The Mexicans and Texan vaqueros followed his lead, and, circling about the red men, soon closed in upon them from three sides. Rifles began to ring out, and, with a wild yelping, the Indians started to retreat. As they did so, Henry Shane waved his sombrero in the air, and all raced after the red men, on the dead gallop.

Now was a beautiful running fight. The Indians could not aim at all well, from the backs of their ponies. Their bullets went very wide. The whites, on the other hand, shot two of the Indian mustangs; and, although their owners fell to the ground, both swung themselves to the backs of other ponies and safely rode off, hanging to the waists of the riders. Finally they all got away in a deep canyon, and ambuscaded themselves so well behind rocks and boulders that the plainsmen decided to withdraw. The Indians had not hit a single white man.

Soon after this event Henry Shane purchased some sheep and took them up on the Foris River to graze. He lived in a tent, with one companion. They pitched their canvas behind a brush fence.

One night Henry was sitting with his back to this fence, boiling some coffee, with no thought that any redskins were within twenty miles of him. But at this very moment several were prowling around his camp and had noticed the position which he was in. One of them — bolder than the rest — slipped up to the opposite side of the fence with the intention of poking his gun through the brush and shooting the pioneer in the back. As he shoved the muzzle of his gun through the dry twigs, he made so much noise that the plainsman heard him. Turning to his Mexican herder, Felipe Flores, he cried out:

"Felipe! What is that noise?"

"It is a rat," replied Felipe. "I saw one running through the brush."

As he ceased speaking the Indian attempted to shoot, but his gun snapped and hung fire. The frontiersman heard the noise and jumped to his feet. When he did so, the gun went off, as the Indian attempted to jerk it back through the brush, and the ball passed through Shane's hat. The Indian ran away, before the startled sheepman could seize a rifle and shoot in return.

The frontiersman had certainly had a narrow escape, and he determined in future to be more careful. Next morning he rode to a neighboring ranch and discovered that the Indians had been there and had carried off twenty-five horses. The ranchers were anxious to get back their stock, so a force was immediately raised to pursue the thieving redskins. They rode out — thirteen in all — and soon overtook the Indians upon the west branch of the river Neuces. The redskins were in camp, but saw the white men as they came up a mountain, and moved off in a great hurry. With a wild shout, the plainsmen, vaqueros, and Mexicans started to gallop after the red men, who crowded through a gap in the mountains and ran away, carrying the captured horses with them. But their pursuers gained rapidly, and pressed the Indians so close that they dropped seven head of the Adams horses. These were quickly seized by the whites, who followed up the fleeing redskins until their own mounts were exhausted.

" Reckon we'll have to give up," said Henry Shane. " Boys, there's some good beef stewing at the Indian camp. Let's go back and get some!"

All turned towards the deserted Indian encampment, and, when they arrived there, found some shields and head-dresses which the Indians had left in their flight. They then camped for the night.

Next morning Henry Shane was anxious to get back home, as the scout was practically over. Saddling up his broncho, he started out over the plain accompanied by a Mexican named Leal, who was the "boss" of a neighboring ranch. They travelled on together for about two miles, when suddenly and very unexpectedly they met a band of Indians in the road driving a bunch of horses before them. When these saw the two ranchmen they turned their bronchos away from the road, and kept on, without molesting the whites.

" Well," said Shane to his companion, " we should go back and tell the other men that here is a chance to fight Indians."

" No," answered Leal. " I'm going home. But you can do as you wish."

Shane bade the " boss " good-by and started for the place which he had just left. The plainsmen were still in camp at the bluff, but they had their horses saddled and were preparing to mount just as the excited Henry rode up.

" Boys! " he cried, " I've just met a band of Indians with some stolen horses. You come along with me and we'll get these fellows, sure."

" Lead on! " cried his men. " Lead on! "

They were anxious for a fight.

The ranchers were soon galloping forward, and it was not long before they had overtaken the Indians, who quickly started off, waving their blankets at the captured horses in order to stampede them. Firing commenced, and Shane had a piece shot from the horn of his saddle. Two of the Indians were killed, but their horses carried them into the brush. Finally the redskins made a stand upon the top of a round mountain, but as soon as the whites charged them they ran. They left three saddled pintos behind them.

The plainsmen made a rapid pursuit, and soon captured thirty horses and seven mules. The red men seemed to give up all hope of ever defeating the whites, and scurried off like so many rabbits. They dodged behind boulders and sage-brush. So quickly did their ponies get away that they were soon out of sight. Henry Shane and his companions were well satisfied with the day's work and gave up the pursuit, for their own mounts were badly winded.

Life upon the frontier of Texas in those days was certainly exciting for any one engaged in the sheep or cattle business. In spite of the continued danger from redskins, Henry Shane did not give up his interest in sheep. One of his brothers — named Constance — lived with him and helped to herd the flock, although he kept continually upon his guard and was never without his rifle. He, himself, was soon to have a narrow escape from death.

One morning Constance was about two hundred yards from the house carefully watching a number of sheep. He was sitting near the bank of a creek, when he heard horses' hoofs knocking the rocks under the bluff. He stepped up to the edge of the bank and looked over, expecting to see some cattlemen from a neighboring ranch. To his surprise and dismay he saw nine Indians, with the chief in the lead. They were riding up the bank in an old cow trail.

Young Constance was too startled to move. He stood there trembling, and allowed the redskins to come right up to him. The chief had a heavy quirt in his hand, with which he struck Shane a stinging blow over the head and knocked him down. He then dismounted and stripped him. The red men now gathered around their captive, making a great screeching and howling.

Henry Shane saw the Indians collected in a group, and, seizing his rifle, went to a corner of a fence to watch them. He could not see his brother, and was all prepared to fire, should the redskins make a move in his own direction. The Indians saw him standing there, and, shooting Constance with an arrow, they rode away, yelping derisively.

Henry followed the redskins in order to see which course they took, and then came back to camp, still unaware that anything had happened to his brother. The Indians had apparently determined to withdraw entirely, which was fortunate for the lone sheep herder. Constance finally crawled to his feet and came back to the camp, declaring that there were eight bucks and one squaw in the party and that the squaw had shot him. He was grievously wounded, — so grievously that every one who saw him said that he would die. But he fooled them all and became perfectly well again, — much to the joy of Henry, who loved him dearly.

Exciting adventures were still in store for the daring Henry Shane, who continued to herd his sheep in this border country, in spite of the fact that the cruel redskins were all around him. Not long after the wounding of Constance, Henry went up the river, which ran near his ranch, and entered the ranch-yard of a sheepman called Joe Brown, who owned a sheep vat and a furnace. The ranch was then vacant, as Mr. Brown had moved to Uvalde and had told Shane that he could use his vat and furnace for dipping sheep. It was Henry's intention to start a fire in the furnace for the purpose of boiling tobacco, which was used in dipping the sheep, to cure them of a disease called " the scab," or to prevent them from catching this dread complaint.

A Mexican named Bernaldo was with the sheepman, and rode forward in order to get some horses which were in a small pasture not far distant. He soon came back upon the dead run, whipping his horse furiously with his hat.

" Hello, there! What's the trouble?" shouted Shane.

The Mexican was so excited that he passed on without seeing or hearing the plainsman, although he was not far from him as he raced recklessly by. He was certainly well frightened at something.

Shane was not armed. This was unusual, as he seldom left the house without a gun, because of the possibility of an Indian attack. Hearing a great commotion in the pasture, where the horses were, he walked up to the fence only to see — to his dismay — that there were seven Indians in the field after the horses. They saw him at once and three of them left the enclosure in order to give him chase.

The plainsman was in a tight position, but his courage did not desert him at this crucial moment. As luck would have it, he carried a long stick in his hand, which he had used in order to punch the fire in the furnace. He turned and ran, but the Indians were upon the backs of their ponies and soon came very close to him. He pointed his stick at them, as if about to shoot. Every redskin dodged and swung himself upon the off side of his horse. "Ugh! Ugh! He have shooting-stick!" cried one.

This gave the courageous frontiersman another opportunity to run, and he made off as fast as his legs would carry him. A man named Patterson had a ranch near by and to this sheltering abode the plainsman now bent his footsteps. The Indians were hot on his trail and soon caught up with him, but he again pointed his stick at them. They dodged, and this gave him a second start, so that he reached the ranch-yard and jumped over the fence into the cow-pen. Uttering loud and vociferous cries, the Indians shot some arrows at him, and then turned back in order to secure the horses from the pasture. This they did and were soon galloping away with them.

The pioneer climbed out of the cow-pen, ran up to the ranch house, and called to the owner, who happened to be there:

"Come on, Patterson. If you will assist me, we will get back the horses."

"I'm your man," Patterson replied. "Here's a rifle of mine. I will take a six-shooter."

"All right," said Shane. "We'll see if we cannot do something to these crafty fellows. Come on!"

The two ranchmen soon met the Indians coming down the road, driving the horses before them. The valiant two stepped to one side in order to ambush the red thieves, Shane hiding behind a large cactus plant. As the foremost Indian came near, Shane took good aim at him, and pulled the trigger of his rifle. But it refused to go off. The Indians heard the noise and galloped away with their captured horses, while the two ranchmen made after them. They, themselves, were ambushed and had to ride hard in order to get away from the redskins, who were reinforced by a considerable band. After their retreat the plainsmen again followed with additional numbers, but the Indians were well ahead, and the pursuit had to be abandoned.

In 1872 Mr. Shane decided to make a sheep camp about two and a half miles from where he lived, so drove down there in a wagon one morning, in order to pitch a tent and fix things for the comfort of his Mexican herder, who was off with a band of sheep. The camp was beneath the fork of a live-oak tree. The frontiersman left his wagon about a dozen yards from where he was at work, and started to put a small board between the forks of the live-oak, to serve as a shelf. Two guns were in his wagon.

While thus occupied, he suddenly heard a wild war-whoop, and found that he had been attacked by the Indians. A redskin came up behind the wagon, on horseback, and shot at the ranchman with a six-shooter, the ball striking the right-hand fork of the tree and knocking the bark into his face and eyes. The pioneer turned, in order to get his guns out of his wagon, and faced the levelled revolver of the savage. He kept cool — in spite of this danger — and, as he walked to the wagon, received two more shots from the Indian. As the redskin was behind the conveyance, his shots went high, passing over the head of the frontiersman, who soon reached his wagon and looked for his guns. The Comanche saw what the white man was after, and, when he perceived that his shots had failed to take effect, he wheeled his horse and ran away. Shane seized a rifle and fired at him, killing his horse when he did so. As the pinto rolled upon the ground eight more Indians showed themselves and began to charge the lone white man. The gun which he had just discharged was a Mississippi yager, and he had no more balls for it.

But the frontiersman had another weapon: a new, single-shot Ballard rifle, and he only had two cartridges for it; one in the gun and one in his pocket. In leaving home that morning he had left his belt behind, which was full of cartridges for the Ballard. He was in a close place, but he had — as you know — been in close places before, and he was determined to make the best fight that he could. He resolved not to waste a shot. Using his wagon as a breastwork he awaited the onset of the Indians, and when they came nearer he raised his gun and aimed at them. The redskins dodged behind the prickly pear and mesquite bushes, from which they opened fire, hitting the wagon and the ground around it repeatedly.

Now occurred a lively battle. The frontiersman had tied a fat mule about one hundred feet from the wagon, where he could eat grass. A daring redskin concluded to risk his chances and get the animal, so, leaving the cover of the mesquite bushes, he advanced across open ground in order to steal the unsuspecting beast. When Shane saw the Indian coming with his knife ready to sever the rope which held the mule, he determined to risk a crack at him. He was an excellent shot, and he knew that he could kill the Indian if he did not dodge too quickly. Taking a quick but accurate aim, he fired. The Comanche brave jumped high in the air, and then fell in a sheep trail and lay there. The other Indians set up a terrible howling when they saw that their companion had been killed, and several of them ran quickly, seized him by the hair and dragged him out of sight behind the prickly pear bushes. The pioneer still crouched low and waited for the Comanches to come on, but, dreading to expose themselves to such marksmanship, the Indians did not again show themselves.

Certainly things looked bad for Henry Shane, but help was at hand. The Mexican attendant heard the fight, and from the number of shots that were fired supposed that his employer had been killed. He ran to the ranch in order to inform Mrs. Shane of this fact. The lady sent four Mexicans out to see if they could not assist her husband. When they neared the scene of action the Indians decamped, leaving their dead comrade behind. The ranchers buried the Comanche brave where he had fallen in the sheep trail.

When the lucky sheepman returned to his ranch from the scene of this thrilling little battle he found that a strange happening had come to pass. The Mexican sheep-herder who had rushed home to warn his wife that the Indians had surrounded him, was found to be in a serious condition, through over-exertion in carrying the news of Henry's supposed death. The poor fellow was in great pain, and, although he was placed in a wagon and was carried to San Antonio, where he could see the best physicians, he died soon afterwards.

As for the gallant Shane, he continued to have exciting adventures with the redskins, and, not long after the lucky escape which I have just narrated, had another brush with the roving Comanches. He had made a sheep camp three miles from his house, at a place called Long Hollow, and had his Mexican herder with him. This was the faithful Felipe Flores.

Early one morning Shane heard rocks rattling in the hollow below the camp, so he and Flores went out a short distance in front in order to investigate the matter. Felipe went slightly in advance, and to Shane's questioning as to what he saw, replied:

"It is Mr. Dilliard, whom we have been expecting to help us hunt for some lost sheep."

Shane kept on, but suddenly started back in dismay. Ten Comanches were coming for him upon the dead run.

In an instant the sheepman turned and hastened to the tent in order to seize his rifle. The Indians were right after him, and crowded Felipe so closely that he ran backward towards the fire. As a Comanche endeavored to thrust a lance into his body he fell into the flames. When this occurred the Indians opened fire upon Henry Shane, endeavoring to hit him before he could get his gun. Several balls struck the tent, but the Ranger was unscathed.

A COMANCHE WARRIOR.

Now the plainsman seized his rifle, and, wheeling around, fired at his enemies. They retreated at once and dashed into the thick brush. As they scampered away, two Indians on the same horse were seen to ride behind a thick bunch of prickly pears, only one of whom came out upon the other side.

"That second redskin is still behind the pears," said Flores. "He is waiting there in order to shoot any one who may come out to look around."

"I think that I'll stir him up a bit," said Shane, and, aiming at the bunch of pears, he let drive. Sure enough, he routed an Indian, who ran off, screeching loudly. When the spot was afterwards examined a bullet hole was seen in the pears. The redskin had had a narrow escape.

This was not Henry's last adventure with the redskins by any means, for, about a month later he went down the river, less than a mile from his ranch, to a place called the "Indian Crossing." There were two Mexicans with him, who had a wagon and a pair of mules. Their intention was to saw cypress logs in order to make boards and shingles for a new ranch house.

The plainsmen finished their work of loading logs and were soon ready to return home. One of the Mexicans, called Antonio, had a gun which had been resighted. He wished to have Shane try it, and therefore called out:

"Come here, Señor, and try my rifle. It can shoot well I know, but I would like to have your opinion of it. There is a tree which will make a good mark."

"I'm agreeable," replied Henry, taking up the gun. He fired two shots at the tree. When he had finished, the Mexican went over to see where he had hit the bark.

Over forty Indians were crossing the ford of the river near by at about this moment. They heard the rifle shots, and, learning from a scout that three white men were there, determined to surround and capture them. So they spread out like a fan in order to completely annihilate the little party. Half of the redskins came up on the bluff upon the east side, opposite Shane and his two Mexicans; the balance went to the old crossing above, so as to come around the frontiersmen upon the west side and thus cut off their retreat in both directions. Henry Shane was now in another tight box. Let us see how he fared.

A sudden rattling of rocks warned the pioneer and his companion that some one was near by. His friend (the Mexican) mounted a stump, so that he could see the crossing, and said:

"There are soldiers coming up the river."

As he jumped down, Henry, himself, climbed up on the stump in order to have a look.

"Soldiers!" he cried. "Why, man, those are Indians!"

He immediately seized his rifle and stood prepared for action.

Antonio, as you know, had gone to look at the bullet marks upon a tree. When the Indians came down the bank of the river they encountered this Mexican and opened fire upon him. Antonio attempted to run back to Shane, but, as he started forward, he was struck by a bullet, and fell into some high weeds. The Indians closed in upon the other two sheepmen, uttering wild cries of delight, for they felt that they had them, and they bore no love for Henry Shane. They were armed with Spencer carbines and commenced a rapid fire upon the bold frontiersman and his companion.

The bullets began to rain in from both sides of the creek, as Shane took shelter behind a huge cypress log and commenced the unequal battle. He was now in the tightest place that he had ever been in in his life, but he kept cool, and only fired at long intervals, and with careful aim. The redskins were uncertain as to the force they were attacking and were afraid to come down into the bed of the river and to fight at close quarters. The second Mexican crawled into a tree-top, so that only his feet were visible. He was of no assistance to the gallant frontiersman.

After shooting away for some time, the Indians decided to send a warrior on horseback below (where Shane was crouching), in order to see if all were killed, or if there were any still left. The frontiersman was on the alert, and, as the redskin approached, he caught the first motion of the reeds as he slipped through. The rest of the red men had ceased firing and were all under cover.

There was a moment of breathless anxiety. Shane held a large revolver in his hand, as he lay close to the ground, watching around the end of the log, as the fellow came in view. At once he aimed at the

redskin's breast and pulled the trigger. The Comanche reeled and fell to one side of his horse, clutch-
ing the mane of the animal as it ran up a bluff. The
other redskins now rose from the grass and endeavored to stop the startled beast; but he kept running
around in a circle, for some time, with the Indian
still hanging to his mane. At last he was captured,
and a loud wailing cry told the frontiersman that the
shot which he had fired had done its deadly work.

The Indians now held a council of war. They could
be easily seen by Shane, where he lay. Apparently
they had had sufficient fighting, for they mounted
and rode off. As they disappeared from view, the
happy frontiersman mounted a stump and counted
forty warriors. How many he had killed besides this
last one he could not tell. He took no time to investigate the matter and prepared to leave at once.

The sides of the log, behind which he had lain,
were perforated with bullets. One bullet hole was in
his boot leg, one was in his hat, two were in his shirt,
three were in the wagon bed, and one of the mules was
badly wounded. In spite of this, the animal was able
to draw the wagon home with him, in which was
placed the wounded Antonio. The other Mexican had
crawled from his hiding-place after the fight was over.
He was certainly not made of the same stern stuff as
was Henry Shane.

The bold rancher and frontiersman had had a narrow escape, but he had a still narrower escape, some
time later. It was upon a winter's day, and he had
gone out to a place called "Griner's Bottom" in

order to listen to turkeys as they flew up to roost, for he wished to kill some of them for dinner on Christmas Eve. He found the place, and had not been there long before he heard the sound of horses' feet. Looking around, he saw five Indians riding towards him. They seemed to be unaware of his presence.

There was no time for anything but quick action. Henry hugged the live-oak tree, against which he had been leaning. As he did so, the Indians came jogging along on both sides of him: two on one side — three on the other. It was rapidly getting dark, so they did not see the lone frontiersman. Luckily they did not look back after they had gone past. Had they done so, they would have seen Henry pressing himself flat against the tree trunk, grasping his muzzle-loading shotgun very tightly and trying to keep his teeth from chattering. Sometimes this antiquated gun missed fire. Oh, fortunate Ranger! The redskins were soon trotting onward in the darkness.

This was not the last adventure which the daring Henry had with the savages by any means, but it was the most exciting. He lived for many years upon his ranch in Uvalde County; prospered, and became one of the solid citizens of the state. Truly his was an adventurous soul. It was to such men as these, who dared to take any chance and assume any risk, that the West owes its settlement, its civilization, and upbuilding.

All honor, then, to Henry Shane, — the Texan pioneer for whom the Indian had no terrors. He passed through so many hairbreadth escapes that one would think him often thankful that he was alive. Hail to this stout German who helped to make history upon the Mexican frontier!

POOR JERRY LANE:

THE LOST TRAPPER OF WYOMING

[This is the story of a young frontiersman, whom I knew, myself]

.   .   .   .

JACKSON'S HOLE, Wyoming, was named after one Jackson, a pioneer, explorer, ranchman, and horseman. Jackson's Hole was also the home of horse thieves who, gathering up their captured steeds, would run them into this peaceful valley to feed them on the rich, natural hay until they could be driven out at a different angle and sold to some one who knew nothing of their former ownership. Jackson's Hole was also the home of desperadoes who had fled from justice. Jackson's Hole was the place that I was going to in the summer of 1899.

"Goin' to Jackson's Hole, be yer?" said a fellow in a big sombrero, on the train to Idaho Falls. "Young man, you'll never get out alive. Young man, it's a desperate place."

He winked at me, shook his finger in my face, and dropped back into the seat from which he had arisen. "Young man," he continued, "the Injuns will get you, sure. Young man, look out!"

I confess that I felt somewhat disconcerted.

" I'll take care of my scalp," said I.

Here the companion of my friend in the sombrero spoke. This one had a red handkerchief knotted about his tawny neck, and wore a corduroy waistcoat.

" Yes, son," said he, " haven't you heard about the Injuns in Jackson's Hole two years ago? They stampeded th' settlers, ran off a lot of stock, murdered an' burned, until rounded up by the U. S. Cavalry. Reckon there be some more loose in thar now. An' panthers! Why, boy, they're as thick as peas in a pod. An' dangerous, too, by gravy! "

The first speaker guffawed.

" 'Tain't nawthin' to th' grizzlies," said he. " They be monstrous pestiferous. Why, they pull you from your horse they be so unafraid of men."

I squirmed uneasily in my seat, for I saw that they knew me to be a tenderfoot.

" Boy, you'll be eaten alive an' scalped to boot," continued the fellow in the sombrero. " The good Lord have mercy on your soul."

" Amen! " echoed his companion.

And I wriggled again, for I saw that they knew me to be an Easterner, and were having fun in their own way.

At any rate, I was bound for Jackson's Hole and would get there somehow or other in spite of horse thieves, " Injuns " and grizzly bears.

We met at Idaho Falls. When I say we, I mean our party, for we were surveyors, bent upon exploration of Uncle Sam's possessions, and upon making an accurate map of the somewhat unknown country near Jackson's Hole. We knew that it was a great land for game and fish and that it was the home of monster bands of elk, but we also knew that it had an unsavory reputation as the haunt for " bad " men of the hills. As I had come up on the train, certain placards in the stations showed that these same " bad " men were still around and had been operating at the expense of the Express Companies.

The placards read:

> " $40,000 REWARD
> For the Capture, Dead or Alive, of the
> Men who robbed the Union Pacific
> Express near Rawlins, Wyoming, on
> the Evening of June 4th."

Then followed an inaccurate description of those who had been seen to enter the mail car, seize the box containing valuable mail and expressage, and decamp across the prairie with their plunder on their ponies' backs.

At Pocatello, Idaho, I looked from the window and saw beneath me a light-haired, blue-eyed Swede. He was standing there nonchalantly, dressed in a corduroy suit, blue handkerchief knotted about his neck, and wide sombrero.

" That's the sheriff," said a man at my elbow.

" Where's he bound? " I asked.

" Into the hills after the train robbers," he answered. " He has a *posse* with him and they ought to be able to capture a few of the bandits who held up the Union Pacific Express."

The train rolled on, but I always remembered that sturdy little figure, standing carelessly on the platform, in corduroys. In a week he had been ambushed, with his entire *posse,* and two had escaped out of the eleven. The little sheriff was buried in the hills.

To get into Jackson's Hole was then a rather difficult affair, for it meant a long journey by pack-train from either Market Lake or Idaho Falls. But the surveyor and the sons of the pioneer, whom he engaged to pilot him, were not adverse to pushing into a wild country. It took a week to outfit the party, secure the necessary horses, engage the men, and whip the fractious range-animals into some kind of submission for carrying saddles, pack equipment, and heavy bags of food and tenting. Then, in a cloud of alkali dust, and with a crowd of Blackfeet children gazing open-mouthed at the curious caravan, we were off for the blue hills which lay to the northeast.

The plains of Idaho are not only arid and parched, but they are covered with sage-brush, which emits a strong, pungent odor that is delicious. The alkali dust arises in clouds, and chokes one, as one proceeds, but that is not the only difficulty, for — strange as it may seem — the mosquito breeds by the millions in the irrigating ditches, and had it not been for the thick gauntlet gloves and netting attached to our sombreros, we would have been fairly eaten alive by the black swarms which followed us in clouds.

Every now and again — afar off on the prairie —

we would see a whirling cloud of moving alkali dust.

"Wild horses running to water," said one of the cowboys. "That's the way they always go, on the dead gallop."

Occasionally we came near enough to see some of them and they were lean, gaunt and rangy creatures, which had escaped from the ranches, had run off to the prairie and had found pleasure in the free and untrammelled life of the plains. They would snort, as we approached, throw their heads high in the air, and then — turning around — would be off like the wind.

As we rode along, hot, dusty, and thirsty, I heard about Jerry Lane.

"This here Lane," said Jack (a lean, little cowboy) "is a Noo Yorker. He came out here three years ago, sayin' that life was too tame for him back East, an' he wanted to be right in the Rocky Mountains, where the wolves, bears, and antelope could be seen, just th' same as in th' time of Kit Carson an' Bill Bent. Some says that he's a millionaire. Some says that he isn't. Leastways he has about all th' money one needs in this here country, an' they tell me his cabin in th' Rockies is full of th' best kind of rifles, of steel traps, books, an' all that's nice."

"He found life too tame for him back East."

This sentence stuck in my mind and I knew — in a moment — what kind of a youth was Jerry Lane. He had the same spirit as the old explorers. He possessed the imagination of a Lewis or a Clarke; a

Champlain, or a La Salle. To him the spirit of the wilderness was all absorbing, and, shaking off the trammels of civilization, he loved to live out his days amidst the towering mountains, which, even then, stretched before us, jutting high from the sage-brush plateau. I immediately felt a sympathetic interest for Jerry Lane.

To cross into the valley of Jackson's Hole requires one's utmost exertions, for one must climb up the Teton Pass in order to get over the mountains which surround this paradise of fish and game. For a man and a horse to pass up and across is easy work, but we were unfortunate enough to have a wagon with us. As we neared the bottom of the trail, which led almost perpendicularly up in the air, we saw a broken vehicle of a pioneer.

" The Top of Teton Pass, or Bust," some one had written on a board and placed upon the battered spokes.

It had " Busted."

Now climbing, pushing, blowing, we yoked four horses to our wagon and gradually worked it to the summit of the Pass. It was July, but snow was on the ridges, and the air was like Labrador as it swept across the hemlock-covered mountains. When once on top of the Pass, what a view! We gazed down into a peaceful little vale with log houses and thatched roofs, fields of green grass with stacks of yellow hay, and bluish gray rivers curving gracefully across the plain. Hereford cattle, with their brown bodies and white faces, grazed contentedly upon the wide sweep of natural grass, and the barking of dogs sounded indistinctly from the barnyard of a new-made home.

Down we pushed into the valley, then onward, across the Snake River at Moeners' Ferry, and then to the Buffalo Fork of the Grosventre. Antelope began to appear upon the plain and danced about us like yellow and white rubber balls. Two of the cowboys dismounted and fired at them, resting their rifles upon their knees. They could not duplicate the marksmanship of Kit Carson or Buffalo Bill. Not an antelope was even wounded.

We camped in a beautiful spot near the Grosventre River, and, just as we were lighting the fire for supper, a cry went up from some one:

"Elk! Elk!"

I was busy pouring some coffee, and, looking up, saw a cowboy pointing to a high bank opposite our camp. Sure enough, there stood a noble bull elk, his spreading antlers standing out on either side, giving him a calm and majestic appearance. He was gazing curiously at the animated scene below.

Why is it that the average man's first instinct when he sees a wild animal is to kill it? I was satisfied with watching this magnificent child of the forest, but not so with the rest of the party. Three of them ran immediately to get their rifles and a fusillade of bullets soon whistled in the direction of the big elk. He turned, galloped off into the timber, and left the cowboys to bemoan their lack of ability with the shooting-iron.

" By gracious," said one, " I can't hit a barn door at fifty yards! "

The elk was but one of the many which ranged the Jackson Hole country and whose deep trails could be seen on every hand. Their bleaching antlers, which they had shed, were also upon many a hill, and frequently we would pass a rancher's cabin, where a fence would have been constructed of the white twisted horns of the old bulls. I knew that we would soon see a quantity of elk, and we did.

Not many evenings later, as we were again boiling our coffee for dinner, the most unearthly scream that I have ever heard echoed from the canyon just to our right. It was answered by another, and — if I can make you believe it — the sound was as if a woman were being strangled.

" Mountain lion screeching," said Jack, with a grim smile. " Awful noise, ain't it? "

I confessed that it was.

" Makes me always feel skeery. Kind uv makes th' gooseflesh creep up my back. Heard 'em a thousand times but always frightens me."

The cowboy drew closer to the fire and I noticed that he was shivering.

The mountain lion is a great coward and is afraid to attack a human being. Unless cornered and extremely hungry, he will not fight. He has — in spite of this — the most unearthly scream, which would make one believe that he was one of the fiercest and most bloodthirsty of beasts. Welling up upon the clear night air — in the very heart of the wilderness

— it is enough to freeze one's blood to hear their wailings. It takes strong nerves to listen to their gruesome noise without shaking.

I heard the lions again about a week later, when I and a cowboy called Jim, were making our way up the side of a beautiful little tributary to the Grosventre. We were following a deep-rutted elk trail which led up the edge of a mountain to and from their summer feeding grounds, upon one of the higher plateaus. There was a log cabin nestling at the foot of the opposite hill — used by one of the game wardens — and, in the rear of this, a deep bank of hemlocks clothed the side of the cliff. Here the lions were concealed, and, seeing us riding in the open, shrieked out their defiance at the trespassers upon their demesne.

Although a startling and nerve-racking sound, we kept upon our way, and I confess that I looked to the shells in my rifle — fearing that one of the screechers might consider us excellent bait for their dinner. Soon we had advanced far up the canyon and then the lions ceased their caterwauling.

We were now in the heart of gameland. The tracks of bear were extraordinarily thick, and every now and again we would come to fresh sign, not an hour old. Once I reached a stream through which a big grizzly must have just passed, for the water was still muddy, and the print of his feet could easily be seen in the soft bank. In spite of their apparent numbers we could not even catch a glimpse of one of them, and, although I was constantly hoping to meet with a specimen of these monsters of the glen, I was never to catch even a fleeting glimpse of one.

Not so with the rest of the party. Not a week later one of the cowboys rode into camp with a wild yelping, and there — behind him — were two of his companions, lugging in the body of a brown bear. He was a little fellow and his fur was all rubbed away in places, where he had scratched himself against the rocks. In spite of this he was good eating and his haunches were enjoyed by most of the party. Personally, I did not care for the meat and preferred canned tongue.

The elk trails were most abundant, and I knew that we would soon see these brown deer, for we gradually moved up to the summit of the Rockies, where were vast plateaus covered with millions of beautiful flowers. These the noble animals lived upon in summer and slept among them too, for I would often find round holes in the grass, where some of them had bedded down a short time before. One evening two of the horse-wranglers returned to camp with the haunch of a cow elk, and stated — with much glee — that they had run upon a band of six, coming through some fallen timber. Two had fallen before their rifles, and, after cutting off enough for the use of our camp, they had placed the bodies in a position that could be easily approached, at a later date, when bear would undoubtedly be feeding upon the venison.

A week later we had a glorious view of a large herd of elk.

While traversing a high belt of timber my companion — a surveyor — called out to me to hurry over and see something on the other extremity of the ridge, upon which he had just taken his position. When I reached his side I saw that he was looking in the direction of a high plateau, upon which fully a thousand elk were feeding. No bulls seemed to be there — they were all cows and calves — and were grazing like a herd of cattle. The little calves were butting at each other and frisking about in great glee, while their fond mammas watched them with loving and tender glances of affection. It was a beautiful and moving vista.

My companion had a field-glass, and we stood watching the changing mass of elk for at least an hour. They apparently had no knowledge of our presence, for the wind was blowing from them to us, so that no strange " scent of the trespassing man " came to their keen nostrils. There — in that beautiful mountain pasture — the baby elk were growing to maturity, — while far below in the valley the settlers were gathering the natural hay which usually fed them, for the use of their own cattle during the long and cruel winter. There would be much suffering and distress among the band, when they had left these mountain meadows for the valley.

A week later we met the trapper and plainsman: Jerry Lane. I had already come upon his cabin and had stopped there for luncheon, leaving a neat piece of paper on the door to the effect that, —

" Pardner, we used your tin plates, spoons, knives, and one can of potted tongue."

High up in the hills the little log hut was situated near a stream of icy water. It was about sixteen by twenty feet, the floor covered with bear and wolf skins, and four rifles in the rack. Great steel traps hung upon the walls outside, and antelope hides were tacked against it. There were good books within: stories of hunting and adventure, — and upon the floor — were numerous copies of the Sunday *New York Journal*. Jerry Lane had lived well upon the summit of the Rockies.

I will never forget the view of the young trapper which came to me that morning. All around were the towering Rockies: an occasional fleck of snow upon the brown surface of the high cliffs; a gushing stream over on the right; the sage-brush plateau stretched away on every side, brown, bare, parched. A puff of dust first appeared in the far distance, then two figures rode up on horseback. They drew nearer and nearer. In front was the youthful personification of Buffalo Bill. It was Jerry Lane.

He was riding a magnificent half-bred animal — a roan. His bridle and saddle, as I remember — were silver mounted. A big pair of Mexican spurs were on his heels. With a close-fitting suit of tawny buckskin, a wide sombrero, cartridge-belt around the waist, and a long rifle hung neatly under the left leg he was a perfect picture of a plainsman, — such a picture as one sees in dime novels.

Behind him was an evil-looking customer, dressed in a slovenly manner, and scowling beneath a rather battered-in slouch hat. His horse, too, had nowhere

near the breeding of the other. He frowned as he
approached: the other smiled.

" Hello! " said Jerry Lane. " Dusty, isn't it? "

" You bet," said I. " Where you bound? "

" Montana."

" Hunting? "

" No, just taking life easy."

That was all the conversation that we had. He
waved his hat to me, touched the spurs to his horse's
flanks, and was soon off down the divide. For a long
time I stood and gazed after the lithe figure: young,
beautiful, brimming over with health and exuberance,
— the man who had found New York too tame for
his hot blood. Could you blame him?

Three days later a cow-puncher rode into our camp,
threw his saddle on the ground, hobbled his pony, and
drew near the mess table.

" Too bad about Jerry, warn't it? " said he, as he
seated himself.

" Why, what's the matter with him? " I asked.

" Shot."

" W-h-a-a-t! "

" Yes, got into a row over the Montana line. They
say it was accidental. Some one dropped his six-
shooter on the floor. It exploded. No more Jerry
Lane."

. . . .

That night I walked out to a lonely rock and gazed
at the brilliant stars. It was the true West, after all,
the West that I had always read about but had never
seen until now. I thought of the sandy-haired, blue-

eyed sheriff who had gone to the Great Beyond. I
thought of poor Jerry Lane: that lithe, active figure
in buckskins; that devil-may-care manner; that fresh,
pink-cheeked face. Yes, the West still held her trag-
edies, and the low wail of a coyote far off on the plain
sounded ominously dreary, while the hand of death
lay over the great wild wastes of the rolling, sage-
brush-covered prairie.

THE SONG OF THE MOOSE

THIS is the song which the trapper heard,
Heard in the gloom of the forest dark,
Heard while the embers snapped and snarled,
To the growl and glare of the glimmering spark.
Heard while the lucivee cried from the pines,
And the ribboned splash of a startled loon,
Crystalled the rim of the lake, as it lay
Soft in the gleam of the hunter's moon.
This is the song of the moose.

Near the amber drip of the torrent's rip,
  Where the lean wolf howls at the blinding spray,
Where the sleeted pine is riven and rent,
  By stress and strain of the mist-bank gray;
We struggled and fed through the reedling's bed,
  Where the sheldrake croons to her fledglings brown,
And the otter mewed to its hungry brood,
  As the osprey peered from the hemlock's crown.

Our moosling day was a rapturous play,
  We browsed where the partridge drummed a song,
Where the brown bear hid in the tamarack,
  Where the days were short and the nights were long.
We roamed 'neath the arch of the drowsy larch,
  Where the beaver bred in the inky pool,
We splashed in the foam of the cataract,
  In the frothing spume and the ripples cool.

351

We hid 'neath the pine of the Serpentine,
   As the red fox barked to his sleek-fed mate;
We ate of the birch of the Restigouche,
   Where the goldfinch whisper and undulate.
Oh, bright were the days, with surcease of care,
   As we fed and grew from our clumsy birth;
While the woods were green with a shimmering sheen,
   And the sun shone hot on the moss-grown earth.

Then came the prod from the fleet-flying squad,
   As the gray goose sped to the Chesapeake;
The leaves grew sere at the slow, dying year,
   And the salmon raced from their spawning creek.
Our mothers fled from our marsh-sunken bed,
   We browsed no more on the soft lilies' pad;
From the distant blue came the caribou,
   Rank upon rank — and their temper was bad.

Their eyes were bad, as they fought for our feed,
   When the air grew chill in the Northern blast,
And the white flakes fell from the sodden sky,
   On the sleeted lakes, soon frozen hard fast.
Pure white was the cowl of the arctic owl,
   And soft was his voice from the cedar deep;
As we ploughed our yard 'neath the mountain's guard,
   And marked our birch for the long winter's keep.

Now, sharp came the clang, as the wood-axe rang,
   " 'Tis man," said our kin, " you must wander afar
From the sound of his voice and reach of his arm,
   For his song is death and his hand is war."

The blue wisps curled from the lone logger's hut,
  Far down in the depths of the silent wood;
And shouts came loud from the boisterous crowd,
  As they sapped the strength of the forest's blood.

We were taught to fend, with a lunge and bend,
  The spring of the lynx, with his snarling yelp;
We were shown to ride, with a single stride,
  The charge of the wolf and his whining whelp.
We saw how to strip the birch with our lip,
  And to trample the shoots with our fore-leg weight;
We learned how to tell a foe by the smell,
  That law in the wood was the law of hate.

Another year, and the wide ridge was clear,
  As the snow grew less, and the day grew long;
With a start of the sap we swung from our trap,
  While the chickadee whispered his mating song;
And the robin came, with feathers of flame,
  To carol a psalm from the budding spray,
While the chewink's flute, like a minstrel's lute,
  Trilled clear in the balm of the softening day.

Oh, that life was good in the opening wood,
  As our brothers' horns turned velvet to bone,
We wandered at will over hummock and hill,
  'Till we found out — alas — we were never alone.
Man found us there, in our deep, forest lair,
  And plunge as we would in the thicket's gloom,
We ran on his track and the sign of his pack,
  As he close hunted us down to our doom.

There, oft in the dark, we trembled to hark
　To his muffled call, by bank of the pond,
And to those who lacked in spirit of fear,
　It was death to inquire, and death to respond.
Oft have we trod on the ranks of the slain,
　As prostrate they lay near some crystal stream;
Lured to their end by the low, soothing cry,
　Mocking the mate of a love-longing dream.

To the whispering rest of the trackless West,
　We travel to live where the range-land is clear,
Where wolf and bear keep their sheltering lair,
　Where silence is deep and man is not near.
Few — few are there left from 'merciless war,
　Waged on our ranks, now broken and gone,
Yet, struggle we must 'gainst slaughtering lust,
　Our end is in view — race-driven, forlorn.

This is the song which the trapper heard,
　Heard in the gloom of the forest dark,
Heard of an ancient and vanishing race,
　By the growl and glare of the glimmering spark.
Heard of the mannish blood-lust and greed,
　Of the withering waste in the rifle's path,
Song of the steel-clad bullet's speed,
　This is the song of the moose.

"LURED TO THEIR END BY THE LOW, SOOTHING CRY."

RETROSPECT

NO longer moves the wagon train through clouds of
    rolling dust,
No longer speaks the musket, foul caked with yellow rust,
Wild days have passed; the yelping brave has vanished in
    the mists of time,
Wild fights are o'er, the valiant scout has ceased to cheer
    the firing line.
The brutish bison herds are gone — the lean coyote sneaks
    here and there,
Where once the pronghorn fed in peace, and shyly roamed
    the grizzly bear.
The elk are dead — the puma, too, no longer shrieks his
    wailing cry,
Where trapper's fires are blazing clear, and sharply light
    the dark'ning sky.
From out the past, pale forms arise, the shapes of those who
    fought and bled
On treeless plains of alkali, and bravely found a gory bed.
The ghostly shapes go riding past; scout, voyageur, and
    priest,
Chief, warrior, and squaw, who gathered at the trader's
    feast.
No more their laughter echoes loud, no more their voices rise
    and fall,
By bed of stream, 'neath aspen's bough, where clumsy Indian
    children sprawl.

The chatter of the dance is hushed; the yells of warrior
    bands are gone,
As — gathering for the dance of death — they held high
    revelry 'till dawn.
We gaze upon the written page, we marvel that such tales
    are truth,
Of fighting fierce, of wrangling rude, of scalp-dance and the
    cries of youth.
Then thankfully we tread the paths, which voyageur and
    trapper bold
Were wont to tread in olden times, when passions fierce were
    uncontrolled.
Yes — blood was shed — yes — men were brave, who con-
    quered and who won the West,
Now there is love where once was strife — the scouts have
    reached their Heavenly rest.

THE END.

INDEX